Choral Connections...
Enhancing the Choral Experience

D1378603

GLENCOE
McGraw-Hill

CHORAL CONNECTIONS...

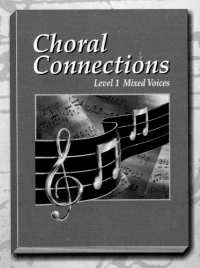

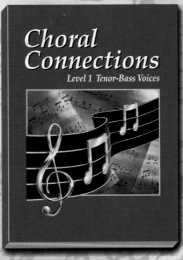

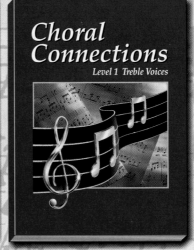

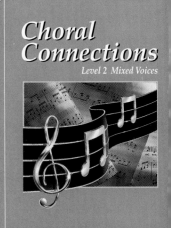

Sets a new standard for choral music

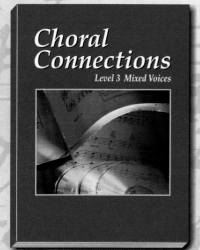
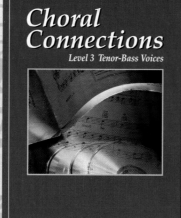
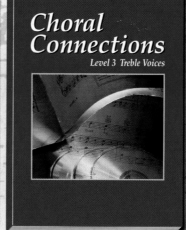
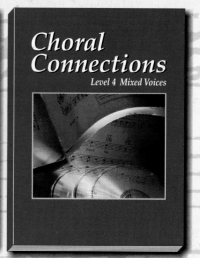

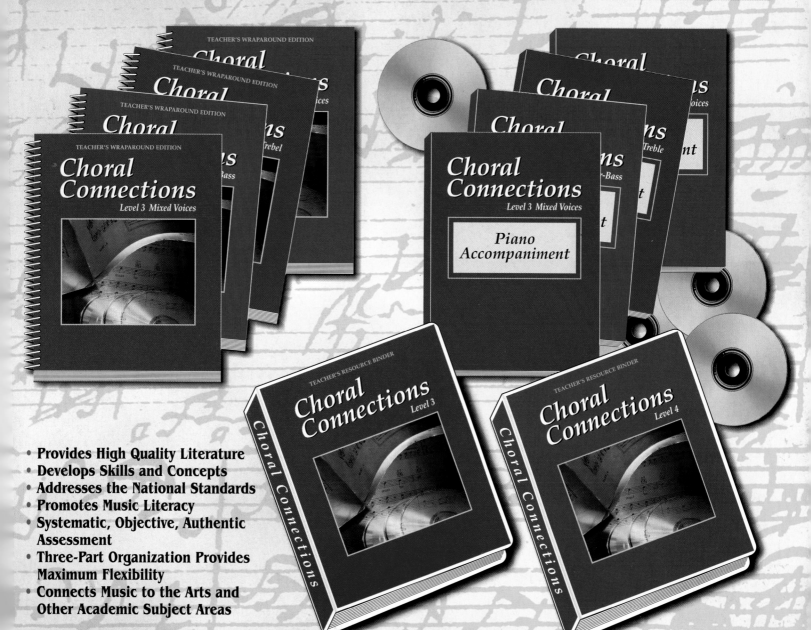

- **Provides High Quality Literature**
- **Develops Skills and Concepts**
- **Addresses the National Standards**
- **Promotes Music Literacy**
- **Systematic, Objective, Authentic Assessment**
- **Three-Part Organization Provides Maximum Flexibility**
- **Connects Music to the Arts and Other Academic Subject Areas**

STUDENT MATERIALS
STUDENTS SUCCEED WITH RICH MATERIALS, APPROPRIATE ACTIVITIES, AND VARIED LEARNING OPPORTUNITIES

A *four-level* series of eight books:

Level 1 - Mixed, Tenor-Bass, or Treble Voices
Level 2 - Mixed Voices
Level 3 - Mixed, Tenor-Bass, or Treble Voices
Level 4 - Mixed Voices

El Progreso H

For my colleague, Paul Garcia

Dindirin, Dindirinda
Anonymous
Arranged by Franc

South African Suite
I. Tshotsholoza

Stormy Weather
Music by Harold Arlen
Arranged by Jay Alth

Merrily We Sing Noel
(Celebrate a Happy Hanukkah)
SAB Voices and Piano with Opt

👁 **Sight-Singing**

Sight-sing this exercise on solfège and hand signs or numbers, then on *doom*. Use your usual lighter tone, then sing with a heavier tone. Do a step-touch motion, alternating first to the right, then to the left, as you sing.

🎵 **Singing: "Have Your Lamps Gone Out?"**

Many spirituals and African-American folk songs originated during the slavery period. The slaves used code words in songs to represent freedom and the land of freedom.

Tell what you know about how slaves escaped on the Underground Railroad. Then read the text of "Have Your Lamps Gone Out?" to discover the meaning of the song.

Now turn to the music for "Have Your Lamps Gone Out?" on page 22.

HOW DID YOU DO?
Reading music on your own gives you the freedom to share music with others whenever you want. Think about your preparation and performance of "Have Your Lamps Gone Out?"
1. Was your part mostly melody, mostly accompaniment, or a combination of the two. Are both important? Tell why you gave the answer you did.
2. Describe heavier and lighter tone. Can you sing equally well both ways? Sing a phrase from this lesson both with lighter and heavier tone.
3. There are solos and group parts in this piece. Which do you prefer to sing? Tell how it feels to sing solo or as part of a group.
4. How well do you think your ensemble performed this piece? What was good? What could be better? What should you work on next?

LESSON 3

Have Your Lamps Gone Out?

CHORAL MUSIC TERMS
accompaniment
melody
tone
solo/group

Based on a traditional African-American folk song
ARRANGER: Malcolm Dalglish

VOICING
SAB

PERFORMANCE STYLE
Swaying naturally
Accompanied by dulcimer or piano

FOCUS
• Read and sing melody and accompaniment parts.
• Sing with heavier tone.
• Sing solo and group parts.

Warming Up

🎵 **Rhythm Drill**
Read and clap the rhythm, then say it on *doom*. Notice the grace notes.
Try this:
• Sing the rhythm on D, or *do*.
• Sing it again on A, or *so*.
• Sing it using D and A, switching as you wish.
• Sing the rhythm on B, or *la*.
• Sing it using D, A and B, or *do, so,* and *la,* improvising a melody using just these pitches.

🎵 **Vocal Warm-Up**
Sing these pitches using solfège and hand signs or numbers, tuning the chords carefully. Now sing the exercise on *oo*.

Have Your Lamps Gone Out?

Based on a traditional African-American folk song
Malcolm Dalglish

Voices and Hammer Dulcimer

Baroque Period

After completing this lesson, you should be able to:
• Describe the general characteristics of Baroque visual arts.
• Discuss the most important differences between Renaissance music and Baroque music.
• Identify at least five new musical forms of the Baroque period.
• Identify at least four major composers of the Baroque period.

The artworks of the Renaissance reflect the ideas and ideals of the period. They are balanced and restrained, they communicate a sense of calm. The next period of European history—the Baroque period which lasted from about 1600 until around 1750—was an age of reaction against the restraint and balance of the Renaissance. Baroque artists expressed the ideals of their own time by adding emotion, decoration, and opulence to their works.

A Time of Continued Development
The explorations and developments ...
into the Baroque period ...
and Europe ...

1600–1750

COMPOSERS
Claudio Monteverdi (1567–1643)
Arcangelo Corelli (1643–1713)
Henry Purcell (1659–1713)
Antonio Vivaldi (1678–1741)
Georg Philipp Telemann (1681–1767)
Johann Sebastian Bach (1685–1750)
George Frideric Handel (1685–1750)

ARTISTS
El Greco (1541–1614)
Michelangelo da Caravaggio
(c. 1565–1609)
Peter Paul Rubens (1577–1640)
Frans Hals (1580–1666)
Artemisia Gentileschi (c. 1597– 1...
Georges de ... (1593–1652)
... (1599–1660)
... (1606–1669)
... (1660)

... tests. They were easy to sing and to ... gation could join in ... collection of compositions with instrumental ... related secular or sacred text segments. The ... er a sacred or a secular work itself marks ... ors at important Protestant churches

Galileo | Henry Hudson explores the Hudson River | Pilgrims land in America | Isaac Newton | Quakers arrive in Massachusetts
1564–1642 | **1609** | **1620** | **1642–1727** | **1656**

1607 | **1618–1648** | **1636** | **1643–1715**
Jamestown, Virginia, established settlement | Thirty Years' War | Harvard College founded | Reign of Louis XIV as King of France

1608
Telescope invented in Holland

During this period, instrumental music gained in importance, both in the church and as music commissioned for the entertainment of the courts of Europe. Vocal music also underwent changes. Instrumental accompaniments were increasingly added to both sacred and secular vocal works, and several new musical forms developed.

Instrumental Forms
As instrumental music grew more important, the musical instruments themselves were refined and their uses changed. The violin, previously a solo instrument, was added to ensemble groups. The harpsichord and the organ became the most important keyboard instruments.

Longer instrumental works were composed during the Baroque period. Often, these compositions consisted of several *movements,* individual pieces that sound fairly complete within themselves but are part of a longer work.

One of the new instrumental forms of the Baroque period was the **concerto grosso.** This composition for a small chamber orchestra consists of several movements.

▲ The ornate interior decor is reflected endlessly in the Hall of Mirrors, designed by François de Cuvilliés (1699–1768). Musical embellishment and ornamentation of the Baroque period provide similar stylistic elements in compositions by Johann Sebastian Bach and his contemporaries.

1716–39, François de Cuvilliés, Hall of Mirrors, Amalienburg, Munich, Germany

and features a moving bass line and an elaborate melody. Most of the major Baroque composers wrote concerti grossi. Among the best known are *The Four Seasons* by Antonio Vivaldi and the set of six *Brandenburg Concertos* by Johann Sebastian Bach.

Another instrumental form that developed was the **suite,** a set of musical movements, usually inspired by dances, of contrasting tempos and styles. Suites and suite-related compositions were very popular during this time; the most famous suites were those composed by Bach.

Vocal and Mixed Forms
Vocal music became more varied and notably more dramatic during the Baroque period. Sacred music continued to be predominantly choral, but new instrumental accompaniment added greater variety and strength to many compositions. One of the new forms of the Baroque period was the **chorale,** or *hymn tune.* Chorales were

▲ Attention to detail, particularly in direct and reflected light in mirrors and doorways, characterizes this work of Diego Velásquez (1599–1660). The challenge to the viewer to find all the images in *Las Meninas* equals the challenge to comprehend the intricacies in a Bach fugue or concerto, representative musical works of the same period.

1651–57, Diego Velásquez, Las Meninas, 10.4 x 9 (125 x 108.7 x 9"), Museo del Prado, Madrid, Spain

38 *Choral Connections Level 3 Mixed Voices*

Johann Sebastian Bach
1685–1750

1682 | First American newspaper established, Boston News-Letter | Handel comes to England
George Frideric Handel | **1704** | **1710**
1685–1759

Publication of Newton's Mathematical Principles
1687

Benjamin Franklin
1706–1790

... 21

Historical Connections Overhead from Resource Binder

140 *Choral Connections Level 3 Mixed Voices*

4

Each text is divided into three sections:

1. Teaching Lessons systematically build skills and concepts

Each lesson includes:

- **Focus**
- **Choral Music Terms**
- **Warm-Up Exercises**
- **Sight-Singing Exercises**
- **Assessment**

LESSON 5

The Road Less Traveled

CHORAL MUSIC TERMS
key changes
phrase release
sixteenth notes

VOICING
SAB

COMPOSER: Carl Strommen
TEXT: Carl Strommen

PERFORMANCE STYLE
With feeling
Accompanied by piano

FOCUS
- Read and clap rhythms, including sixteenth notes an...
- Recognize and sing key changes accurately.
- Perform correct phrase releases.

Warming Up

Rhythm Drill
Practice reading and clapping these rhythms. Use Maelzel's metron...
of ♩=76 as a tempo. Create longer phrases by clapping different combi...
pattern after another.

Vocal Warm-Up 1
Sing this choral warm-up on solfège and hand signs or num...
by half steps. Tune each chord quickly.

Vocal Warm-Up 2
Sing this exercise using solfège or numbers. Repeat, using the last pitch (*ti*) as *do*. After
the first few, do this by ear. Hear the relationships so the new tonic chord is in tune.

Sight-Singing
Sight-sing this exercise using solfège. Notice that when more than one part is written
on a staff, the direction of stems tells you which notoheads are your part.

The Road Less Traveled

SAB Voices and Piano

Words and Music by
Carl Strommen

SOPRANO
ALTO

With feeling (♩ = 76 - 84)

BARITONE

PIANO

♪♪ BAROQUE CONNECTIONS

Listening to...

Baroque Music

CHORAL SELECTION

Handel — Messiah, "Hallelujah" Chorus

George Frideric Handel (c. 1685–1750) was a contemporary of Johann Sebastian Bach. Handel's compositions, great in number, were mostly English oratorios and Italian operas of all of his works. Mes-siah is the most well known. It is also exceptional in that it has no plot and is based on Old and New Testament passages of the Bible. Mes-siah was written in less than a month and was first performed in Ireland in 1741. It did not gain favor in England until a decade after its first performance in 1742. However, since that time it has grown to have tremendous popularity, being one of the favorite musical works of the Christmas and Easter holiday seasons.

INSTRUMENTAL SELECTION

Bach — Organ Fugue in G Minor (Little Fugue)

Johann Sebastian Bach (c. 1685–1750) was born into a family of musicians. Through his lifetime, he held many positions as organist and church musician. During his employment at Weimar, Cothen, and Leipzig, Bach composed mostly secular works (at the request of the prince. His benefactor). For nearly all of his career as a composer he wrote music for the organ. His organ music has a characteristic use of the obbligato pedals, contributing yet again to the elaborate style that we associate with music from the Baroque period.

♪♪ BAROQUE CONNECTIONS

Introducing...

"Werfet Panier Auf Im Lande"

Georg Philipp Telemann

Setting the Stage

"Werfet Panier Auf Im Lande," attributed to Georg Philipp Tele-mann, is based on Jeremiah's prophecy in the Bible predicting the destruction of Babylon because of its sinful ways. Keep this theme in mind so that you don't become carried away with the dancelike qual-ity of the music. If Telemann meant for there to be any joy in the music, it is in troops marching to war accompanied by the stirring music of a military band with its trumpet calls.

Meeting the Composer

Georg Philipp Telemann

In his own time, Georg Philipp Telemann (c. 1681–1767) was one of the most highly esteemed of all German musicians. Although he was one of the most prolific composers of all time, he composed in the sha-dows of Bach and Handel. Perhaps for this reason, this great Baroque composer is hardly more than a name in the twentieth century. Telemann's vast output of music includes some 40 operas, 700 church cantatas, 44 Passions, 600 French overtures, and innumerable other orchestral, chamber, and harpsichord compositions.

Singing: "Werfet Panier Auf Im Lande"

Music is often played when people gather for special events. Describe the music you would expect to hear at a football game. What kind of music would you expect to hear at a wedding? Describe the music you would expect to hear at a funeral. If selected appropriately, music can enhance the mood of any occasion.

Now turn to the music for "Werfet Panier Auf Im Lande" on page 146.

Now turn to the music for "Werfet Panier Auf Im Lande" on page 146.

HOW DID YOU DO?

Think about your preparation and performance of "Werfet Panier Auf Im Lande."
1. Describe how you perform 6/8 meter.
2. Describe the mood of "Werfet Panier Auf Im Lande" and tell how you performed the music to enhance the mood.

3. Where might you suggest that this piece be performed?
4. Tell why this piece is considered an exemplary model of Baroque vocal music. Give specific musical characteristics.

---

2. Making Historical Connections

- **Historical narrative**
- **Listening selections accompanied by listening maps**
- **Historical literature**

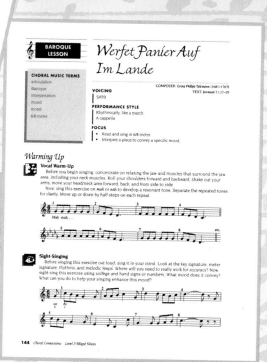

BAROQUE LESSON

Werfet Panier Auf Im Lande

CHORAL MUSIC TERMS
articulation
Baroque
interpretation
mood
motet
6/8 meter

COMPOSER: Georg Philipp Telemann (1681–1767)
TEXT: Jeremiah 51:27–29

VOICING
SATB

PERFORMANCE STYLE
Rhythmically, like a march
A cappella

FOCUS
- Read and sing in 6/8 meter.
- Interpret a piece to convey a specific mood.

Warming Up

Vocal Warm-Up
Before you begin singing, concentrate on relaxing the jaw and muscles that surround the jaw area, including your neck muscles. Roll your shoulders forward and backward, shake out your arms, move your head/neck area forward, back, and from side to side.
Now, sing this exercise on *mah* or *nah* to develop a resonant tone. Separate the repeated tones for clarity. Move up or down by half steps on each repeat.

Mah mah . . .

Sight-Singing
Before singing this exercise out loud, sing it in your mind. Look at the key signature, meter signature, rhythms, and melodic leaps. Where will you need to really work for accuracy? Now sight-sing this exercise using solfège and hand signs or numbers. What mood does it convey? What can you do to help your singing enhance this mood?

144 *Choral Connections   Level 3 Mixed Voices*

---

3. Additional Performance Selections

- **Patriotic**
- **Holiday**
- **Multicultural**
- **Proven Audience Pleasers**

38

...al Connections   Level 3 Mixed Voices

TEACHER WRAPAROUND EDITIONS
SAVE TIME, BUILD SKILLS, DELIVER EXCELLENT PERFORMANCE

1. Flexible Lesson Design

Clear, logical, yet flexible directions.

Each lesson, linked to one musical selection, includes:

- **Focus**
- **Objectives—clear and measurable**
- **Choral Music Terms**
- **Warm-Ups develop rhythm, vocal, and sight-singing skills**
- **Suggested Teaching Sequence builds skills and concepts**
- **Assessments match objectives**

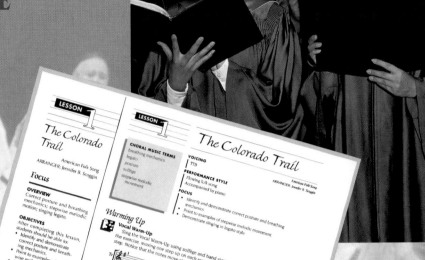

2. Three Assessment Options

- **Allow informal checkpoints and formal assessments**
- **Can be compiled to create a portfolio showing growth**
- **May be done by teacher, student, peers, or a combination**

3. Extending the Learning

The Extension section of each lesson offers:

- **Teaching strategies**
- **Background information**
- **Vocal development strategies**
- **Music literacy activities**
- **Enrichment Extensions**
- **Curriculum Connections**

ADDITIONAL RESOURCES
- ## ADD DEPTH, ALTERNATIVES AND OPTIONS
- ## INVOLVE STUDENTS IN THEIR OWN LEARNING
- ## DEVELOP LISTENING, NOTATION, AND CRITICAL THINKING SKILLS

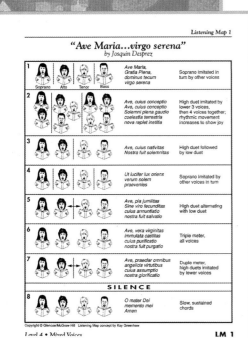

The Listening Program

Correlated with the historical section, the listening selections include:

- Two selections from each historical period, accompanied by listening maps
- Cross references to an optional CD program

The Teacher's Resource Binder

A separate set of teaching tools involve students in their own learning. The binder, which accompanies each level, includes:

- **Four-color fine art transparencies to enhance the historical narratives.**
- **Reproducible blackline masters providing:**
  - **basic resource information**
  - **music theory worksheets**
  - **pronunciation guides**
  - **listening maps**
  - **assessment masters**

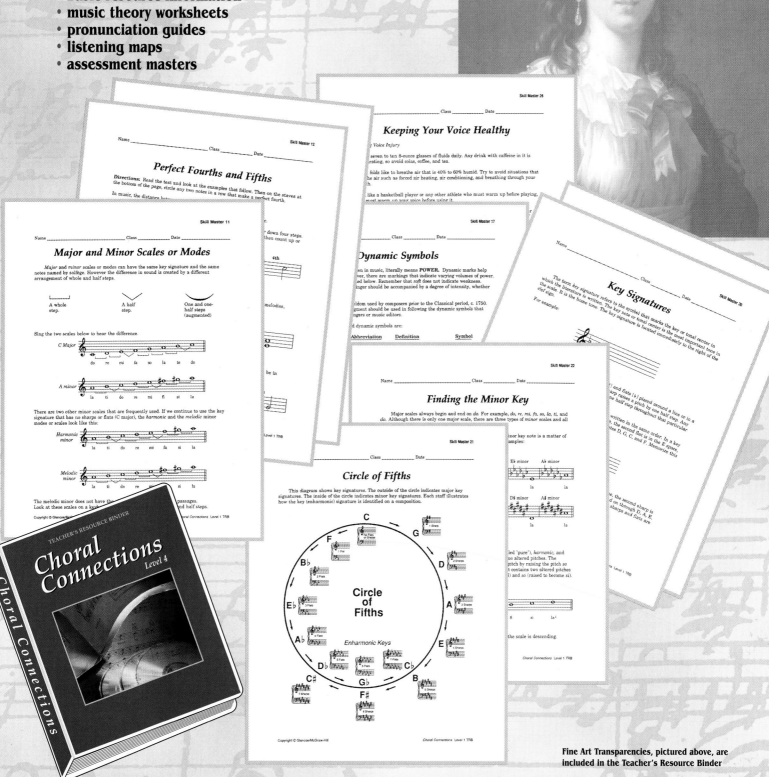

Fine Art Transparencies, pictured above, are included in the Teacher's Resource Binder

PERFORMANCE LITERATURE AND TEACHING LESSONS

LEVEL 1 MIXED VOICES
24 selections

LESSONS
1. Bound for Jubilee-*Joyce Elaine Eilers*
2. A Red, Red Rose-*Daniel Burton*
3. Over There-*Jerry Ray*
4. Dare to Dream!-*Niel Lorenz and Mary Lynn Lightfoot*
5. The Tiger-*Sherri Porterfield*
6. Shalom, My Friends-*Douglas E. Wagner*
7. Whisper! Whisper!-*Jay Althouse*
8. Mansions in the Sky-*Carl Strommen*
9. Down by the Riverside-*Brad Printz*
10. Something Told the Wild Geese-*Sherri Porterfield*
11. Praise Ye the Lord, All Nations-*Johann S. Bach*
12. Wiegenlied-*Johannes Brahms and Sherri Porterfield*
13. Nightfall-*Lou Williams-Wimberly*
14. Riu, Riu, Chiu-*Linda Steen Spevacek*

MAKING HISTORICAL CONNECTIONS
Renaissance Period
  Kyrie Eleison-*Antonio Lotti*

Baroque Period
  Alleluia from *For Us a Child Is Born*-*Johann S. Bach*

Classical Period
  Dies Irae from *Requiem*-*Wolfgang A. Mozart*

Romantic Period
  In Stiller Nacht-*Johannes Brahms*

Contemporary Period
  River, Sing Your Song-*Eugene Butler*

ADDITIONAL PERFORMANCE SELECTIONS
  I Hear Liberty Singing-*Greg Gilpin*
  It's Time to Fly Away-*Joyce Elaine Eilers*
  Shenandoah-*Arranger Brad Printz*
  Three Yoruba Native Songs of Nigeria-
    Arrangers Henry Leck and Prince Adeniyi
  The Tree of Peace-*Arranger Fred Bock*

FEATURED LISTENING SELECTIONS
  Cantate Ninfe-Luca Marenzio
  Saltarello-Anonymous
  Cantata No. 80, A Mighty Fortress is Our God, No. 8
  Brandenburg Concerto No. 2, First Movement-
    Johann S. Bach
  Non So Pui from *The Marriage of Figaro*, Act 1,
    Scenes 6 and 7-*Wolfgang A. Mozart*
  Eine kleine Nachtmusik, First Movement-
    Wolfgang A. Mozart
  Habanera from *Carmen*, Act 1-*Georges Bizet*
  The Great Gate of Kiev and The Hut on Fowl's Legs
    from *Pictures at an Exhibition*-
    Modest Mussorgsky
  Mister Tambourine Man-*Bob Dylan*
  *The Young Person's Guide to the Orchestra-
    Benjamin Britten*

LEVEL 1 TENOR-BASS VOICES
26 selections

LESSONS
1. The Colorado Trail-*Arranger Jennifer B. Scoggin*
2. Lord, In the Morning-*R. Paul Drummond*
3. Me Gustan Todas-*Arranger Donald W. Crouch*
4. Drink to Me Only with Thine Eyes-
    Arranger Robert Lawrence
5. I'm Bound Away-*Donald Moore*
6. Viva Tutti-*Ralph Hunter*
7. My Love Is Like a Rose-*Eugene Butler*
8. Emmanuel's Birth-*Arranger Bobby L. Siltman*
9. My Highland Lassie, O!-*Tullye B. Norton*
10. Bound for Jubilee-*Joyce Elaine Eilers*
11. Masters In This Hall-*Chartres/Arranger David Burger*
12. Scarborough Fair-*Arranger Harry Swenson*
13. Something Told the Wild Geese-*Sherri Porterfield*
14. Sing Me a Song of a Lad That Is Gone-
    Sherri Porterfield
15. Steal Away-*Arranger Bobby L. Siltman*

MAKING HISTORICAL CONNECTIONS
Renaissance Period
  Ah, Robin, Gentle Robin-*William Cornysh*

Baroque Period
  Praise the King-*George Frideric Handel*

Classical Period
  Praise We Sing to Thee-*Franz Joseph Haydn*

Romantic Period
  Abendlied-*Felix Mendelssohn*

Contemporary Period
  Jubilate Deo-*Linda Steen Spevacek*

ADDITIONAL PERFORMANCE SELECTIONS
  Old Dan Tucker-*Arranger Pat Willet*
  Medley for Christmas-*Arranger Bobby L. Siltman*
  Vive l'Amour-*Arranger Bobby L. Siltman*
  Now Is the Month of Maying-*Thomas Morley*
  My Lord, What a Morning-*Arranger Lois B. Land*
  I Want to Be a Sailor-*Joseph M. Martin*

FEATURED LISTENING SELECTIONS
  Kyrie from *L'homme armé* Mass-*Guillaume Dufay*
  Saltarello-Anonymous
  Cantata No. 80, A Mighty Fortress is Our God,
    No. 5-*Johann S. Bach*
  Water Music, No. 6-*George Frideric Handel*
  Trio from *The Marriage of Figaro*, Act 1, Scenes
    6 and 7-*Wolfgang A. Mozart*
  Piano Concerto in G Major, First Movement-
    Wolfgang A. Mozart
  Children's Chorus from *Carmen*, Act I-
    Georges Bizet
  Symphonie fantastique, Fifth Movement-
    Hector Berlioz
  Mister Tambourine Man-*Bob Dylan*
  Symphonic Dances from *West Side Story*-
    Leonard Bernstein

LEVEL 1 TREBLE VOICES
27 selections

LESSONS
1. This Train Goes Marching In-*Arranger Sandy Feldstei*
2. Lift Up Your Voice, Alleluia-*Sally K. Albrecht*
3. No Well, No Well!-*Steve Kupferschmid*
4. Peace in Twelve Languages-*Thomas Knight*
5. Sing a Joyful Song-*Sally K. Albrecht*
6. Kwanzaa-*Teresa Jennings*
7. We Sing Feliz Navidad-*Carl Strommen*
8. In the Meadow-*Arranger Beatrice P. Krone*
9. Dear Nightingale, Awake-*Arranger Gerhard Track*
10. The First Noel/Pachelbel's Canon-*Johann Pachelbel*
11. Annabel Lee-*Edna Lewis and John Mitri Habash*
12. A la Nanita Nana-*Arranger David Eddleman*
13. For the Beauty of the Earth-*John Rutter*
14. Joshua Fit the Battle of Jericho-
    Arranger Warren Williamson
15. The Ash Grove-*Arranger Thurlow T. Steffy*

MAKING HISTORICAL CONNECTIONS
Renaissance Period
  Non Nobis, Domine-*William Byrd*

Baroque Period
  Sound the Trumpet-*Henry Purcell*

Classical Period
  Ave Verum Corpus-*Wolfgang A. Mozart*

Romantic Period
  Evening Song (Abendlied)-*Felix Mendelssohn-
    Bartholdy*

Contemporary Period
  Linden Lea-*Ralph Vaughan Williams*

ADDITIONAL PERFORMANCE SELECTIONS
  Alexander's Ragtime Band-*Irving Berlin*
  America, of Thee I Sing!-*Mary Donnelly and
    George L. O. Strid*
  Let Freedom Sing!-*Mary Lynn Lightfoot*
  'Round the Riverside-*Arranger Saundra Berry Musse*
  Chumbara-*Arranger Aden G. Lewis*
  The Kalanta of the New Year-*Malcolm Dalglish*
  Three Sephardic Folk Songs
    I. Irme Quiero-*Arranger The Western Wind*
    II. Rahelica Baila-*Arranger Lawrence Bennett*
    III. Xinanáy-*Elliot Z. Levine*

FEATURED LISTENING SELECTIONS
  Fair Phyllis-*John Farmer*
  Saltarello-Anonymous
  There Were Shepherds from *Messiah*-
    George Frideric Handel
  Prelude and Fugue in C Minor, from *The Well-
    Tempered Clavier*, Book 1-*Johann S. Bach*
  Non So Pui from *The Marriage of Figaro*, Act 1,
    Scenes 6 and 7-*Wolfgang A. Mozart*
  Piano Sonata in C Minor (*Pathétique*), First
    Movement-*Ludwig van Beethoven*
  Dans l'Air from *Carmen*, Act I-*Georges Bizet*
  A Midsummer Night's Dream, Overture-
    Felix Mendelssohn
  My Funny Valentine-*Richard Rodgers*
  Music for Strings, Percussion and Celesta, Fourth
    Movement-*Béla Bartók*

LEVEL 2 MIXED VOICES

27 selections

LESSONS

- The Lord of All Creation-*Johann Michael Haydn*
- In These Delightful Pleasant Groves-*Henry Purcell*
- Have Your Lamps Gone Out?-
  Arranger Malcolm Dalglish
- O Won't You Sit Down-*Arranger Arthur Hardwicke*
- The Road Less Traveled-*Carl Strommen*
- Carol of the Bells-*Mikola D. Leontovich*
- Cantate Domino-*John Carter*
- Agnus Dei-*Wolfgang A. Mozart*
- Early One Morning-*Arranger Noble Cain*
- Domine Deus-*Jacob Regnart*
- Sanctus-*Franz Joseph Haydn*
- Scarborough Fair-*Arranger Willard A. Palmer*
- Agnus Dei-*Audrey Snyder*
- Zamba for You-*Ariel Ramirez*

MAKING HISTORICAL CONNECTIONS

Renaissance Period
- My Heart Is Offered Still to You-*Orlande de Lassus*

Baroque Period
- Gloria in Excelsis-*Antonio Vivaldi*

Classical Period
- Gloria from *Heiligmesse*-*Franz Joseph Haydn*

Romantic Period
- Song of the Lark-*Felix Mendelssohn*

Contemporary Period
- The Snow-White Messenger-*Arranger Lloyd Pfautsch*

ADDITIONAL PERFORMANCE SELECTIONS
- Ezekiel's Wheel-*Philip Kern*
- Like an Eagle-*Carl Strommen*
- Merrily We Sing Noel-*B. Dardess*
- Stormy Weather-*Harold Arlen*
- South African Suite-*Henry Leck*
  - **I.** Tshotsholoza
  - **II.** Siyahamba
  - **III.** Gabi Gabi
- Dindirin, Dindirindaña-*Anonymous*
- Freedom Is Coming-*Henry H. Leck*
- Hymn of Promise-*Natalie Sleeth*

FEATURED LISTENING SELECTIONS
- Gloria from *Pope Marcellus* Mass-
  Giovanni Pierluigi da Palestrina
- Two Dances-*Tylman Susato*
- Hallelujah! from *Messiah*-*George Frideric Handel*
- Spring, from *The Four Seasons*, Third Movement-
  Antonio Vivaldi
- Credo from *Lord Nelson Mass*-*Franz Joseph Haydn*
- Symphony No. 100 in G Major (*Military*), Second
  Movement-*Franz Joseph Haydn*
- *The Song of the Earth*, Third Movement-
  Gustav Mahler
- Symphony No. 5 in C Minor, First Movement-
  Ludwig van Beethoven
- *Alexander Nevsky*, Seventh Movement-
  Sergei Prokofiev
- Street in a Frontier Town from *Billy the Kid*,
  Scene 1-*Aaron Copland*

LEVEL 3 MIXED VOICES

25 selections

LESSONS

1. Dream a Dream-*Ed Robertson*
2. The Road Less Traveled-*Carl Strommen*
3. Nginani Na-*Arranger Caroline Lyon*
4. Music, When Soft Voices Die-*Philip Young*
5. Cantaremos-*Ramón Noble*
6. Laudate Nomen Domini-*Christopher Tye*
7. Pål På Haugen-*Arranger Bradley Ellingboe*
8. It Was a Lover and His Lass-*Michael Larkin*
9. I Hear a Sky-Born Music-*Lois Land*
10. Four Spanish Christmas Carols-
    Arranger Noe Sanchez
11. Alleluia-*Will James*
12. Flow Gently, Sweet Afton-*Arranger John Leavitt*
13. Jesu Dulcis Memoria-*Tomás Luis de Victoria*
14. May the Road Rise to Meet You-*David Hamilton*
15. In Memoria Aeterna-*Antonio Vivaldi*

MAKING HISTORICAL CONNECTIONS

Renaissance Period
- O Domine Jesu Christe-*Giovanni
  Pierluigi da Palestrina*

Baroque Period
- Werfet Panier Auf Im Lande-*Georg Philipp Telemann*

Classical Period
- Sanctus-*Luigi Cherubini*

Romantic Period
- If I Should See You All Alone-*Felix Mendelssohn*

Contemporary Period
- Still, Still, Still-*Arranger John Rutter*

ADDITIONAL PERFORMANCE SELECTIONS
- Shut De Do-*Randy Stonehill*
- The River-*Garth Brooks and Victoria Shaw*
- Look-A That Star-*Jay Althouse*
- A Holiday Wish-*Jay Althouse*
- El Progreso Honduras-*Elliot Z. Levine*

FEATURED LISTENING SELECTIONS
- As Vesta Was Descending-*Thomas Weelkes*
- Ricercar in the Twelfth Mode-*Andrea Gabrieli*
- Hallelujah Chorus from *Messiah*-
  George Frideric Handel
- Organ Fugue in G Minor (*Little Fugue*)-
  Johann S. Bach
- Lá Ci Darem la Mano from *Don Giovanni*, Act I-
  Wolfgang A. Mozart
- Symphony No. 40 in G Minor, First Movement-
  Wolfgang A. Mozart
- La Donna è Mobile from *Rigoletto*, Act III-
  Guiseppe Verdi
- *Symphonie fantastique*, Fourth Movement (March to
  the Scaffold)-*Hector Berlioz*
- Tonight from *West Side Story*-*Leonard Bernstein*
- Theme and Variations on Simple Gifts from
  Appalachian Spring, Section 7-*Aaron Copland*

LEVEL 3 TENOR-BASS VOICES

26 selections

LESSONS

1. An Irish Blessing-*Donald Moore*
2. Ah, Robin, Gentle Robin-*William Cornysh*
3. Blow, Blow, Thou Winter Wind-*Sherri Porterfield*
4. Who Are the Brave-*Joseph M. Martin*
5. Streets of Laredo-*Arranger Merrilee Webb*
6. Two Folk Songs for Male Voices-*Arranger John Rutter*
7. Down in the Valley-*Arranger George Mead*
8. Sanctus-*Franz Schubert*
9. Ya Viene la Vieja-*Arranger Jim Leininger*
10. There Comes a Ship Full-Laden-*Heinrich Schütz*
11. Workin' on the Railroad!-*Arranger Donald Moore*
12. My Love for You-*Ludwig van Beethoven*
13. Two Humorous Songs-*Joseph Haydn/
    Christian Felix Weisse*
14. Come, Praise the Lord-*William Crotch*
15. Gloria-*Franz Schubert*

MAKING HISTORICAL CONNECTIONS

Renaissance Period
- Let Thy Merciful Ears, O Lord-*Thomas Weelkes*

Baroque Period
- Exsultate Justi-*Lodovico Viadana*

Classical Period
- Come, O Jesus, Come to Me-*Maria Luigi Cherubini*

Romantic Period
- Schön Blümelein-*Robert Schumann*

Contemporary Period
- Do You Fear the Wind?-*Leland B. Sateren*

ADDITIONAL PERFORMANCE SELECTIONS
- Hail to Our Audience!-*Ralph Wilkinson*
- Dance of the One-Legged Sailor-*Brent Pierce*
- Deshi-*Brent Pierce*
- The Crawdad Song-*Arranger Aden Lewis*
- O Mary, Don't You Weep-*Arranger Raymond Rhea*
- Echo Carol-*Arranger Paul Royer*

FEATURED LISTENING SELECTIONS
- As Vesta Was Descending-*Thomas Weelkes*
- Ricercar in the Twelfth Mode-*Andrea Gabrieli*
- For unto Us a Child Is Born from *Messiah*-
  George Frideric Handel
- *Brandenburg* Concerto No. 5 in D Major, Third
  Movement-*Johann S. Bach*
- Catalog Aria from *Don Giovanni*, Act I-
  Wolfgang A. Mozart
- Trumpet Concerto in E Flat Major, Third Movement-
  Franz Joseph Haydn
- Erlkönig (Erlking)-*Franz Schubert*
- *Transcendental Étude No. 10 in F Minor*-*Franz Liszt*
- Tonight from *West Side Story*-*Leonard Bernstein*
- *Concerto Grosso 1985*, First Movement-
  Ellen Taafe Zwilich

PERFORMANCE LITERATURE AND TEACHING LESSONS
(continued)

LEVEL 3 TREBLE VOICES

25 selections

LESSONS
1 The Rainbow Comes and Goes-*Lois Land*
2 Behold, a Tiny Baby-*Arranger Mary Lynn Lightfoot*
3 Whispering Pine-*Eugene Butler*
4 Joseph's Lullaby-*Russell Schulz-Widmar*
5 Welcome Now in Peace-*Arranger Judith Herrington*
6 Silent the Forests-*Eugene Butler*
7 My Beloved-*Johannes Brahms*
8 Fresh Is the Maytime-*Johann Hermann Schein*
9 Who Has Seen the Wind?-*Robert E. Kreutz*
10 I Never Saw a Moor-*Michael Larkin*
11 Arruru-*Ruth Dwyer/Thomas Gerber*
12 Peace Today Descends from Heaven-
   Alessandro Grandi
13 Os Justi-*Eleanor Daley*
14 Dance On My Heart-*Allen Koepke*

MAKING HISTORICAL CONNECTIONS
Renaissance Period
I Go Before, My Charmer-*Thomas Morley*

Baroque Period
O Death, None Could Conquer Thee-
   Johann Sebastian Bach

Classical Period
Holy, Holy, Holy-*Wolfgang A. Mozart*

Romantic Period
Grüss-*Felix Mendelssohn*

Contemporary Period
Nigra Sum-*Pablo Casals*

ADDITIONAL PERFORMANCE SELECTIONS
Gloria-*Joseph Haydn*
I Wonder as I Wander-*Richard Osborne*
Native American Spring Songs-*Nancy Grundahl*
Festival Alleluia-*Allen Pote*
Wisdom and Understanding-*Kent A. Newbury*
Beautiful Yet Truthful-*Lloyd Pfautsch*

FEATURED LISTENING SELECTIONS
As Vesta Was Descending-*Thomas Weelkes*
Ricercar in the Twelfth Mode-*Andrea Gabrieli*
Chorale from Cantate No. 140 (*Wachet auf, ruft uns
   die Stimme*), Seventh Movement-*Johann S. Bach*
Suite No. 3 in D Major, Air-*Johann S. Bach*
Lá Ci Darem la Mano from *Don Giovanni*, Act I-
   Wolfgang A. Mozart
Symphony No. 94 in G Major (*Surprise*),
   Second Movement-*Franz Joseph Haydn*
Quartet from *Rigoletto*, Act III-*Giuseppe Verdi*
Romance in G Minor for Violin and Piano No. 2-
   Clara Schumann
Lost Your Head Blues-*Bessie Smith*
The Firebird, Scene 2-*Igor Stravinsky*

LEVEL 4 MIXED VOICES

29 selections

LESSONS
1 The One Who Stands Alone-*Joseph Martin*
2 Siyahamba-*Donald Moore*
3 The Prayer of Saint Francis-*René Clausen*
4 Starlight Lullaby-*Philip Lane*
5 God Rest You Merry, Gentlemen-
   James Neal Koudelka
6 Papillon, Tu Es Volage-*Jonathan Thompson*
7 I Saw Three Ships-*Edwin Fissinger*
8 African Noel-*André J. Thomas*
9 The Lord Is My Shepherd-*Allen Pote*
10 Forest Cool, Thou Forest Quiet-*Johannes Brahms*
11 Keep Your Lamps!-*André J. Thomas*
12 Blessed Are the Pure of Heart-*Woldemar Voullaire*
13 V'amo di Core-*Wolfgang A. Mozart*
14 I Will Lay Me Down in Peace-*Healey Willan*
15 The Cloths of Heaven-*Adolphus Hailstork*
16 Ave Maria-*Franz Biebl*

MAKING HISTORICAL CONNECTIONS
Renaissance Period
Ave Regina Coelorum-*Orlande de Lassus*

Baroque Period
Alleluia-*Giovanni Battista Pergolesi*

Classical Period
Come, Lovely Spring-*Franz Joseph Haydn*

Romantic Period
So Wahr die Sonne Scheinet-*Robert Schumann*

Contemporary Period
I Hear America Singing-*André J. Thomas*

ADDITIONAL PERFORMANCE SELECTIONS
Over the Rainbow-*Harold Arlen*
Three Canticles for Treble Voices-*Paul Liljestrand*
Who Is He in Yonder Stall?-*Robert H. Young*
42nd Street-*Harry Warren*
Blue Moon-*Richard Rodgers*
Desde el Fondo de Mi Alma-*Domingo Santa Cruz*
Georgia on My Mind-*Hoagy Carmichael*
Love Never Ends-*Elizabeth Volk*

FEATURED LISTENING SELECTIONS
Ave Maria-*Josquin Desprez*
The Most Sacred Queene Elizabeth, Her Galliard-
   John Dowland
Zion Hört die Wächter Singen from Cantate
   No. 140 (*Wachet auf, ruft uns die Stimme*),
   Fourth Movement-*Johann S. Bach*
La Primavera from *The Four Seasons*, First
   Movement-*Antonio Vivaldi*
Dies Irae from *Requiem*-*Wolfgang A. Mozart*
Piano Concerto No. 23 in A Major: First Movement-
   Wolfgang A. Mozart
A German Requiem, Fourth Movement-
   Johannes Brahms
The Moldau-Bedrich *Smetana*
Symphony of Psalms, First Movement-
   Igor Stravinsky
Sacrificial Dance from *Le Sacre du printemps*-
   Igor Stravinsky

GLENCOE
McGraw-Hill

MU91312-8

Choral Connections

Level 3 Treble Voices

Teacher's Wraparound Edition

Teacher's Manual

GLENCOE

McGraw-Hill

New York, New York   Columbus, Ohio   Mission Hills, California   Peoria, Illinois

Meet the Authors

SENIOR AUTHOR

Mollie G. Tower - As Coordinator of Choral and General Music of the Austin Independent School District, Mollie Tower was recently nominated as "Administrator of the Year." She is very active in international, national, regional, and state music educators' organizations. Ms. Tower was contributing author, consultant, and reviewer for the elementary programs *Share the Music*, and *Music and You*. Senior author of *Música para todos*, *Primary and Intermediate Dual Language Handbooks for Music Teachers*, she has also written and consulted for many other publications. A longtime advocate of music education, Mollie is a popular clinician who conducts workshops across the country.

Milton Pullen

Professor of Music and Director of Choirs

After attending Texas A & I University where he acquired a Bachelor of Music Education in voice, Milton Pullen attended the University of Houston, where in 1976 he received a Master of Music in conducting. He has taught at the middle and high school level for 24 years and for the last seven years has taught at the university level. He is now Professor of Music and Director of Choirs at Pepperdine University in Malibu, California.

Ken Steele

Choral Director

Ken Steele has taught secondary choral music for 22 years, having directed choirs at the middle school and high school levels. He received the Bachelor of Music degree from Stetson University in DeLand, Florida, and went on to the University of Texas in Austin to earn the Master of Music in Choral Literature and Conducting in 1971, studying with Dr. Morris J. Beachy. A member of Texas Music Educators Association, Texas Choral Directors Association, Texas Music Adjudicators Association, and a lifetime member of the American Choral Directors Association, he is currently the choral director at L. C. Anderson High School, in Austin, Texas.

Gloria J. Stephens

Director of Choral Activities

With 23 years of teaching experience, Gloria Stephens is presently the Director of Choral Activities at Ryan High School in Denton, Texas. Mrs. Stephens earned her Bachelor of Music Education and Master of Music Education degrees from the University of North Texas in Denton. She has also done post-graduate work at Texas Woman's University in Denton, the University of Texas at Arlington, and Westminster Choir College in Princeton, New Jersey.

Contributing Writers

Dr. Susan Snyder has taught all levels of vocal music over the last 25 years. She holds a B.S. in music education from the University of Connecticut and an M.A. from Montclair State College. She holds a Ph.D. in curriculum and instruction from the University of Connecticut and advanced professional certificates from Memphis State University and the University of Minnesota. Teaching at Hunter College and City University of New York, Dr. Snyder was coordinating author of the elementary music program, *Share the Music*, and a consultant on *Music and You*. She has published many articles on music education and integrated curriculum and is an active clinician, master teacher, and guest conductor.

Vocal Development, Music Literacy
Katherine Saltzer Hickey, D.M.A.
University of California at Los Angeles
Los Angeles, California
Choir Director
Pacific Chorale Children's Choruses
Irvine, California

The National Standards for Music Education are reprinted from *National Standards for Arts Education* with permission from Music Educators National Conference (MENC). Copyright ©1994 by MENC. The complete National Standards and additional materials relating to the Standards are available from Music Educators National Conference, 1806 Robert Fulton Drive, Reston, Virginia 22091. (Telephone 800-336-3768.) A portion of the sales of this material goes to support music education programs through programs of the Music Educators National Conference.

Glencoe/McGraw-Hill

A Division of The McGraw-Hill Companies

Send all inquiries to:
Glencoe/McGraw-Hill
15319 Chatsworth Street
Mission Hills, California 91345

ISBN 0-02-655534-4 (Student's Edition)
ISBN 0-02-655557-3 (Teacher's Wraparound Edition)

Printed in the United States of America.

1 2 3 4 5 6 7 8 9 MAL   02 01 00 99 98 97 96

Curr. Lab.
Sec.
MT
935
.T69
1997
Level 3
treble
t.e.

Table of Contents

SECTION		National Standards									Teacher's Resources
Selection	Concepts and Skills	1	2	3	4	5	6	7	8	9	
TEACHING LESSONS											
The Rainbow Comes and Goes	Posture; breath support; rhythms; intervals.	a, c				a, b	b				
Behold, a Tiny Baby!	Minor tonality; independent two-part singing; melismatic and syllabic use of text.	a, c				a, b	a, b, c	a			📁
Whispering Pine	3/4 meter; tonic triad; tuning chords in three parts; altered tones.	a, c		b		a, b	a, b	a			📁
Joseph's Lullaby	Characteristics of choral blend; legato style; sight-singing in F major.	a, c, f		b		a, b	b	a			📁
Welcome Now in Peace	Vowel formation; read and sing in D minor; distinguish between major and minor chords.	a, c		b		a, b	b	a	c		📁
Silent the Forests	Breath control; half steps and altered tones; chromatic passages.	a, c, f				a, b	a, b	a	c		📁
My Beloved	3/4 meter; phrases; form.	a, c, f				a, b	a, b, c	a, b	c		📁
Fresh Is the Maytime	Bright vocal tone quality; part independence; German pronunciation.	a, c, f				a, b	a, b, c	a, b, c	a, c		📁
Who Has Seen the Wind?	Sizzle rhythms; changing meters; strophic form.	a, c, f			a	a, b	a, b, c	a, b, c	a, c		
I Never Saw a Moor	Stepwise melodies; major tonality; sight-singing; musical characteristics that enhance mood.	a, c, f			a	a, b	a, b, c	a, b, c	c		📁
Arruru	Harmony in thirds; staccato and legato articulation; characteristics of Spanish music.	a, c, f				a, b	a, b, c	a, b, c	c	a	
Peace Today Descends from Heaven	2/2 and 3/2 meter; syllabic melismatic, and imitative treatment of text.	a, c, f		b	a	a, b	a, b, c	a, b	c	a	📁
Os Justi	Dark tone quality; correct diction.	a, b, c		b	a	a, b	a, b, c	a	c	c	📁
Dance on My Heart	Mixed meter; syncopated rhythms; two keys.	a, b, c				a, b	a, b, c	a, b	c	c	

T4

SECTION		National Standards									Teacher's Resources	
Selection	Concepts and Skills	1	2	3	4	5	6	7	8	9		
HISTORICAL LESSONS												
Renaissance Period	Understanding the devel-opment of choral music during the Renaissance period.						c		a, b, c, d, e	a, c, d	🎧 📽 📁	
I Go Before, My Charmer	Independent singing; imitative style; mixed meter (4/4 and 3/2).	a, c				a, b	b, c	a, b	c	a, c, d		
Baroque Period	Understanding the devel-opment of choral music during the Baroque period.			b			c		a, b	a, b, c	🎧 📽 📁	
O Death, None Could Conquer Thee	Minor key; independent singing; imitative; woven parts; German text; musi-cal enhancement of text.	a, c		b		a, b	a, b, c	a, b, c	c	a, c, d	📁	
Classical Period	Understanding the devel-opment of choral music during the Classical period.						a, b, c	a	a, b, c, d, e	a, c, d, e	🎧 📽 📁	
Holy, Holy, Holy	Contrasting dynamics; Latin text.	a, c, f				a, b	a, b	a	c	a, c, d	📁	
Romantic Period	Understanding the devel-opment of choral music during the Romantic period.						a, b, c	a	a, b, c, d, e	a, c, d, e	🎧 📽 📁	
Gruss	Melodic steps and leaps; melodic repetition; German language.	a, c, f		b		a, b	a, b	a	c	a, c, d	📁	
Contemporary Period	Understanding the develop-ment of choral music during the Contemporary period.		c		b, c		a, c		a, b		🎧 📽 📁	
Nigra Sum	Reading rhythm and pitch; rich tone quality; posture and breathing; Latin language.	a, c				a, b	a, b	a	c	a, c	📁	

ADDITIONAL PERFORMANCE SELECTIONS
Gloria
I Wonder as I Wander
Native American Spring Songs
Festival Alleluia
Wisdom and Understanding
Beautiful Yet Truthful

 The folder icon indicates that Teacher Resources (such as listening maps, blackline masters, etc.) are available to support the learning process.

 The transparency projector icon indicates that there are overhead transparencies available to enhance learning.

 The headset icon indicates that there are listening selections specifically chosen to aurally illustrate the music of the period.

The National Standards for Music Education were developed by the Music Educators National Conference. Reprinted by permission.

MUSIC

The study of music contributes in important ways to the quality of every student's life. Every musical work is a product of its time and place, although some works transcend their original settings and continue to appeal to humans through their timeless and universal attraction. Through singing, playing instruments, and composing, students can express themselves creatively, while a knowledge of notation and performance traditions enables them to learn new music independently throughout their lives. Skills in analysis, evaluation, and synthesis are important because they enable students to recognize and pursue excellence in their musical experiences and to understand and enrich their environment. Because music is an integral part of human history, the ability to listen with understanding is essential if students are to gain a broad cultural and historical perspective. The adult life of every student is enriched by the skills, knowledge, and habits acquired in the study of music.

Every course in music, including performance courses, should provide instruction in creating, performing, listening to, and analyzing music, in addition to focusing on its specific subject matter.

1. **Content Standard:** Singing, alone and with others, a varied repertoire of music

   Achievement Standard, Proficient:
   Students
   a. sing with *expression and *technical accuracy a large and varied repertoire of vocal literature with a *level of difficulty of 4, on a scale of 1 to 6, including some songs performed from memory
   b. sing music written in four parts, with and without accompaniment
   c. demonstrate well-developed ensemble skills

   Achievement Standard, Advanced:
   Students
   d. sing with expression and technical accuracy a large and varied repertoire of vocal literature with a level of difficulty of 5, on a scale of 1 to 6
   e. sing music written in more than four parts
   f. sing in small ensembles with one student on a part

2. **Content Standard:** Performing on instruments, alone and with others, a varied repertoire of music

   Achievement Standard, Proficient:
   Students
   a. perform with expression and technical accuracy a large and varied repertoire of instrumental literature with a level of difficulty of 4, on a scale of 1 to 6
   b. perform an appropriate part in an ensemble, demonstrating well-developed ensemble skills
   c. perform in small ensembles with one student on a part

   Achievement Standard, Advanced:
   Students
   d. perform with expression and technical accuracy a large and varied repertoire of instrumental literature with a level of difficulty of 5, on a scale of 1 to 6

3. **Content Standard:** Improvising melodies, variations, and accompaniments

   Achievement Standard, Proficient:
   Students
   a. improvise stylistically appropriate harmonizing parts
   b. improvise rhythmic and melodic variations on given pentatonic melodies and melodies in major and minor keys
   c. improvise original melodies over given chord progressions, each in a consistent *style, *meter, and *tonality

   Achievement Standard, Advanced:
   Students
   d. improvise stylistically appropriate harmonizing parts in a variety of styles
   e. improvise original melodies in a variety of styles, over given chord progressions, each in a consistent style, meter, and tonality

4. **Content Standard:** Composing and arranging music within specified guidelines

   Achievement Standard, Proficient:
   Students
   a. compose music in several distinct styles, demonstrating creativity in using the *elements of music for expressive effect
   b. arrange pieces for voices or instruments other than those for which the pieces were written in ways that preserve or enhance the expressive effect of the music
   c. compose and arrange music for voices and various acoustic and electronic instruments, demonstrating knowledge of the ranges and traditional usages of the sound sources

   Achievement Standard, Advanced:
   Students
   d. compose music, demonstrating imagination and technical skill in applying the principles of composition

5. **Content Standard:** Reading and notating music

   Achievement Standard, Proficient:
   Students
   a. demonstrate the ability to read an instrumental or vocal score of up to four *staves by describing how the elements of music are used

Students who participate in a choral or instrumental ensemble or class

   b. sightread, accurately and expressively, music with a level of difficulty of 3, on a scale of 1 to 6

Achievement Standard, Advanced:
Students

   c. demonstrate the ability to read a full instrumental or vocal score by describing how the elements of music are used and explaining all transpositions and clefs

   d. interpret nonstandard notation symbols used by some 20th-century [sic] composers

Students who participate in a choral or instrumental ensemble or class

   e. sightread, accurately and expressively, music with a level of difficulty of 4, on a scale of 1 to 6

6. Content Standard: Listening to, analyzing, and describing music

Achievement Standard, Proficient:
Students

   a. analyze aural examples of a varied repertoire of music, representing diverse *genres and cultures, by describing the uses of elements of music and expressive devices

   b. demonstrate extensive knowledge of the technical vocabulary of music

   c. identify and explain compositional devices and techniques used to provide unity and variety and tension and release in a musical work and give examples of other works that make similar uses of these devices and techniques

Achievement Standard, Advanced:
Students

   d. demonstrate the ability to perceive and remember music events by describing in detail significant events[3] occurring in a given aural example

   e. compare ways in which musical materials are used in a given example relative to ways in which they are used in other works of the same genre or style

   f. analyze and describe uses of the elements of music in a given work that make it unique, interesting, and expressive

7. Content Standard: Evaluating music and music performances

Achievement Standard, Proficient:
Students

   a. evolve specific criteria for making informed, critical evaluations of the quality and effectiveness of performances, compositions, arrangements, and improvisations and apply the criteria in their personal participation in music

   b. evaluate a performance, composition, arrangement, or improvisation by comparing it to similar or exemplary models

Achievement Standard, Advanced:
Students

   c. evaluate a given musical work in terms of its aesthetic qualities and explaining the musical means it uses to evoke feelings and emotions

8. Content Standard: Understanding relationships between music, the other arts, and disciplines outside the arts

Achievement Standard, Proficient:
Students

   a. explain how elements, artistic processes (such as imagination or craftsmanship), and organizational principles (such as unity and variety or repetition and contrast) are used in similar and distinctive ways in the various arts and cite examples

   b. compare characteristics of two or more arts within a particular historical period or style and cite examples from various cultures

   c. explain ways in which the principles and subject matter of various disciplines outside the arts are interrelated with those of music[4]

Achievement Standard, Advanced:
Students

   d. compare the uses of characteristic elements, artistic processes, and organizational principles among the arts in different historical periods and different cultures

   e. explain how the roles of creators, performers, and others involved in the production and presentation of the arts are similar to and different from one another in the various arts[5]

9. Content Standard: Understanding music in relation to history and culture

Achievement Standard, Proficient:
Students

   a. classify by genre or style and by historical period or culture unfamiliar but representative aural examples of music and explain the reasoning behind their classifications

   b. identify sources of American music genres,[6] trace the evolution of those genres, and cite well-known musicians associated with them

   c. identify various roles[7] that musicians perform, cite representative individuals who have functioned in each role, and describe their activities and achievements

Achievement Standard, Advanced:
Students

   d. identify and explain the stylistic features of a given musical work that serve to define its aesthetic tradition and its historical or cultural context

   e. identify and describe music genres or styles that show the influence of two or more cultural traditions, identify the cultural source of each influence, and trace the historical conditions that produced the synthesis of influences

Terms identified by an asterisk (*) are explained further in the glossary of *National Standards for Arts Education*, published by Music Educators National Conference, © 1994.

3. E.g., fugal entrances, chromatic modulations, developmental devices

4. E.g., language arts: compare the ability of music and literature to convey images, feelings, and meanings; physics: describe the physical basis of tone production in string, wind, percussion, and electronic instruments and the human voice and of the transmission and perception of sound

5. E.g., creators: painters, composers, choreographers, playwrights; performers: instrumentalists, singers, dancers, actors; others: conductors, costumers, directors, lighting designers

6. E.g., swing, Broadway musical, blues

7. E.g., entertainer, teacher, transmitter of cultural tradition

INTRODUCTION

Choral Connections is a four-level series designed to build music literacy and promote vocal development for all students and voice categories in grades 6–12. The series is a multi-textbook program supported with print materials and audio listening components. This enables students to develop music skills and conceptual understanding, and provides teachers with a flexible, integrated program.

Choral Connections presents beginning, intermediate, and advanced-level literature for various voice groupings: mixed, treble, and tenor-bass. This comprehensive choral music program includes student texts, teacher's wraparound editions, teacher's resource binders, and optional audio recordings designed to enhance student learning while reducing teacher preparation time.

Choral Connections is a curriculum that provides your students with a meaningful, motivating choral music experience, and will help you and your students make many connections. This choral music program …

Connects to . . . the National Standards

The National Standards are correlated to each lesson for quick-and-easy identification and reference. The performance standards related to singing and reading notations are explicit in each lesson, and by using the extension activities, teachers can connect the musical elements through improvisation and composition. Analysis and evaluation are an active and consistent component of lessons throughout the series. Additional student activities connect the lessons to the other arts, as well as provide a consistent historical and cultural context.

Connects to . . . Skill Development

Through vocal warm-ups and sight-singing exercises, students build vocal skills and master the vocal and sight-reading skills necessary to perform each piece. Rhythmic melodic and articulation skills are developed as needed for expressive interpretation. Students are encouraged to develop listening skills and use their perceptions to improve individual and group performance.

Connects to . . . Performance

Fundamental to a quality choral music program is the student performance of the literature. Student performance provides opportunities for young musicians to demonstrate musical growth, to gain personal satisfaction from achievement, and to experience the joy of music making. To help develop skills, *Choral Connections* provides exercises in warming-up and sight-singing which help prepare students to successfully sing each piece.

Conceptual understanding is built throughout the teaching/learning sequence, as the performance is prepared.

Connects to . . . the Arts and Other Curriculum Areas

Choral music provides a rich opportunity to connect the musical experience to other art disciplines (dance, visual arts, theatre), and to enhance the learning in other subject areas. It also provides a vehicle to help students gain knowledge and understanding of historical and cultural contexts across the curriculum.

PROGRAM PHILOSOPHY

Responding to Trends in Choral Music Education

Choral Connections is consistent with current educational philosophy that suggests:

- Performance is a product which should be the end result of a sound educational process, building conceptual understanding and skills as the performance is prepared.

- Students are motivated through materials and concepts that are connected to their own lives and interests, and they should be exposed to high-quality, challenging musical literature.

- Students learn best when they are active participants in their learning, and when they clearly understand and help set the goals of the learning process.

- Students understand concepts better when they have background information and skills which allow them to place their learning into a larger context.

- Students need to actively manipulate musical concepts and skills through improvisation and/or composition in order to fully assimilate and understand them.

- Students improve when they receive fair, honest, and meaningful feedback on their success and failures.

- Students should be encouraged to assess themselves individually and as a group, learning to receive and process constructive criticism, which leads to independent self-correction and decision making.

Scope and Depth of Music Literature

Most students are capable of performing more difficult material than they can sight-sing. Therefore, the literature in *Choral Connections* is drawn from many periods and styles of music. The wide range of composers and publishers ensures variety, and allows for various skills and concepts to be developed as each new piece is encountered. The high standards set in *Choral Connections* provides selections that are inherently powerful and exciting for students. Rather than working with contrived songs to teach skills or concepts, students learn through discovery and interaction with quality literature.

Addressing the National Standards

The National Standards for Arts Education, published in 1994 and reprinted with permission on pages T6–T7, launched a national effort to bring a new vision to arts education for all students. The National Standards provides a framework for achievement in music, with outcomes suggested for grades 4, 8, and 12. *Choral Connections* addresses the National Standards in several ways.

The most obvious and predominant National Standards addressed in choral ensemble are: (1) singing and (5) reading notation. However, good performance requires musical understanding which only occurs when all aspects of musical experience are incorporated. The preparation of vocal performance is enriched and deepened by involvement in all nine of the National Standards.

As you teach with *Choral Connections*, there will be frequent opportunities to deepen or extend student learning through: (2) playing through and creating accompaniments, (3) improvisation, (4) composition and arranging, (6) analyzing, (7) assessing, (8) linking with other arts and other academic disciplines, and (9) understanding historical and cultural contexts. The National Standards identified for each lesson and the Teacher's Wraparound extension activities help you become aware of the National Standards, and the depth of learning that will occur as you implement this choral music program.

Promoting Music Literacy

Choral Connections promotes music literacy. Literacy includes oral and aural aspects of music communication— reading, writing, singing, and listening. Each lesson begins with a *vocal warm-up* during which the student builds vocal skills through singing and listening. The lesson then proceeds to *sight-singing exercise(s)*, emphasizing reading development. These exercises may be rhythmic, melodic, harmonic, or a combination thereof; and emphasize the musical elements which are the objectives of the lesson. The sight-singing exercises lead directly into the *musical selection*. Students are encouraged to sight-sing in every lesson, and are assessed in an increasingly rigorous way as the text progresses from lesson to lesson. Sight-singing is approached as a challenge, and a means to the student's musical independence.

Literacy goes beyond reading pitch and rhythm and extends to the expressive elements of music and appropriate interpretation. Students are frequently asked to explore interpretive aspects of music making, and encouraged to suggest their own ideas for phrasing, dynamics, and so on. Through careful listening and constructive critique of their own work, they will gradually become more discriminating about the quality of performance, and the impact of that performance on the audience.

Including Authentic Student Assessment

The assessment in *Choral Connections* is systematic, objective, and authentic. There is ongoing *informal assessment* by teacher observation throughout the lessons. The text is written as a series of action steps for the student, so there are many opportunities for the director to hear and see the level of accomplishment.

Students will find objectives at the beginning of each lesson, and two types of assessment questions at the end. First, factual questions that check for understanding of concepts and skills are presented. Next, there are questions which require higher-level thinking through analysis, synthesis, and/or evaluation. The questions are always related directly to the lesson objectives, and allow students to demonstrate their understanding. By answering the questions, and demonstrating as suggested, students are involved in *self-assessment*. Many times students are involved in their own assessment, constructing rubrics or critiquing their performance, and identifying their next challenge.

The Teacher's Wraparound Edition includes lesson objectives and each lesson is taught so the concepts and skills are experienced, labeled, practiced, and reinforced, then measured through *formal assessment*. These assessment tasks match the lesson objectives, allowing students to demonstrate understanding of concepts and skills through performance, composition, or writing. Students are frequently required to produce audio or video tapes. This authentic assessment technique keeps testing of rote learning to a minimum, and allows measurement of higher-level application of knowledge and skills. A portfolio can be constructed for individual students, groups, or the whole ensemble; demonstrating growth over time.

Connecting the Arts and Other Curriculum Areas

Lessons in *Choral Connections* integrate many appropriate aspects of musical endeavor into the preparation of a piece. Students compose, improvise, conduct, read, write, sing, play, listen/analyze, and assess on an ongoing basis that builds understanding, as well as high standards. In this way, the many aspects of music are integrated for deeper learning.

As one of the arts, music can be linked to other arts through similarities and differences. Throughout the text, and particularly in the historical section, music is compared and contrasted with other arts to determine aspects of confluence, and the unique features of each art.

As one way of knowing about the world, music can be compared with concepts and skills from other disciplines as seemingly different as science or mathematics. The integrations between music and other disciplines are kept at the conceptual level, to maintain the integrity of both music and the other subjects. For example, mathematical sets of 2, 3, 4, 5, and 6 might be explored as a link to pieces with changing meter; or the text of a piece might become a starting point for exploration of tone painting. In Making Historical Connections, a time line connects music to social studies, and a list of authors for each period provides a link to language and literature.

Providing a Variety of Student Activities

Choral Connections begins with the choral experience, and builds understanding through active participation in a range of activities including singing, playing, improvising, composing, arranging, moving, writing, listening, analyzing, assessing, and connecting to cultures, periods, or disciplines. Lessons are written with the heading "Have students ... ," so there is always an emphasis on learning by doing.

Fitting Your Classroom Needs

Effective classrooms are characterized by many features, including student participation, a positive environment, clear sense of purpose, challenging content, high motivation, and a sense of sharing between teacher and student. These probably describe your choral ensemble classroom, and Choral Connections will allow you to make the most of these characteristics.

With Choral Connections, your students will be clear about purpose and direction, have multiple routes to success, and be involved in their own learning. The lessons will guide you and your students to share in the excitement of music making, and help you to grow together. The lessons are written the way you teach, and allow you to maintain and strengthen your routines, while adding flexibility, variety, and depth.

ORGANIZATION AND FLEXIBILITY

Each Choral Connections text is divided into the following sections:
- Preparatory Materials
- Lessons
- Making Historical Connections
- Additional Performance Selections

Preparatory Materials

Preparatory Materials introduce such basic concepts as notes and their values, rests and their values, rhythm patterns, breathing mechanics, solfège and hand signs, frequently found intervals, and pitch. Activities provided in the Teacher's Wraparound Edition suggest ways to use these materials as beginning exercises if your students have little or no music background. If your students are familiar with choral music, these Preparatory Materials can be both a quick review and a convenient reference.

Lessons

The Lessons are designed to be taught over a period of time. Each lesson is developed around a piece of quality authentic music literature. The lesson includes warmups, sight-singing, and rhythmic or melodic drills, all of which are directly related to preparation of the piece. Objectives are clearly stated, and a motivational opening activity or discussion is provided. The Teacher's Wraparound Edition outlines a carefully sequenced approach to the piece, with multiple entry points, and clear assessment opportunities to document achievement and growth.

Making Historical Connections

Making Historical Connections provides narrative, listening, and choral experiences for each of the five main historical periods. A narrative lesson provides a brief and interesting exposition of the main characteristics of the period, leading from the previous period, and outlining the achievements and new styles that emerged. A time line guides the student to place the musical characteristics into a larger historical and cultural context. The listening lesson includes both vocal and instrumental listening selections from the period, with listening maps and teacher wraparound lessons to guide student listening. The third component, a literature lesson, rounds out the student experience through a preparation of a piece to be sung from the period.

Additional Performance Selections

Additional Performance Selections provide a range of additional literature featuring popular pieces and multicultural selections that can be used to enhance the repertoire of your choral music performance. Warm-up exercises and suggestions to help you guide your students through the score are given, as well as program tips.

Lesson Objectives

Each lesson has objectives that emphasize and build conceptual understanding and skills across the lessons. The objectives in this book are:

LESSON OBJECTIVES	
LESSON 1 The Rainbow Comes and Goes	• Read and clap rhythms. • Use correct posture and breath support. • Aurally and visually identify and sing intervals of a major second, major third, perfect fourth, perfect fifth, major sixth, and an octave.
LESSON 2 Behold, a Tiny Baby!	• Read and sing in minor tonality. • Identify and sing melismatic and syllabic use of text. • Sing in two independent parts.
LESSON 3 Whispering Pine	• Read rhythms in 3/4 meter. • Identify, read, and sing pitches of the tonic triad. • Tune chord tones in three parts, including altered tones.
LESSON 4 Joseph's Lullaby	• Identify and sing using characteristics of choral blend. • Sing in a legato style. • Sight-sing using solfège and hand signs or numbers in F major.
LESSON 5 Welcome Now in Peace	• Sing, forming vowels correctly. • Identify, read, and sing in D minor. • Visually and aurally distinguish major and minor chords.
LESSON 6 Silent the Forests	• Sing softly with control. • Identify half steps and altered tones. • Sing descending chromatic passages.
LESSON 7 My Beloved	• Read and sing in 3/4 meter. • Identify parts of a phrase. • Sing, shaping phrases correctly. • Identify sections and form of a piece.
LESSON 8 Fresh Is the Maytime	• Sing with a bright vocal tone quality. • Sing a part independently with two other parts. • Sing with correct German pronunciation.
LESSON 9 Who Has Seen the Wind?	• Read and sizzle rhythms in changing meters. • Identify characteristics and sing in strophic form.
LESSON 10 I Never Saw a Moor	• Identify and sight-sing stepwise melodies. • Sight-sing in major tonality. • Identify musical characteristics that enhance the mood of a poem.
LESSON 11 Arruru	• Sing a harmony part in thirds. • Use staccato and legato articulation. • Identify some characteristics of Spanish music.
LESSON 12 Peace Today Descends from Heaven	• Read and perform in 2/2 and 3/2 meter. • Identify and perform syllabic, melismatic, and imitative passages.
LESSON 13 Os Justi	• Sing with a dark tone quality. • Sing with correct diction.

	LESSON OBJECTIVES (continued)
LESSON 14 Dance on My Heart	• Read rhythms in mixed meter. • Identify and perform syncopated rhythms. • Read and sing in two keys.
RENAISSANCE PERIOD	• Describe some characteristics of Renaissance architecture, fine art, and music. • Explain the difference between sacred music and secular music. • Discuss the major musical forms of the Renaissance period. • Identify some of the key composers of the Renaissance period.
I Go Before, My Charmer	• Sing one part independently with another part. • Identify and sing in imitative style. • Read and sing rhythms in mixed meter, with 4/4 and 3/2 meter.
BAROQUE PERIOD	• Describe the characteristics of Baroque architecture, fine art, and music. • Discuss the most important differences between Renaissance music and Baroque music. • Identify at least five new musical forms of the Baroque period. • Identify at least four major composers of the Baroque period.
O Death, None Could Conquer Thee	• Read and sing in a minor key. • Sing imitative and interweaving lines independently. • Sing using correct German pronunciation. • Identify musical enhancement of text.
CLASSICAL PERIOD	• Describe characteristics of architecture, fine art, and music of the Classical period. • Discuss the most important musical forms of the Classical period. • Identify the key Classical composers.
Holy, Holy, Holy	• Identify and perform contrasting dynamics. • Sing in three parts with homophonic and polyphonic (imitative) textures. • Sing correct Latin pronunciation.
ROMANTIC PERIOD	• Describe the characteristics of architecture, fine art, and music of the Romantic period. • Identify the major musical forms of the Romantic period. • Explain the importance of nationalism in Romantic music. • Identify at least three major Romantic composers.
Gruss	• Identify and sing melodic steps and leaps. • Identify melodic repetition between voice parts and sections of a piece. • Sing using correct German pronunciation.
CONTEMPORARY PERIOD	• Describe characteristics of architecture, fine art, and music of the Contemporary period. • Discuss at least five musical forms of the Contemporary period. • Identify at least four Contemporary composers. • Explain the importance of fusion in Contemporary music.
Nigra Sum	• Read and sing familiar rhythms and pitches using a rich tone quality. • Use correct posture and breathing. • Sing using correct Latin pronunciation.

Student Text

Lessons

The lessons, through which students systematically build musical skills and conceptual understanding, comprise the majority of the text. These lessons are structured as follows:

- **FOCUS** . . . tells the student the main concepts and skills addressed in the lesson. By having only a few main goals, students and teacher will keep focused on these objectives as work progresses.

- **SIGHT-SINGING EXERCISES** . . . build rhythmic, melodic, and expressive sight-singing skills through exercises that are directly related to some aspect of the upcoming musical selection. Through sight-singing practice every day, students gain confidence and skills to become independent readers.

- **CHORAL MUSIC TERMS** . . . give the students an opportunity to build a musical vocabulary essential for clarity of thought in communicating about music to others.

- **WARM-UP EXERCISES** . . . allow the students to warm-up their bodies, voices, and minds at the beginning of every class, while immediately exploring the main rhythmic, melodic, and skill issues that will arise in preparing the piece. These exercises are designed to sequentially build skills.

- **SINGING** . . . provides a motivating introduction to the piece of music, related to the student's perspective, which begins with a familiar idea and asks the student to think about or explore some concept or skill. Through interest and active participation, the student is then led logically into the piece.

- **STUDENT SELF-ASSESSMENT—HOW DID YOU DO?** . . . gives the student ways to assess accomplishment, growth, and needs, for both self and group. Beginning with recall, comprehension and application questions, the final questions ask for analysis, synthesis, and evaluation, guiding the student to higher-level thinking and the ability to self-assess.

Making Historical Connections

The Historical section of the text provides a survey of Western music history through exploration of the culture and music of the five overarching periods: Renaissance, Baroque, Classical, Renaissance, and Twentieth Century. Each period is addressed in the following ways:

- **Historical Narrative Lesson** . . . provides a brief, student-oriented historical context of the period through visual art, architecture, historical events, musical developments, artistic characteristics, musical personalities, and listening selections. Students are encouraged to imagine this time period as if they were living in it, and experience the music from the perspective of the period.

- **Historical Listening Lesson** . . . provides one choral and one instrumental listening selection, to give students an aural experience with the styles, sounds and forms of the period. Listening maps are provided in the Teacher's Resource Binder so the student can follow along as a visual guide to listening.

- **Historical Literature Lesson** . . . is paired with the narrative lesson for each period, and provides the opportunity to perform a piece with appropriate characteristics and performance style. The selected materials reflect the period, and provide a concrete example of those characteristics introduced in the previous narrative.

Additional Performance Selections

Each book provides additional performance selections which meet the various needs of the ensemble and director. Each selection is accompanied by a specifically designed warm-up to build appropriate vocal skills.

- **Patriotic Selections** . . . provide excellent openers and closers for concerts, and are particularly useful when performing at patriotic celebrations.

- **Holiday Selections** . . . acknowledge the need for performance literature appropriate for winter holidays and during the spring season.

- **Multicultural selections** . . . provide an opportunity for performance of music that has different criteria than Western art music, allowing exploration of different languages, vocal tone color, styles, movement, and cultural characteristics.

- **Proven Audience-Pleaser Selections** . . . allow you to round out your programs with appropriate rousing or sentimental pieces that provide a change of pace or variety.

Glossary

The glossary provides brief, accurate definitions of musical terms used in the text.

TEACHER'S WRAPAROUND EDITION

National Standards Connections

Choral Connections affords multiple opportunities to address the National Standards. Correlations between both lesson content, extension activities, and bottom-page activities are listed to show the relationship between lesson activities and the standards.

Teaching Sequence

Each lesson is organized to follow a logical progression from warm-ups through assessment, while providing maximum flexibility of use for your individual situation. Each lesson is linked to one musical selection, and provides learning opportunities based on the inherent concepts and skills required to understand and perform the piece. The lessons of the Teacher Wraparound Edition are structured as follows:

- **Focus** . . . gives the teacher a brief overview of concepts and skills which form the content of the objectives and assessments in the lesson.

- **Objectives** . . . provides concrete, measurable objectives allowing an interconnected approach to lesson segments. Each objective will be assessed in three ways during the lesson.

- **Choral Music Terms** . . . identifies the terms used during the lesson to build understanding and skills.

- **Warming Up** . . . includes rhythm and vocal warm-up exercises, as well as sight-singing exercises. The vocal warm-ups are designed to sequentially develop vocal skills, and start each class immediately with singing. The sight-singing exercises are designed to systematically build sight-singing skills, and lead directly into the upcoming piece. The purpose of each exercise is stated clearly for the teacher and student at the beginning of the lesson. These exercises may all be done before the piece is introduced, or they may be presented cumulatively, one each day, and concurrent with developing understanding of the piece.

- **Singing** . . . provides motivation and an entree to the piece of literature. Many different approaches are utilized, but they all draw the student into the piece through active learning and thinking.

- **Suggested Teaching Sequence** . . . returns to each warm-up activity and reviews, then guides you directly from the warm-up into the piece of literature. In this way, you have multiple entry points, so your approach is new and different each day the ensemble works on the piece. Specific rehearsal techniques, based on sight-singing, sectional work, and analysis of difficulties build skills and conceptual understanding as the performance is refined day after day. Each lesson includes recommended steps for organizing students into small groups by voice part to sight-sing the song separately before coming together in full ensemble to perform the selection.
- **Assessment** . . . provides Informal Assessment, Student Self-Assessment, and Individual Performance Assessment. There is appropriate assessment for each lesson objective.

Assessment

Informal Assessment is accomplished through teacher observation during the lesson. Each objective is observable, and the text indicates the checkpoint for teacher assessment.

Student Self-Assessment is accomplished through oral or written response to questions in the Student Text.

Individual Performance Assessment requires the student to demonstrate a skill or understanding through individual assessment. This is frequently done through audio or video taping, creation of rubrics to assess the quality of the performance, or a written exercise to demonstrate understanding. Individual Performance Assessment can be done by the teacher, student, peers, or a combination thereof. The tapes may be compiled into a portfolio which shows growth and development of understanding.

Extensions and Bottom-Page Activities

Extensions and bottom-page activities in each lesson afford a plethora of background information, teaching strategies, and enrichment opportunities.

- **Enrichment activities** in the side columns provide opportunities for movement, improvisation, composition, and analysis based on lesson and selection content.
- **Vocal development strategies** give detailed information about specific techniques that facilitate vocal production, style, and negotiation of difficult passages within the piece.
- **Music literacy strategies** help students expand their ability to read and analyze music.
- **Teaching strategies** are available to reinforce concepts or skills that may be difficult for students,

or elaborate on classroom management techniques suggested within the lesson.

- **More about** boxes provide background historical, cultural, and/or biographical information to give deeper understanding of the piece.
- **Curriculum connections** provide strategies to help students build bridges between music and other disciplines.

Performance Tips

In the Additional Performance Selection section, you are provided with performance suggestions that identify specific strategies that have worked successfully for choral music teachers, and potential "hot spots" you may need to address. Each selection is accompanied by a suggested program, including selections from the book. These recommendations should be extremely helpful for the beginning choral director, and provide many interesting alternatives for the experienced conductor.

TEACHER'S RESOURCE BINDER

The Teacher's Resource Binder contains teaching materials designed to reduce teacher preparation time and maximize students' learning. The following categories are provided to assist with meeting the individual needs and interests of your students.

Skill Masters. The *Skill Masters* provides sequential musical concepts that can be used to review and reinforce musical concepts in the areas of rhythm and pitch, music literacy, vocal development, and pronunciation guides.

Blackline Masters. The *Blackline Masters* are designed to enhance the concepts presented in the student text lessons.

Assessment. Assessment activities provide performance assessment criteria, rubrics, and other activity pages to help teachers with individual and group assessment.

Fine Art Transparencies. Full color overhead transparencies of the visual art pieces that introduce each of the historical sections are provided.

Listening Maps. Blackline masters of listening maps are provided and feature choral and instrumental selections. These help reinforce learning about the five major historical periods. Teachers may wish to make a transparency of the blackline master and have students follow along as the teacher points to the overhead transparency.

FEATURED LISTENING SELECTIONS

The Listening Program provides rich resources of sound to reinforce learning about the five major Western historical periods. Two selections for each period, one choral and the other instrumental, are accompanied by listening maps. At first, students listen as observers, watching the teacher guide their listening with a transparency of the map on the overhead projector. In the next listening, they then follow their own copies of the map, showing their ability to hear specific musical features. The Teacher's Wraparound Edition provides the CD number and track at point of use for each selection. Many more historical period examples are included on the CD sets than are referenced in the text. You're invited to use them to supplement and extend your lessons, or to have students create their own maps to creatively demonstrate understanding of musical and/or historical elements.

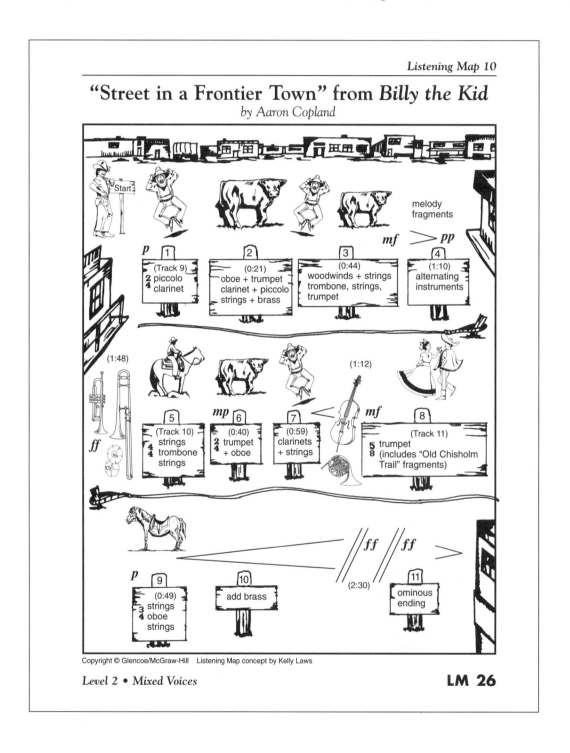

"Street in a Frontier Town" from *Billy the Kid*
by Aaron Copland

melody fragments

mf > *pp*

p

1
(Track 9)
2/4 piccolo clarinet

2
(0:21)
oboe + trumpet
clarinet + piccolo
strings + brass

3
(0:44)
woodwinds + strings
trombone, strings,
trumpet

4
(1:10)
alternating
instruments

(1:48)

ff

5
(Track 10)
4/4 strings
trombone
strings

mp

6
(0:40)
2/4 trumpet
+ oboe

7
(0:59)
clarinets
+ strings

(1:12)

mf

8
(Track 11)
5/8 trumpet
(includes "Old Chisholm
Trail" fragments)

ff *ff*

p

9
(0:49)
3/4 strings
oboe
strings

10
add brass

(2:30)

11
ominous
ending

Level 2 • Mixed Voices

LM 26

Choral Connections

Teacher's Wraparound Edition

LEVEL 3
TREBLE VOICES

GLENCOE

McGraw-Hill

New York, New York
Columbus, Ohio
Mission Hills, California
Peoria, Illinois

Cover Photos: Peter Samels Photography

Glencoe/McGraw-Hill

A Division of The McGraw-Hill Companies

Send all inquiries to:
Glencoe/McGraw-Hill
15319 Chatsworth Street
Mission Hills, California 91345

ISBN 0-02-655534-4 (Student's Edition)
ISBN 0-02-655557-3 (Teacher's Wraparound Edition)

Printed in the United States of America.

1 2 3 4 5 6 7 8 9   MAL   02 01 00 99 98 97 96

Meet the Authors

Senior Author

Mollie G. Tower—As Coordinator of Choral and General Music of the Austin Independent School District, Mollie Tower was recently nominated as "Administrator of the Year." She is very active in international, national, regional, and state music educators' organizations. Ms. Tower was contributing author, consultant, and reviewer for the elementary programs *Share the Music* and *Music and You.* Senior author of *Música para todos, Primary and Intermediate Dual Language Handbooks for Music Teachers,* she has also written and consulted for many other publications. A longtime advocate of music education, Mollie is a popular clinician who conducts workshops across the country.

Milton Pullen
Choir Director

After attending Texas A & I University where he acquired a Bachelor of Music Education in voice, Milton Pullen attended the University of Houston, where in 1976 he received a Master of Music in conducting. He has taught at the middle and high school level for 24 years and for the last seven years has taught at the university level. He is now Professor of Music and Director of Choirs at Pepperdine University in Malibu, California.

Ken Steele
Choir Director

Ken Steele has taught secondary choral music for 22 years, having directed choirs at the middle school and high school levels. He received the Bachelor of Music degree from Stetson University in DeLand, Florida, and went on to the University of Texas in Austin to earn the Master of Music in Choral Literature and Conducting in 1971, studying with Dr. Morris J. Beachy. A member of Texas Music Educators Association, Texas Choral Directors Association, Texas Music Adjudicators Association, and a lifetime member of the American Choral Directors Association, he is currently the choral director at L. C. Anderson High School, in Austin, Texas.

Gloria J. Stephens
Choir Director

With 23 years of teaching experience, Gloria Stephens is presently the Director of Choral Activities at Ryan High School in Denton, Texas. Mrs. Stephens earned her Bachelor of Music Education and Master of Music Education degrees from the University of North Texas in Denton. She has also done post-graduate work at Texas Woman's University in Denton, the University of Texas at Arlington, and Westminster Choir College in Princeton, New Jersey.

Consulting Author

Dr. Susan Snyder has taught all levels of vocal music over the last 25 years. She holds a B.S. in music education from the University of Connecticut and an M.A. from Montclair State College. She holds a Ph.D. in curriculum and instruction from the University of Connecticut and advanced professional certificates from Memphis State University and the University of Minnesota. Teaching at Hunter College and City University of New York, Dr. Snyder was coordinating author of the elementary music program, *Share the Music*, and a consultant on *Music and You*. She has published many articles on music education and integrated curriculum and is an active clinician, master teacher, and guest conductor.

Consultants

Choral Music
Stephan P. Barnicle
Choir Director
Simsbury High School
Simsbury, Connecticut

Vocal Development, Music Literacy
Katherine Saltzer Hickey, D.M.A.
University of California at Los Angeles
Los Angeles, California
Choir Director
Pacific Chorale Children's Choruses
Irvine, California

Music History
Dr. Kermit Peters
University of Nebraska at Omaha
College of Fine Arts
Department of Music
Omaha, Nebraska

Contributors/Teacher Reviewers

Dr. Anton Armstrong
Music Director and Conductor, St. Olaf Choir
St. Olaf College
Northfield, Minnesota

Jeanne Julseth-Heinrich
Choir Director
James Madison Middle School
Appleton, Wisconsin

Caroline Lyon
Ethnomusicologist
University of Texas at Austin
Austin, Texas

Caroline Minear
Supervisor
Orange County School District
Orlando, Florida

Judy Roberts
Choir Director
Central Junior High School
Moore, Oklahoma

Dr. A. Byron Smith
Choir Director
Lincoln High School
Tallahassee, Florida

Table of Contents

Preparatory Material

Using the Preparatory Material

The preparatory material found on these pages is designed to build a basic rhythmic, melodic, and sight-singing vocabulary. By working through the challenges, students will build the skills required for successful work in the upcoming lessons.

- If your students have little or no music background, take a day or two to introduce this musical vocabulary. Have them singing a few rounds to get them familiar with basic conducting, breathing, and working together.
- If your students have a rich music background, and have participated in a solid elementary and/or middle-school music program, review these challenges quickly, stopping to answer questions and clarify any misunderstandings. Then proceed to Lesson 1. Refer back to these pages during lessons when necessary.

Notes and Rests

The alignment of notes and rests on this page show the relationship between notes or rests of different value. Encourage students to learn these concepts early.

viii

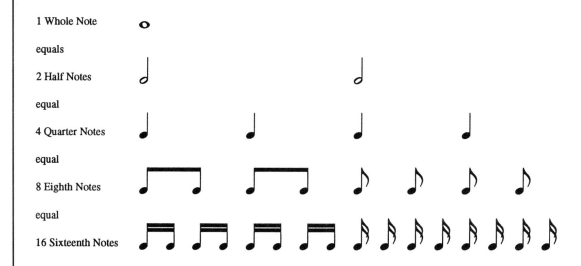

viii

Rhythm Challenge in 4/4 Time

Directions: Accurately count and/or perform the following rhythms without stopping!

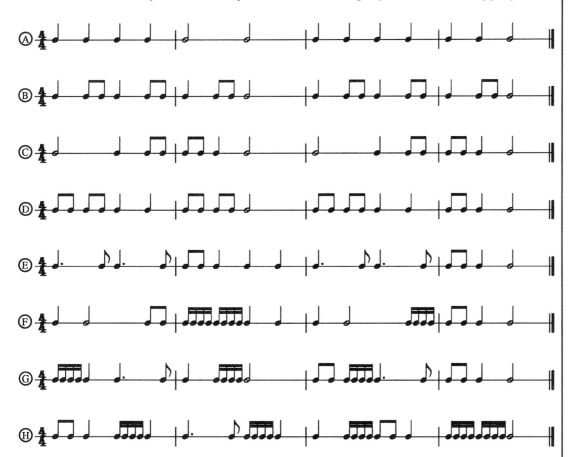

When presenting a rhythm challenge, allow students the chance to read through the whole challenge first, answering any questions, and helping them resolve any concerns. Then offer students the opportunity to perform the challenge without pressure.

At the beginning of the year, too much pressure for those with little or no previous experience might discourage them for the rest of their lives! Some techniques to consider are:

- Have students design a chart in the form of a graph with approximately 15 columns that represent the same number of trials. One or more trials can be attempted at the beginning of each class. After each trial, each student should record the number of the measure where the first mistake was made. After fifteen trials, most students should show, by a line graph, considerable improvement.
- Encourage students to design their own method of tracking their improvement. Students with access to computer programs might take it upon themselves to create a personalized chart for individuals or one for the entire class.

More Rhythm Challenges

To increase students' skill at reading rhythms, have them:

- Speak or clap each rhythm challenge as a group or in small ensembles, isolating and practicing measures and phrases that pose difficulty.
- Practice in small groups for a predetermined amount of time, such as 5 minutes. At the end of that time, assess rhythmic reading in one of the following ways: each student speaks and claps the pattern; each group speaks and claps the pattern; the whole class speaks and claps the pattern.
- Students should keep a record of their progress by recording the first measure where an error is made on each successive attempt.

Rhythm Challenge in 6/8 Time

Directions: Accurately count and/or perform the following rhythms without stopping!

x

Breathing Mechanics

Singing well requires good breath control. Support for singing comes from correct use of the breathing mechanism. Deep, controlled breathing is needed to sustain long phrases in one breath. Also, correct breathing will support higher, more difficult passages.

Posture
Posture is very important in breath support.
- Keep your body relaxed, but your backbone straight.
- To stretch your back: Bend over and slowly roll your back upward until you are standing straight again. Do this several times.
- Hold your rib cage high, but keep your shoulders low and relaxed.
- Facing front, keep your head level. Imagine you are suspended by a string attached to the very top of your head.
- When you stand, keep your knees relaxed, but do not "lock" them by pushing them all the way back. Keep your feet slightly apart.
- When you sit, keep both feet flat on the floor and sit forward on the edge of your chair.

Inhaling
- Expand the lungs out and down, pushing the diaphragm muscle down.
- Inhale silently without gasping or making any other noise.
- Keep the throat and neck muscles relaxed to maintain a feeling of space in the back of the mouth (picture a reverse megaphone).
- Imagine taking a cool sip of air through a straw, lifting the soft palate.
- Expand your entire waistline, keeping the chest high, and the shoulders relaxed, feeling the breath low in the body.

Breath Control
To help you develop breath control do the following:
- Hold one finger about six inches from your mouth imagining that your finger is a birthday candle. Now blow out a steady stream of air to blow out the flame of the candle.

Summary

STANDING
Feet slightly apart, one
slightly forward
Knees relaxed
Backbone straight
Rib cage high
Shoulders low
Head level

SITTING
Feet on the floor
Sit on edge of chair
Backbone straight
Rib cage high
Shoulders low
Head level

Breathing Mechanics
Remind students that vocal tone, resonance, and intonation are affected by posture and breathing. Basic singing posture is a relaxed, but firm, body stance. Have students read through the text on this page and practice correct posture and breathing.

Diaphragmatic Breathing
Have students:
- Feel the sensation of muscle expansion by placing thumbs above the small of the back with fingers pressing the top of the hips. Sip a long, deep breath and feel the action of the muscles.
- Feel the action of the diaphragm muscle by pressing the fingertips of both hands into the midsection of the torso just below the rib cage. Take a startled, quick surprise breath and feel the action of the muscle. Ask: Which way did it react?
- Feel the diaphragm muscle expand outward as they sip a long, cool breath.
- Pant like a dog or bark like a dog (arf and woof). Feel the action of the diaphragm.
- Use unvoiced consonants, such as sh, f, p, t, and k in different rhythms and tempo to create the diaphragmatic action.

What is Signing?

Signing in music describes the use of hand signals to represent relative sounds of pitches. The signs were used by Reverend John Curwen from a method developed by Sarah Glover of Norwich in the nineteenth century. The *do* is movable and was intended to teach beginners to sing accurate pitches. The system has been adopted by the Kodaly approach and Tonika-Do system in Germany.

Intervals

Help students remember intervals by relating them to the first two pitches of the following familiar songs:

Major 2nd —"Frère Jacques"
Major 3rd —"Taps"
Perfect 4th—"Here Comes the Bride"
Perfect 5th—"Twinkle, Twinkle Little Star"
Major 6th—"My Bonny Lies Over the Ocean"
Octave—"Somewhere, Over the Rainbow"

Have students:

- Challenge one another in pairs, one singing an interval, the other telling what interval was heard.
- Check any disagreements with another pair.
- Take turns singing intervals.

Composing with Frequently Found Intervals

Have students:

- Compose an exercise of eight measures, using at least three different intervals shown on this page.
- Notate their melodies.
- Describe their piece and perform it to a classmate.

xii

Solfège and Hand Signs

Solfège is a system designed to match notes on the staff with specific interval relationships. Hand signs provide additional reinforcement of the pitch relationships.

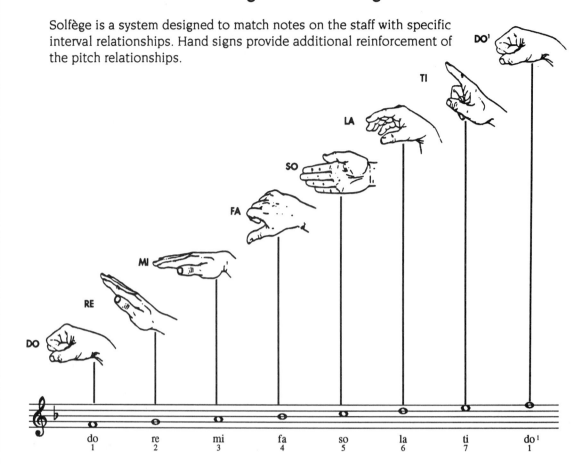

Frequently Found Intervals

An interval is the distance between two notes.

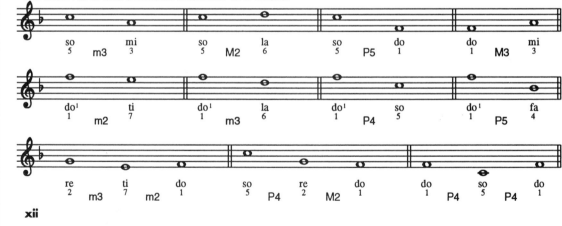

Pitch Challenge

Directions: Accurately sing each measure on solfège using hand signs and without stopping! During the measure of rest, look ahead to the next challenge.

Testing Pitch Accuracy

The best way to get better at pitch accuracy is to get feedback about which pitches are sung flat or sharp. The following activity is excellent for both the singer and listener. However, use confident volunteers only, as students will be critiqued openly in front of peers.

Have students:

- Listen to volunteers who are willing to have their pitch accuracy assessed as they perform the Pitch Challenge on this page with a partner.
- If the pitch is accurate, listeners should point thumbs to the side; if sharp, point thumbs up; and if flat, point thumbs down.
- Repeat this activity with as many volunteers as time permits.

Lessons

The Rainbow Comes and Goes

COMPOSER: Lois Land
TEXT: William Wordsworth

Focus

OVERVIEW
Posture; breath support; rhythms; intervals.

OBJECTIVES
After completing this lesson, students should be able to:
- Read and clap rhythms.
- Use correct posture and breath support.
- Aurally and visually identify and sing intervals of a major second, major third, perfect fourth, perfect fifth, major sixth, and an octave.

CHORAL MUSIC TERMS
Define the Choral Music Terms for students, giving pronunciation, and answering any questions that may arise.

Warming Up

Rhythm Drill
This Rhythm Drill is designed to prepare students to:
- Speak and clap known rhythms.
- Clap three independent parts.
- Be precise and accurate.

Have students:
- Read through the Rhythm Drill directions.
- Perform the drill.

2

The Rainbow Comes and Goes

CHORAL MUSIC TERMS
andante
breath support
intervals
major second
major sixth
major third
octave
perfect fifth
perfect fourth
posture
rhythm

COMPOSER: *Lois Land*
TEXT: *William Wordsworth (1770–1850)*

VOICING
SSA

PERFORMANCE STYLE
Andante
A cappella

FOCUS
- Read and clap rhythms.
- Use correct posture and breath support.
- Aurally and visually identify and sing intervals of a major second, major third, perfect fourth, perfect fifth, major sixth, and an octave.

Warming Up

Body Warm-Up
Use your imagination to do this warm-up. Stand, pretending a birthday cake is balanced on each shoulder. Be sure the cakes don't fall to the ground as you walk carefully around the room. You are demonstrating the correct posture for singing.

Rhythm Drill
Speak and clap each line separately. Then divide into sections and perform all three lines at the same time. Strive for precision and accuracy.

TEACHER'S RESOURCE BINDER

National Standards
Through involvement with this lesson, students should develop the following skills and concepts:
1. Singing, alone and with others, a varied repertoire of music. **(a, c)**
5. Reading and notating music. **(a, b)**
6. Listening to, analyzing, and describing music. **(b)**

Vocal Warm-Up

Sing this pattern on *loo*. Be sure to follow the dynamic markings to help connect the pitches.

Loo loo loo loo loo.

Sight-Singing

Sight-sing this exercise using solfège and hand signs or numbers. For variety, read the exercise in reverse after you have mastered reading it in the usual manner. Starting with the end pitch, sing the pitches going to the left until you reach the beginning pitch. Identify the intervals of major third, perfect fourth, perfect fifth, and an octave. Which are easy to sing in tune? Which are difficult?

Singing: "The Rainbow Comes and Goes"

A piano tuner is a technician who tunes a piano. By playing two pitches at the same time that are a fourth apart, the technician is able to tell whether the strings need tightening or loosening.

When you read music, the notes tell you how far apart the sounds are. This distance is called an interval. Just like the technician, you need to know what the interval sounds like to decide whether your pitch is in tune, or needs adjustment. When you use your voice as an instrument, you are your own technician.

Now turn to the music for "The Rainbow Comes and Goes" on page 4.

HOW DID YOU DO?

You have begun to learn how to "play your voice." Think about your preparation and performance of "The Rainbow Comes and Goes."

1. Define how good posture and good breath support are related. Can you have one without the other? Why or why not?

2. How would you describe your ability to perform rhythms? Demonstrate by clapping one line of the Rhythm Drill, first alone, then in a trio.

3. Describe an interval, then tell the difference between a major second, major third, perfect fourth, perfect fifth, major sixth, and an octave.

4. Working with a partner, arrange for one of you to sing the first pitch of an interval, in the sight-singing exercise; then point to the interval. Your partner will sing the second pitch to complete the interval. Both of you check the accuracy of the second pitch, adjusting it until it is correct. Switch roles after several ntervals.

5. What did you like about performing the piece "The Rainbow Comes and Goes"? Tell what you would change if you had the chance.

Composer Lois Land

Presently the organist and director of music at an Episcopal church in Garland, Texas, Lois B. Land is also an adjunct professor at Texas Christian University. She has published choral compositions and textbooks in music education. Her background also includes teaching music at both the high school and elementary levels.

Body Warm-Up

This Body Warm-Up is designed to prepare students to:
- Use correct posture for singing.

Have students:
- Read through the Body Warm-Up directions.
- Perform the excercise.

Vocal Warm-Up

This Vocal Warm-Up is designed to prepare students to:
- Sing with good breath support.
- Follow dynamic markings.
- Sing with legato articulation.

Have students:
- Read through the set of Vocal Warm-Up directions.
- Sing, following your demonstration.

Sight-Singing

This Sight-Singing exercise is designed to prepare students to:
- Sight-sing using solfège and hand signs or numbers.
- Identify and sing primary intervals.

Have students:
- Read through the Sight-Singing exercise directions.
- Read through each voice part rhythmically, using rhythm syllables.
- Sight-sing through each part separately using solfège and hand signs or numbers.
- Sight-sing the exercise in reverse for variety.
- Sing all parts together.

Singing: "The Rainbow Comes and Goes"

Identify concept of tuning and intervals. Have students:
- Read the text on page 3.
- Use Skill Master 9, *Intervals*, in the TRB to identify and practice hearing, writing and singing intervals of a major second, major third, perfect fourth, perfect fifth, major sixth, and an octave.

Suggested Teaching Sequence

1. Review Rhythm Drill.

Have students:

- Review the Rhythm Drill on page 2.
- Discuss ways to sustain the whole and half notes when clapping; for example, slide hands in a circular motion for the duration.
- Clap the patterns alone, and then together, striving for accuracy, precision, and balance.
- Clap the rhythm of "The Rainbow Comes and Goes" in sections, noticing when the meter changes.

2. Review Body Warm-Up.

Have students:

- Review the Body Warm-Up on page 2.
- Discuss correct posture for singing.

3. Review Vocal Warm-Up.

Have students:

- Review the Vocal Warm-Ups on page 3.
- Discuss correct breathing techniques for singing.
- Sing the Vocal Warm-Up, practicing these techniques and following the dynamic markings for a legato tone.

4. Review Sight-Singing.

Have students:

- Review the Sight-Singing exercise on page 3.
- Try it backward after mastering it forward.
- Identify the intervals, relating them to Skill Master 9, *Intervals,* in the TRB.
- Decide which intervals are easiest to sing and which require extra effort to sing in tune.

5. Sight-sing "The Rainbow Comes and Goes" using solfège and hand signs or numbers.

Have students:

- Divide into voice sections (SSA) and read each part using rhythm syllables.

4

The Rainbow Comes and Goes

Lois Land
William Wordsworth

SSA, U.I.L. Sight Reading Selection for Class AAA (SSA)

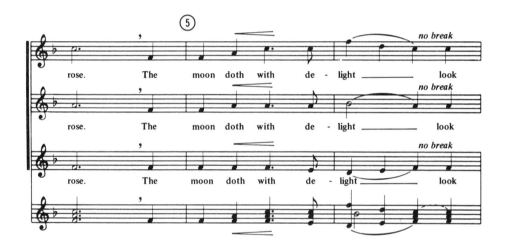

 VOCAL DEVELOPMENT

Have students:

- Modify the vowel sounds in *comes, lovely, sunshine, pass'd,* and *from.*
- Energize sustained tones by increasing the breath support and dynamic level.
- Enjoy the vowel resonance on *goes, rose, moon, know,* and *go.*
- Sustain phrases by staggering their breathing through the phrases.

- The *r* consonant after a vowel should be almost silent, as in *are, bare, waters, starry, glorious, birth, earth,* and *there.*
- Consider a single flip on the *r* consonant in *rainbow* and *rose.*
- Listen for diphthongs in *delight, round, night,* and *I.*
- Identify intervals and chords between the parts and tune them carefully.

- Still in sections, sing with solfège and hand signs or numbers, identifying and working on problem areas.
- Discuss proper posture and breathing.
- Sing the piece through using solfège and hand signs or numbers with full ensemble.
- Divide into sections and recite the text rhythmically for each voice part.
- Sing the piece through with text as a full ensemble, focusing on accurate rhythms, intervals, posture, and breathing.

Assessment

Informal Assessment

During this lesson, students showed the ability to:
- Read and clap rhythms with precision.
- Use correct posture and breathing for singing.
- Identify, read, and sing intervals.
- Sing accurate rhythms and intervals, using correct posture and breath support, in "The Rainbow Comes and Goes."

Student Self-Assessment

Have students:
- Evaluate their performance with the How Did You Do? section on page 3.
- Answer the questions individually. Discuss them in pairs or small groups and/or write their response.

Individual Performance Assessment

Have each student:
- Visually and aurally identify intervals of M2, M3, P4, P5, M6, and an octave that you write on the board.
- In a trio, clap the rhythm of each line of the Rhythm Drill, showing accuracy and rhythmic independence.
- In a double trio, sing measures 1–19 of "The Rainbow Comes and Goes," demonstrating correct posture, breathing, and rhythmic and intervallic accuracy.

CONNECTING THE ARTS
Creative Dance

If some ensemble members are familiar with modern or creative dance, have them:
- Create a dance that matches the mood and phrases of the piece.
- First explore possible movements that flow with the piece, using the rainbow, rose, moon, and waters on a starry night as images for impressionist or abstract interpretation.

- Move as the piece is sung (perhaps using an audio tape), exploring the phrase lengths and mood. Avoid movements that are too literal.
- Allow each phrase to rise and fall with the pitch and dynamics that shape it.
- Create a dance by choosing the best of their explored movements.
- Perform the dance with the piece.

Extension

Changing Meters

Have students:

- Read the rhythm of the piece as they tap the quarter note pulse throughout.
- Discuss which beats of each measure are accented in 4/4 (1st or 1st and 3rd), 6/4 (usually 1st and 4th, but sometimes 1st, 3rd, and 5th), and 5/4 (either 1st and 3rd or 1st and 4th).
- Look at specific measures in the piece to see which accented quarter notes make the most sense in each measure.
- Sing the piece with accuracy when changing meters.

Transferring the Rhythms to Unpitched Instruments

Have students:

- Review the three lines of rhythm in the Rhythm Drill, and then decide on an arrangement of these rhythms into a piece; for example: part 1, part 2, part 3, parts 1 and 2, parts 1 and 3, parts 2 and 3, all parts together.
- Clap this arrangement.
- Choose contrasting unpitched instrument sounds for this arrangement. (triangle, cabasa, hand drum)
- Practice until the arrangement is rhythmically accurate.

Writing a Melody to Wordsworth's Poetry

Have students:

- Discuss the general mood and meaning of the text.
- Discuss ways that the musical setting reinforces the poem's mood and message.
- Choose a Wordsworth poem, and first write a rhythm that fits the words, and then a melody for it.
- Add chords to harmonize their melody.

National Standards

The following National Standards are addressed through the Extension and bottom-page activities:

1. Singing, alone and with others, a varied repertoire of music. **(a, c)**
3. Improvising melodies, variations, and accompaniments. **(a)**
4. Composing and arranging music within specified guidelines. **(a, b)**
5. Reading and notating music. **(a)**
6. Listening to, analyzing, and describing music. **(a, c)**
8. Understanding relationships between music, the other arts, and disciplines outside the arts. **(a, b, d)**

Behold, a Tiny Baby!

Thirteenth Century Plainsong
ARRANGER: Mary Lynn Lightfoot

CHORAL MUSIC TERMS
independent singing
melismatic
minor tonality
syllabic

VOICING
SA

PERFORMANCE STYLE
With growing intensity
Accompanied by piano

FOCUS
- Read and sing in minor tonality.
- Identify and sing melismatic and syllabic use of text.
- Sing in two independent parts.

Warming Up

Body Warm-Ups
Do these exercises mirroring your teacher or a classmate. Warming up your body will help you produce a relaxed, full sound.
- Neck rolls: With a very, very loose and relaxed neck, slowly roll your head from side to side.
- Shoulder rolls: Very slowly and deliberately roll both shoulders forward five times, then backward five times.
- Head massage with shoulders: Pull shoulders up until they touch the bottom of your ears. Hold for a count of five, then quickly release the shoulders. Do this five times.
- Back massages: Massage the back of the person to your right. Then turn around and have them return the favor.

Vocal Warm-Up
Sing this example on *no*. First sing a separate *no* for each pitch, then sing the whole pattern on one *no*. Which way is syllabic, and which is melismatic? Repeat using *nay, nee, nie,* and *noo*. Keep your jaw relaxed as you form pure vowel sounds.

Lesson 2: Behold, a Tiny Baby! **7**

TEACHER'S RESOURCE BINDER
Blackline Master 1, *Syllabic and Melismatic Texts*

National Standards
Through involvement with this lesson, students should develop the following skills and concepts:
1. Singing, alone and with others, a varied repertoire of music. **(a, c)**
5. Reading and notating music. **(a, b)**
6. Listening to, analyzing, and describing music. **(a, b, c)**
7. Evaluating music and music performances. **(a)**

Behold, a Tiny Baby!

Thirteenth-Century Plainsong
ARRANGER: Mary Lynn Lightfoot

Focus

OVERVIEW
Minor tonality; independent two-part singing; melismatic and syllabic use of text.

OBJECTIVES
After completing this lesson, students should be able to:
- Read and sing in minor tonality.
- Identify and sing melismatic and syllabic use of text.
- Sing in two independent parts.

CHORAL MUSIC TERMS
Define the Choral Music Terms for students, giving pronunciation, and answering any questions that may arise.

Warming Up

Body Warm-Ups
These Body Warm-Ups are designed to prepare students to:
- Physically relax in preparation for singing.
Have students:
- Perform the Body Warm-Ups, following the directions.

Vocal Warm-Up

The Vocal Warm-Up on page 7 is designed to prepare students to:

- Sing in a minor tonality.
- Distinguish between melismatic and syllabic text.
- Sing vowels with a relaxed jaw.

Have students:

- Read through the Vocal Warm-Up directions.
- Sing, following your demonstration.

Sight-Singing

This Sight-Singing exercise is designed to prepare students to:

- Sight-sing using solfège and hand signs or numbers in minor.
- Identify *la* as the tonal center in minor.
- Sing in two parts, tuning intervals.
- Distinguish between melismatic and syllabic use of text.

Have students:

- Read through the Sight-Singing exercise directions.
- Read through each voice part rhythmically, using rhythm syllables.
- Sight-sing through each part separately using solfège and hand signs or numbers.
- Sing all parts together.

Singing: "Behold, a Tiny Baby!"

Identify melismatic and syllabic text. Have students:

- Read the text on page 8.
- Identify melismatic and syllabic use of text.
- Construct texts for the Sight-Singing exercise that are melismatic and syllabic.
- Find examples of syllabic and melismatic text on the first page of "Behold, a Tiny Baby!"

Sight-Singing

Sight-sing this exercise using solfège and hand signs or numbers. What is the tonal center, and what will you call it? First sight-sing the two lines separately, then sing them together. Tune the intervals carefully. Can you think of a text that would make this a melismatic passage? Now think of a different text that would be syllabic.

Singing: "Behold, a Tiny Baby!"

The text of a song can be *syllabic* or *melismatic*. Syllabic text provides one syllable for each pitch. There will be a syllable in the music under each notehead. Melismatic text provides one syllable which is held for over many pitches. You can find this easily in the music, because there is only one syllable in the text, and the notes have a slur connecting them.

Now turn to "Behold, a Tiny Baby!" on page 9 and find examples of syllabic and melismatic use of text.

HOW DID YOU DO?

You have increased your knowledge and skills during this lesson. Think about your preparation and performance of "Behold, a Tiny Baby!"

1. Name the tonal center of "Behold, a Tiny Baby!" and sing the first two phrases using solfège and hand signs or numbers to demonstrate your reading ability in this key.

2. Sing the Sight-Singing exercise with a classmate. How well can you hold your part when there are two different parts being sung? What is easy? What needs more work?

3. Tell the difference between melismatic and syllabic use of text, then sing one of each to demonstrate.

4. Describe your performance of "Behold, a Tiny Baby!" Tell what was good first, then what could use more work. Give examples to support your thoughts. What do you think you should work on next to improve?

5. Now describe the ensemble's performance.

Arranger Mary Lynn Lightfoot

In addition to her responsibilities as the choral editor for Heritage Music Press, Mary Lynn Lightfoot has published over 100 choral compositions. Named the Outstanding Young Woman of America in 1984, she was also the 1994 recipient of the Luther T. Spayde Award for Missouri Choral Conductor of the Year, presented by the Missouri American Choral Directors Association. When not busy with her composing and editorial duties, Mary Lynn frequently travels throughout the United States as a guest conductor and clinician.

Behold, a Tiny Baby!

Mary Lynn Lightfoot
Quoting Veni Emmanuel, Thirteenth Century Plainsong

Two-part Chorus and Piano*
M. L. L.

Duration: approx. 3:03
*Also available for SATB (H327) and Three-part Mixed (15/1028).

©MCMXCIII Heritage Music Press. All rights reserved. Reproduction of this publication
without permission of the publisher is a criminal offense subject to prosecution.
Printed in U.S.A.
Reproduced by permission. Permit # 275772.

Behold, a Tiny Baby! **9**

1. Review Body Warm-Ups.
Relax the body. Prepare to sing.
Have students:
- Review the Body Warm-Ups on page 7.
- Do each of the activities with a teacher or student leader.

2. Review Vocal Warm-Up.
Sing in minor. Distinguish between syllabic and melismatic use of text.
Have students:
- Review the Vocal Warm-Up on page 7.
- Discuss differences between syllabic and melismatic use of text.
- Identify the pure vowel sounds, and listen as they sing to unify the sound between singers.

MUSIC LITERACY

To help students expand their music literacy, have them:
- Analyze the thematic sections of the song (the three different songs combined).
- Conduct the mixed meter of the *Sing gloria!* section at measure 38.

3. Review Sight-Singing.

Sight-sing using solfège and hand signs or numbers. Identify *la* as the tonal center in minor. Sight-sing in two parts. Create melismatic and syllabic texts. Have students:

- Review the Sight-Singing exercise on page 8.
- Identify the tonal center in minor as *la*.
- Create texts that are either melismatic and syllabic.

4. Sight-sing "Behold, a Tiny Baby" using solfège and hand signs or numbers.

Have students:

- Divide into voice sections (SA) and read each part rhythmically, using rhythm syllables.
- Still in sections, sing with solfège and hand signs or numbers, identifying and working on problem areas.
- Sing the piece through using solfège and hand signs or numbers with full ensemble.
- Divide into sections and recite the text rhythmically for each voice part.
- Sing the piece through with text as a full ensemble, focusing on listening to the other part as they sing.

thee, O Is - ra - el!

Part II: *mp* 22

Be - hold _____ a ti-ny ba - by! Be-

hold _____ a ti-ny child! Be - hold _____ him in a

Part I: *mp*

man - ger, so peace - ful and _ so mild! The

CURRICULUM CONNECTIONS
Metaphors for Syllabic and Melismatic Structure

One generalization that can be extracted from syllabic and melismatic use of text is that sometimes there is a one-to-one correspondence between elements, and sometimes one part of an element fits with a whole set of the other element.

Have students:

- Suggest similar concepts in the other arts for syllabic and melismatic structure. For example:
—Visual art: A design that has circles inside boxes, one circle per box, is syllabic.

To encourage vocal development, have students:

- Demonstrate good vocal tone by singing tall vowels and alter (or modify) the vowel sounds when necessary, as in *come, Emmanuel, and, glory,* and *divine* (*dih-* rather than *dee-*).
- Energize sustained tones by increasing the breath support and dynamic level, especially on the word *behold,* sustaining it to its full value.
- Sustain phrases by staggering the breathing and moving forward through the phrases.
- Demonstrate the correct singing of the *r* consonant after a vowel. It should be almost silent, as in *manger* and *shepherds.*
- Listen for diphthongs (two vowel sounds when one vowel is written) in such words as *rejoice, child, mild, sign,* and *light.* Sing or sustain the first vowel sound and barely sing the second vowel sound with the next syllable.
- Identify intervals between the parts and tune them carefully. Note when the voices move from parts to unison singing to adjust the dynamic attack.

A design which has many circles in each box is melismatic.
—Dance: Movement that has one step for each pitch or beat is syllabic. Movement that flows over several pitches or beats is melismatic.

—Drama: The use of melisma provides dramatic effect on the stage. Try ways to say *Oh?* or *Hm,* or *Ooh* melismatically.
- Identify similar metaphors in other disciplines, such as science, math, history, and so on.

CONNECTING THE ARTS

Creative Dance

If some ensemble members are familiar with modern or creative dance, have them:

- Create a dance for each of the melodies in the piece that matches the phrase lengths.
- First explore possible movements as the piece is sung.

- Create a dance by choosing the best of their explored movements and deciding how they will be combined from measure 49 on.
- Perform the dance with the piece.

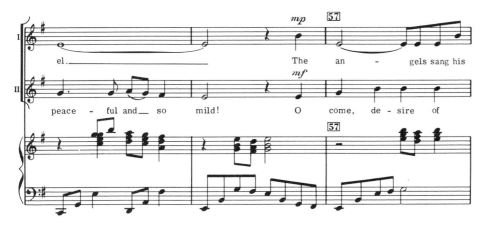

Behold, a Tiny Baby! **13**

Informal Assessment

During this lesson, students showed the ability to:

- Identify and sing melismatic and syllabic use of text in the Vocal Warm-Up exercise.
- Sing in two independent parts in the Sight-Singing exercise.
- Read and sing in minor in both the Vocal Warm-Up and Sight-Singing exercises.
- Sing in two-part harmony, in minor, with both melismatic and syllabic use of text, in "Behold, a Tiny Baby!"

Student Self-Assessment

Have students:

- Evaluate their performance with the How Did You Do? section on page 8.
- Answer the questions individually. Discuss them in pairs or small groups and/or write their responses on a sheet of paper.

Individual Performance Assessment

To further demonstrate accomplishment, have each student:

- Sing her voice part of the Sight-Singing exercise, demonstrating ability to read in minor using solfège and hand signs or numbers.
- In a double duo, sing measures 29–64 of "Behold a Tiny Baby!" demonstrating two-part singing.
- Using Blackline Master 1, *Syllabic and Melismatic Texts,* construct and write down two texts for a given melody, one melismatic and one syllabic.
  or
- Sing from measures 4–18, winking an eye to signal on melismatic segments.

MUSIC LITERACY
Creating a Chordal Accompaniment

Have students:

- Analyze the piano accompaniment for the piece, creating a skeleton of chord tones for each measure.
- Using resonator bells or handbells, play a chordal accompaniment by playing the chord tones once at the beginning of each measure.

- Adjust as necessary, and then add this accompaniment to the piece and piano accompaniment during the whole piece or just from measure 49 on.
- Compose an introduction and coda for bells as well, using a short progression of chords from the piece.

Extension

Phrasing

A phrase in music resembles a phrase of words, encompassing a complete thought. Usually a breath is taken after each phrase. Even among professional musicians, there is much discussion about what constitutes a phrase, and "Behold, a Tiny Baby!" is a perfect case for discussion. Have students:

- Read the text from measures 4–18, and then from 21–29.
- For each section, discuss where they think the word phrases are. (The most logical place for the first example is two phrases, although the first eight measures could be perceived as two shorter phrases. The second example could be seen as phrases of two measures, four measures, or one eight-measure phrase.)
- Sing each section and evaluate whether the musical phrases match the word phrases. (The musical phrases can also be perceived in the above ways.)
- Discuss which phrase organization makes the most sense. (Usually the longer phrases keep the piece from being too choppy, and maintain the integrity of the text and music.)
- Discuss how to shape these phrases. Some possibilities are by breathing only at the beginning and end, and making a small crescendo toward the peak of each phrase. At the section that begins with measure 22, small crescendos/decrescendos on each two measures can build with no new breath after the first and third patterns.

National Standards

The following National Standards are addressed through the Extension and bottom-page activities:

1. Singing, alone and with others, a varied repertoire of music. **(a, c)**
3. Improvising melodies, variations, and accompaniments. **(c)**
4. Composing and arranging music within specified guidelines. **(b)**
5. Reading and notating music. **(a)**
6. Listening to, analyzing, and describing music. **(a, b, c)**
8. Understanding relationships between music, the other arts, and disciplines outside the arts. **(a, b, d)**
9. Understanding music in relation to history and culture. **(a)**

HERITAGE MUSIC PRESS A DIVISION OF THE LORENZ CORPORATION • BOX 802 • DAYTON, OH 45401-0802

Behold, a Tiny Baby! **15**

Understanding Partner Songs

This piece is constructed from a thirteenth-century plainsong, and a newly composed partner song to harmonize with it. Partner songs are an easy way to ease into two-part independent singing. Have students:

- Identify the two songs within this piece.
- Describe how the two songs fit together as partners.
- Compare this organization to a crossword puzzle, with the two songs each making sense on its own horizontal plane, but also having matching chord tones in each measure, creating a vertical match. If they did not have the same harmonic structure, they would not work as partner songs.

Historical and Cultural Use of Syllabic and Melismatic Text

Throughout the history of Western art music, and in the music of all cultures, the use of text is one of the defining elements of style. Have students:

- Listen to vocal music from different periods and cultures as available.
- Analyze and describe the syllabic or melismatic use of text in the music.

Creating Syllabic and Melismatic Text

Have students:

- Choose a metric poem.
- Speak the poem's text syllabically, then melismatically.
- Set the poem as a speech piece, using both syllabic and melismatic segments.
- Allow a melody to emerge as the poem is repeated, until an improvised melody becomes apparent.

Whispering Pine

COMPOSER: Eugene Butler

TEXT: David Davenport

Focus

OVERVIEW
3/4 meter; tonic triad; tuning chords in three parts; altered tones.

OBJECTIVES
After completing this lesson, students should be able to:
- Read rhythms in 3/4 meter.
- Identify, read, and sing pitches of the tonic triad.
- Tune chord tones in three parts, including altered tones.

CHORAL MUSIC TERMS
Define the Choral Music Terms for students, giving pronunciation, and answering any questions that may arise.

Warming Up

Rhythm Drill
This Rhythm Drill is designed to prepare students to:
- Speak and clap rhythms in 3/4 meter.
- Perform parts independently.
- Feel phrases that are four measures long.

Have students:
- Read through the Rhythm Drill directions.
- Perform the drill.

LESSON 3

Whispering Pine

COMPOSER: *Eugene Butler*

TEXT: *David Davenport*

CHORAL MUSIC TERMS
altered tones
flat
sharp
3/4 meter
tonic chord
tonic triad
tuning

VOICING
SSA

PERFORMANCE STYLE
Liltingly
Accompanied by piano

FOCUS
- Read rhythms in 3/4 meter.
- Identify, read, and sing pitches of the tonic triad.
- Tune chord tones in three parts, including altered tones.

Warming Up

Rhythm Drill
Speak and clap the following rhythms, one line at a time. Then, in three groups, clap all three lines together. Notice the crescendo over the last four measures.

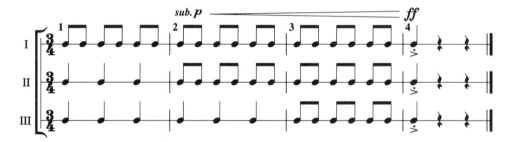

Vocal Warm-Up
Sing this exercise on *loo*. Move up by half steps on the repeats. Feel the tone high in the "mask of the face." Use correct breathing techniques for a steady stream of air under the tone as you sing. The pitches *so*, *mi*, and *do* make a major triad.

Loo, loo loo loo loo.

TEACHER'S RESOURCE BINDER
Blackline Master 2, *Constructing Major Chords*

National Standards
In this lesson, students should develop the following skills and concepts:
1. Singing a varied repertoire of music. **(a, c)**
3. Improvising melodies, variations, and accompaniments. **(b)**
5. Reading and notating music. **(a, b)**
6. Listening to, analyzing, and describing music. **(a, b)**
7. Evaluating music and music performances. **(a)**

Sight-Singing

Notice the altered tone, E♭. Call it *te* instead of *ti*. First all sight-sing each part separately, then divide into three voice parts and sing them together. Sing this exercise slowly, tuning each chord before moving on to the next.

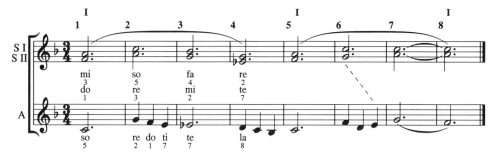

Singing: "Whispering Pine"

The most important tones in most melodies are those of the tonic triad—*do, mi,* and *so.* In the key of F, these are:

do   mi   so   do¹

Sing these pitches as a partner points to them in random order. Keep going until you can hear the sound inside your head before you sing it.

Now choose one pitch for each section of the ensemble to sing. You are making a chord singing all the tones at once. On a signal, change to the pitch of the section to your right. Keep changing and tuning the chords.

Now turn to the music for "Whispering Pine" on page 18.

HOW DID YOU DO?

? ? ?

When you understand the musical concepts within a piece of music, you can make good judgments about how to perform it. Think about your preparation and performance of "Whispering Pine."

1. Tell what the meter of the piece is and what the numbers mean. Clap one line of the Rhythm Drill to show how well you read in this meter.
2. Sing pitches of the tonic triad as a partner points to them in random order. Which intervals are easy to sing? Which are more difficult?

3. Sing measures 5–13 of "Whispering Pine" in a small group, tuning the chords.
4. How well can you sing chord tones when there are other parts being sung? Is it easier by yourself, or with your whole section singing? What might you do to improve this skill?

Lesson 3: Whispering Pine **17**

Vocal Warm-Up
This Vocal Warm-Up is designed to prepare students to:
- Sing the tonic triad.
- Focus the tone in the "mask of the face."
- Use good breath support when singing.

Have students:
- Read through the Vocal Warm-Up directions.
- Sing, following your demonstration.

Sight-Singing
These Sight-Singing exercises are designed to prepare students to:
- Sight-sing in F major and 3/4 meter, using solfège and hand signs or numbers.
- Tune pitches in unison.
- Tune chord tones.
- Identify altered tones.

Have students:
- Read through the Sight-Singing exercise directions.
- Read through each voice part rhythmically, using rhythm syllables.
- Sight-sing through each part separately using solfège and hand signs or numbers.
- Sing all parts together.

Singing: "Whispering Pine"

Identify and sing pitches of the tonic triad. Have students:
- Read the text on page 17.
- Identify the pitches of the tonic chord as *do, mi,* and *so.*
- Sing pitches of the tonic triad as a partner points to pitches randomly.
- Sing the tonic triad as a chord.
- Change pitches, taking the pitch of the section to the right, every time the teacher or a classmate gives a signal such as snapping fingers or clapping hands.

Whispering Pine

Eugene Butler
David N. Davenport

Suggested Teaching Sequence

1. Review Rhythm Drill.

Read and clap rhythms in 3/4 meter. Have students:

- Review the Rhythm Drill on page 16.
- Identify 3/4 meter.
- Clap lines separately and together.
- Add the crescendo on the last four measures, working to get gradually louder.

2. Review Vocal Warm-Up.

Place tone in the head. Identify pitches of the tonic triad. Have students:

- Review the Vocal Warm-Up on page 16.
- Discuss placement of the tone in the "mask of the face," and review good breathing technique.
- Identify the pitches as part of the tonic triad.

SSA Accompanied

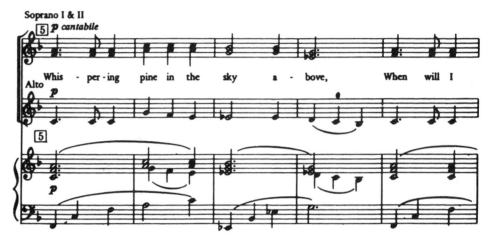

Whis-per-ing pine in the sky a-bove, When will I

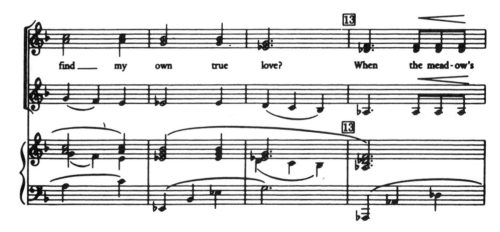

find ___ my own true love? When the mead-ow's

18 *Choral Connections   Level 3 Treble Voices*

TEACHING STRATEGY

Reading the Tones of the Tonic Triad and Rhythms in 3/4 Meter

If students are not accustomed to reading the tones of the tonic triad or rhythms in 3/4 meter, have them:

- Refer to the Skill Master 13, *Pitch Challenge,* in the TRB, and 3/4 meter patterns written on the board.

- Practice these challenges until the pitches and/or rhythms become natural and comfortable.

- Return to "Whispering Pine" and read the piece.

3. Review Sight-Singing.

Read and sing in 3/4 meter, using solfège and hand signs or numbers. Read pitches of the tonic triad. Tune chords. Identify altered tones. Have students:

- Review the Sight-Singing exercise on page 17.
- Tune pitches carefully, both in unison and in chords.
- Discuss altered tones, defining a flat and sharp. (A flat lowers the pitch a half step; a sharp raises the pitch a half step.)
- Review the notation of "Whispering Pine" to find other altered pitches.

4. Sight-sing "Whispering Pine" using solfège and hand signs or numbers.

Have students:

- Divide into voice sections (SSA) and read each part rhythmically, using rhythm syllables.
- Still in sections, sight-sing the pitches on *loo,* working on difficult areas.
- Sing the piece through on *loo* with full ensemble.
- Divide into sections and recite the text rhythmically for each voice part.
- Sing the piece through with text as a full ensemble.

Form

Have students:

- Preview the notation of "Whispering Pine," identifying large sections. (measures 5–20, 21–36, 37–52, 53–end)
- Describe similarities and differences between sections.
- Use these similarities to help learn the piece.

Creating an Accompaniment

Have students:

- Compose a simple chordal accompaniment for melodic instruments, using one triad for each measure of the piece.
- Play the accompaniment as the ensemble sings.

VOCAL DEVELOPMENT

To encourage vocal development, have students:

- Demonstrate good vocal tone by singing tall vowels and alter (or modify) the vowel sounds when necessary, as in *above* and *love*.
- Energize sustained tones by increasing the breath support and dynamic level.
- Sustain phrases by staggering the breathing and moving forward through the eight-bar phrases.
- Increase intensity on repeated notes to feel the forward movement of the melodic lines.
- Demonstrate the correct singing of the *r* consonant after a vowel. It should be almost silent, as in *whispering*, *appear*, *winter*, and *where*.
- Listen for diphthongs (two vowel sounds when one vowel is written) in such words as *pine, sky, I, find, my,* and *mine*. Sing or sustain the first vowel sound and barely sing the second vowel sound with the next syllable.
- Identify intervals and chords between the parts and tune them carefully. Note when the voices move from parts to unison and adjust the dynamic attack.

MUSIC LITERACY
Expressive Elements and Phrasing

To help students expand their music literacy, have them:

- Read the text of "Whispering Pines," identifying where the natural phrase breaks are and, therefore, where they should breathe.
- Look through the notation, finding all dynamic and tempo markings.
- Sing through the phrases, following the dynamic and tempo markings.
- Analyze the thematic sections of the song.
- Contrast the quarter note rhythms against the dotted rhythms in the different parts. Be precise.

Will he be tru - ly mine? _____
Will he _____ be mine? _____

Tell me your se - cret, Whis - per to me,

When will it be, when will it be? _____

Whispering Pine **21**

Informal Assessment

During this lesson, students showed the ability to:

- Speak and clap rhythms in 3/4 meter in the Rhythm Drill.
- Identify and sing pitches of the tonic chord in the Vocal Warm-Up exercise.
- Identify and sing altered tones in the Sight-Singing exercise.
- Sing in three parts in 3/4 meter, including pitches of the tonic triad and altered tones, in "Whispering Pine."

Student Self-Assessment

Have students:

- Evaluate their performance with the How Did You Do? section on page 17.
- Answer the questions individually. Discuss them in pairs or small groups and/or write their responses on a sheet of paper.

Individual Performance Assessment

To further demonstrate accomplishment, have each student:

- In a trio, clap the rhythms of Rhythm Drill in three parts into a tape recorder in an isolated space.
- Sing pitches of the tonic triad as a partner randomly points to the notes.
- In a double trio, sing measures 5–13 into a tape recorder in an isolated space, and then listen individually to the tape and write a self-critique, evaluating what was good and what needs to be improved.

CURRICULUM CONNECTIONS
Creative Writing

Have students:

- Read the text of the piece without the rhythm, and discuss who might be singing these words, recognizing that it is a question that is unanswered.
- Discuss whether they would ask the whispering pine the same question or something different.

- Write a new text in the rhythm of the piece, either constructing a new question or providing a second verse in which the whispering pine provides an answer to the original question.
- Discuss how their text will change the performance parameters of the piece. (funny, cynical, sad, happy)

Extension

Major Chords
Have students:
- Use Blackline Master 2, *Constructing Major Chords,* to identify the characteristics of a major chord.
- Identify the major chords built on major scale tones as I (built on *do*), IV (built on *fa*), and V (built on *so*).
- Sing these chords, one chord tone at a time: *do-mi-so-mi-do; fa-la-do-la-fa;* and *so-ti-re-ti-so.*
- Find the major chords on F, E♭, D♭, and C in "Whispering Pine."

Improvising an Accompaniment to the Sight-Singing Exercise with I, IV, and V Chords
Have students:
- Recall the major chord tones for the I, IV, and V chords in F major.
- Divide into two groups. Half will sing the chord roots, each for one measure, as others sing Sight-Singing exercise 1. (This is experiential, and there will be many mistakes and adjustments.) Switch parts.
- Write the chord roots for each measure on the board.
- Half improvise an accompaniment using chord tones as the other half sings the exercise. Switch.

Composing a Tonic Chord Melody
Have students:
- Listen to a bass line played with just the tonic chord, implying a specific style. (Try a walking bass or a jazzy rhythm in octaves.)
- Begin improvising on just *do,* then add *mi, so,* and high *do,* using all tones of the tonic chord.
- Compose a short melody in the style of the bass line, and write it down.
- Use these as warm-up exercises at the beginning of class.

National Standards
The following National Standards are addressed through the Extension and bottom-page activities:
1. Singing, alone and with others, a varied repertoire of music. **(a, c)**
3. Improvising melodies, variations, and accompaniments. **(a, b, e)**
4. Composing and arranging music within specified guidelines. **(b)**
5. Reading and notating music. **(a)**
6. Listening to, analyzing, and describing music. **(a, b, c)**
8. Understanding relationships between music, the other arts, and disciplines outside the arts. **(c)**

Joseph's Lullaby

COMPOSER: *Russell Schulz-Widmar*
TEXT: *Fred Pratt Green*

CHORAL MUSIC TERMS

choral blend
diction
fermata
intonation
legato style
tone quality

VOICING
| Three-part choir

PERFORMANCE STYLE
| Gently moving
| Accompanied by organ or keyboard

FOCUS
- Identify and sing using characteristics of choral blend.
- Sing in a legato style.
- Sight-sing using solfège and hand signs or numbers in F major.

Warming Up

 Vocal Warm-Up
Sing this Warm-Up using solfège and hand signs or numbers. Hold the tied notes to their full value, slowly raising hands and arms from the center of the body up and out. Next, in three parts, each begin one measure after the other. Hold the *fermata* until all parts get there, then continue to the end together

Lesson 4: Joseph's Lullaby **23**

TEACHER'S RESOURCE BINDER
Blackline Master 3, *Characteristics of Choral Blend*
Blackline Master 4, *Solfège in F Major*
Blackling Master 5, *Assessing Choral Blend*

National Standards
In this lesson, students should develop the following skills and concepts:
1. Singing, alone and with others, a varied repertoire of music. **(a, c, f)**
3. Improvising melodies, variations, and accompaniments. **(b)**
5. Reading and notating music. **(a, b)**
6. Listening to, analyzing, and describing music. **(b)**
7. Evaluating music and performances. **(a)**

Joseph's Lullaby

COMPOSER: Russell Schulz-Widmar
TEXT: Fred Pratt Green

Focus

OVERVIEW
Characteristics of choral blend; legato style; sight-singing in F major.

OBJECTIVES
After completing this lesson, students should be able to:
- Identify and sing using characteristics of choral blend.
- Sing in a legato style.
- Sight-sing using solfège and hand signs or numbers in F major.

CHORAL MUSIC TERMS
Define the Choral Music Terms for students, giving pronunciation, and answering any questions that may arise.

Warming Up

Vocal Warm-Up
This Vocal Warm-Up is designed to prepare students to:
- Read pitches in F major.
- Sing held and tied notes for their full value.
- Sing staggered entrances as they will occur in "Joseph's Lullaby."
Have students:
- Read through the Vocal Warm-Up directions.
- Sing, following your demonstration.

Sight-Singing

This Sight-Singing exercise is designed to prepare students to:
- Identify the syllable names of pitches in F major.
- Sight-sing in F major using solfège and hand signs or numbers.
- Sing with good tuning and balance.
- Sing independently with one or two other parts.

Have students:
- Read through the Sight-Singing exercise directions.
- Read through each voice part rhythmically, using rhythm syllables.
- Sight-sing through each part separately using solfège and hand signs or numbers, listening for tuning and balance.
- Sing all parts together, using a legato style.

Singing: "Joseph's Lullaby"

Identify choral blend. Have students:
- Read the text on page 24.
- Using Blackline Master 3, *Characteristics of Choral Blend,* identify the three characteristics of choral blend as tone quality, diction, and intonation.
- Discuss what each of these characteristics demands of the singer. (tone quality—a well-supported sound; diction—unified vowels and clearly articulated consonants; intonation—correct, in-tune pitch matching)

Sight-Singing

Identify the solfège syllables, then sight-sing in three parts. Listen for tuning and balance. Notice the division of the soprano part in measure 10. Use a legato style.

Singing: "Joseph's Lullaby"

Think about the lullabies you have heard in the past. Many of them have the characteristics of successful choral blend (tone quality, diction, and intonation). Many lullabies you have probably heard are of a gentle, soothing nature. Yet others, such as African lullabies, often have a lively, bouncing nature.

Look at the music for "Joseph's Lullaby" on page 25 and decide whether this piece is soothing or lively.

Now sing the music for "Joseph's Lullaby."

 HOW DID YOU DO?

Were you able to tell the kind of performance the composer had in mind by looking at the music for the piece? Think about your preparation and performance of "Joseph's Lullaby."
1. Did you sing legato? Did the choir? How do you know?
2. Sing from measure 77 to the end of "Joseph's Lullaby" with two classmates demonstrating blended sound.

3. Tell the three characteristics of a blended sound.
4. Can you sight-sing in F major? What pitches or intervals are the most difficult to sing in tune?
5. What did you do well in this lesson? What do you still need to improve?

 "Joseph's Lullaby"

The text for this piece originates from a Christmas card that the author, Fred Pratt Green, sent to the composer, Russell Schulz-Widmar.

Fred Pratt Green

Born in 1903 in Liverpool, England, Fred Pratt Green studied theology at Didsbury Theological College in Manchester, England. In 1928 he was ordained in the Methodist church. With an interest in language arts, he wrote both plays and poetry. Since his retirement in 1969, he has been an active poet and hymn writer.

For Karl

Joseph's Lullaby

Russell Schulz-Widmar
Fred Pratt Green

Three-part Choir (or Choirs)
Any Combination with Organ Accompaniment

*The indications Solo and Ped. apply when this music is performed on the organ.

Joseph's Lullaby **25**

MUSIC LITERACY

To help students expand their music literacy, have them:

- In pairs, write the F major scale on a staff.
- Select one partner to point to the pitches randomly, first in stepwise order, then using some skips, creating melodic fragments or phrases. The other partner will sing the pitches, correcting mistakes using a pitched instrument for reference. Switch roles.
- Both listen for melodic phrases that might become part of a melody they could write for others to sight-sing.
- Analyze the thematic sections.
- Contrast the rhythms of the quarter notes against the dotted rhythms in the different parts. Be precise.

Suggested Teaching Sequence

1. Review Vocal Warm-Up.

Hold out sustained pitches. Practice staggered entrances. Have students:

- Review the Vocal Warm-Up on page 23, using arm motions for sustained and tied notes.
- Sing again in three-part canon, moving on from the fermata as one voice part.

2. Review Sight-Singing.

Practice identifying and singing intervals of thirds and sixths. Have students:

- Use Blackline Master 4, *Solfège in F Major,* to practice singing pitches using solfège and hand signs until they are familiar.
- Review the Sight-Singing exercise on page 24, using solfège and hand signs or numbers.
- Review characteristics of a blended sound and legato articulation.
- Sing again, applying characteristics of a blended sound.

3. Sight-sing "Joseph's Lullaby" using solfège and hand signs or numbers.

Have students:

- Divide into voice sections and read each part rhythmically, using rhythm syllables.
- Still in sections, sing with solfège and hand signs or numbers, identifying and working on problem areas.
- Sing the piece through using solfège and hand signs or numbers with full ensemble.
- Divide into sections and recite the text rhythmically for each voice part.
- Sing the piece through with text as a full ensemble.

4. Sing with legato sound.

Have students:

- Speak the first verse of "Joseph's Lullaby," stopping at the end of each phrase.
- Sing the melody of each phrase on *loo,* connecting each pitch to the next for a legato, smooth style.
- Sing the piece through, attending to legato, smooth singing.

5. Work on the blended sound.

Have students:

- Review the characteristics of choral blend. (tone quality, diction, and intonation)
- Discuss how these characteristics can each be applied to the first phrase of the piece.
- Sing each phrase of the first verse with these three characteristics.
- Discuss any problem areas.

* The soloist should be at the same voice range as the chorus.

Joseph's Lullaby

 TEACHING STRATEGY

Singing A Cappella in Verse 2

Have students:

- Work on parts in separate sections until the pitches are automatic.
- Put the parts together and secure the pitches before addressing any other interpretive ideas.

Joseph's Lullaby

To encourage vocal development, have students:

- Demonstrate good vocal tone by singing tall vowels and alter (or modify) the vowel sounds when necessary, as in *man, son, passing,* and *one* (*awh* vowel sound instead of the *uh* sound).
- Energize sustained tones by increasing the breath support and dynamic level.
- Sustain phrases by staggering the breathing and moving forward through the eight-bar phrases.
- Increase intensity on repeated notes to feel forward movement of the melodic lines.
- Demonstrate the correct singing of the *r* consonant after a vowel. It should be almost silent, as in *winter's, here, there's, where, trav'lers, dark, are, star,* and *manger.*
- Listen for diphthongs (two vowel sounds when one vowel is written) in such words as *sound, now, light,* and *high.* Sing or sustain the first vowel sound and barely sing the second vowel sound with the next syllable.
- Identify melodic (linear) and harmonic (vertical) intervals between the parts and tune them carefully. Note when the voices move from parts to unison singing to adjust the dynamic attack.
- Analyze the coda section (special ending) for the canon.

TEACHING STRATEGY
Diction

Clear pronunciation requires attention to both vowels and consonants. Have students:

- Identify the need for clear diction so the audience will know what the piece is about.
- Discuss what choral techniques will produce clear diction. (unified vowels, crisp beginning and ending consonants, quick mouth movement to shape sounds)
- Sing through slowly with only vowels, keeping the jaw lowered, blending the vowels.
- Add the consonants, keeping the vowels blended.
- Sing through the piece attending to clear diction.

Assessment

Informal Assessment

During this lesson, students showed the ability to:

- Sing held and tied notes in the Vocal Warm-Up exercise.
- Identify pitches and sight-sing in F major in the Sight-Singing exercise.
- Sing, using legato style in the Sight-Singing exercise.
- Sing, using legato style and characteristics of choral blend in "Joseph's Lullaby."

Student Self-Assessment

Have students:

- Evaluate their performance with the How Did You Do? section on page 24.
- Answer the questions individually. Discuss them in pairs or small groups and/or write their responses on a sheet of paper.

Individual Performance Assessment

To further demonstrate accomplishment, have each student:

- In a duet, sing verse 3 into a tape recorder in an isolated space, demonstrating legato style.
- Identify and define the characteristics of a blended choral sound using Blackline Master 5, *Assessing Choral Blend*.
- Sight-sing one of three parts in F major on Blackline Master 5, *Assessing Choral Blend*.

Joseph's Lullaby

CURRICULUM CONNECTIONS

Journalism

Have students:

- Discuss the role of a music critic.
- Review some of the critiques found in the local paper.
- Write a critique of their taped performance or the recorded performance of "Joseph's Lullaby," identifying the good characteristics and making suggestions for improvement.
- Send the best critiques to the school newspaper for publication.

Joseph's Lullaby

National Standards

The following National Standards are addressed through the Extension and bottom-page activities:

1. Singing, alone and with others, a varied repertoire of music. **(a, c)**
3. Improvising melodies, variations, and accompaniments. **(b, e)**
4. Composing and arranging music within specified guidelines. **(a, b)**
5. Reading and notating music. **(a, b)**
6. Listening to, analyzing, and describing music. **(a, b, c)**
8. Understanding relationships between music, the other arts, and disciplines outside the arts. **(d, e)**
9. Understanding music in relation to history and culture. **(c)**

Extension

Expressive Elements and Phrasing

Have students:

- Read the text of "Joseph's Lullaby," identifying where the natural phrase breaks are and, therefore, where they should breathe. (Encourage 8-measure phrases, rather than 4.)
- Look through the notation, finding all dynamic and tempo markings.
- Perform the piece, singing through the phrases and following the dynamic and tempo markings.

Composing in Folk-Song Style

The form and style of "Joseph's Lullaby" are folk-like with even, flowing phrases, stepwise melodies in a narrow range, and AB form. There is unison, part, and solo singing. Have students:

- Identify and list these characteristics.
- With a partner or small group, create their own folk-type melody.
- Add text and/or accompaniment if they wish.
- Perform their pieces.

Finding Well-Blended Skill in Other Disciplines

The skill of vocal blending is essential for a good choral sound. Have students:

- Think of analogies for well-blended sound in other arts, such as dance, visual art, and drama.
- Determine whether there are different criteria for well-blended sound in the music of different periods or cultures.
- Identify times when an unblended sound is desirable.
- Write a paragraph explaining their opinions regarding the well-blended artist.

Welcome Now in Peace

Israeli Folk Song
ARRANGER: Judith Herrington

Focus

OVERVIEW
Vowel formation; read and sing in D minor; distinguish between major and minor chords.

OBJECTIVES
After completing this lesson, students should be able to:
- Sing, forming vowels correctly.
- Identify, read, and sing in D minor.
- Visually and aurally distinguish between major and minor chords.

CHORAL MUSIC TERMS
Define the Choral Music Terms for students, giving pronunciation, and answering any questions that may arise.

Warming Up

Vocal Warm-Ups
These Vocal Warm-Ups are designed to prepare students to:
- Read pitches in F major and D minor.
- Distinguish between major and minor.
- Blend through uniformity of vowels.

Have students:
- Read through the set of Vocal Warm-Up directions.
- Sing, following your demonstration.

30

Welcome Now in Peace

Israeli Folk Song
ARRANGER: Judith Herrington

CHORAL MUSIC TERMS
chord
major
minor
vowels

VOICING
Two-part

PERFORMANCE STYLE
Expressively
Accompanied by piano

FOCUS
- Form vowels correctly for effective diction while singing.
- Identify, read, and sing in D minor.
- Visually and aurally distinguish major and minor chords.

Warming Up

 Vocal Warm-Ups
Sing these Warm-Ups first using solfège and hand signs or numbers, then on the syllable provided. Can you tell which is in major or minor? Work for focused vowels throughout. Move up or down by half steps as you repeat.

Neh   neh   nah   nah   neh   nah   noh   nah   noh   neh. _____

Neh   neh   nah   nah   neh   nah   noh   nah   noh   neh. _____

TEACHER'S RESOURCE BINDER
Blackline Master 6, *Translation of "Welcome Now in Peace"*
Blackline Master 7, *Solfège in D Minor*
Blackline Master 8, *Assessing Major and Minor Chords*

National Standards
1. Singing a varied repertoire of music. **(a, c)**
3. Improvising melodies, variations, and accompaniments. **(b)**
5. Reading and notating music. **(a, b)**
6. Listening to, analyzing, and describing music. **(b)**
7. Evaluating music and performances. **(a)**
8. Understanding relationships between music, the other arts, and disciplines outside the arts. **(c)**

Sight-Singing

Clap the rhythm, then sight-sing this exercise using solfège and hand signs or numbers. Each measure uses tones from the F major or D minor chords. Can you tell which? Sing this exercise in a two-part round, one measure apart.

Singing: "Welcome Now in Peace"

Do you know any words that mean more than one thing? The Hebrew word "shalom" means hello, welcome, farewell, and peace. When you meet a friend or leave a friend, you can use "shalom" as a greeting or a farewell.

Read the text of "Welcome Now in Peace." Discuss the pronunciation of the Hebrew words.

Now turn to the music for "Welcome Now in Peace" on page 32.

HOW DID YOU DO?

? ? ?

Just as you weave friendships, your voices wove together in greetings and wishes for peace. Think about your preparation and performance of "Welcome Now in Peace."
1. Explain how you know if a piece is in D minor or F major? What is the same? What is different? How well can you sight-sing in D minor?
2. Can you hear the difference between major and minor chords? Listen to some chords and signal, pointing your thumb up for major and down for minor, whether they are major or minor.

3. Listen to a small ensemble sing this piece. Describe the criteria you will use to evaluate whether the performance was well done. What will you listen for? What will you look for?
4. Write an assessment of your performance of "Welcome Now in Peace." Tell what you have learned, what you do well, what needs work, and how you feel about your performance of this piece.

Sight-Singing

This Sight-Singing exercise is designed to prepare students to:
- Sing ascending and descending thirds in broken chords.
- Sing major and minor chords.
- Distinguish between major and minor chords.
- Sing in imitative style.

Have students:
- Read through the Sight-Singing exercise directions.
- Read through each voice part rhythmically, clapping the rhythm.
- Sight-sing through each part separately using solfège and hand signs or numbers.
- Sing all parts together.

Singing: "Welcome Now in Peace"

Learn the meaning and pronunciation of the text. Have students:
- Read the text on page 31.
- Identify words that have more than one meaning. *(aloha)*
- Identify the meaning of *shalom.*
- Using Blackline Master 6, *Translation of "Welcome Now in Peace,"* understand the Hebrew text.

TEACHING STRATEGY

Sight-Singing in D Minor

Have students:
- In pairs, write the D minor scale on a staff.
- Select one partner to point to the pitches randomly, first in stepwise order, then using some skips, creating melodic fragments or phrases. The other partner will sing the pitches that are pointed to

as accurately as possible, with both correcting mistakes using a pitched instrument for reference. Switch roles.
- Both listen for melodic fragments or phrases that might become part of a melody they could write for others to sight-sing.

Welcome Now in Peace

Hevenu Shalom A'leychem

Israeli Folksong
Vocal Arr. Judith Herrington
Accompaniment Sara Glick

Suggested Teaching Sequence

1. Review Vocal Warm-Ups.

Read in major and minor. Work on focused vowels. Have students:

- Review the Vocal Warm-Ups on page 30.
- Identify and distinguish between F major and D minor.
- Identify strategies for forming focused, uniform vowels. (lower the larynx, raise the soft palate, keep the throat open, listen to surrounding singers and adjust the vowel tone)
- Create their own vowel combinations to practice uniform vowels.
- Using Blackline Master 7, *Solfège in D Minor,* practice singing pitches using solfège and hand signs until they are familiar.

2. Review Sight-Singing.

Read and distinguish between F major and D minor chords. Sing in canon. Have students:

- Review the Sight-Singing exercise on page 31, using solfège and hand signs or numbers.
- Using Skill Master 11, *Major and Minor Scales or Modes,* in the TRB, learn to identify major and minor chords by sight and sound.
- Tell what chord is used in each measure.
- Sing the exercise in two-part canon.

Two-part, Accompanied

"Welcome Now in Peace"

This arrangement of a well-known Israeli folk song begins with a gesture of welcome, and then moves into a dance of celebration. The piano accompaniment evokes the klezmer instrumental style that contrasts with the weaving of the vocal lines. Tell students that *shalom* has several meanings in the Hebrew language: hello, welcome, farewell, and peace.

Welcome Now in Peace **33**

3. Sight-sing "Welcome Now in Peace" using solfège and hand signs or numbers.

Have students:

- Divide into voice sections and read each part rhythmically, using rhythm syllables.
- Still in sections, sing with solfège and hand signs or numbers, identifying and working on problem areas.
- Identify the key as D minor, and the first pitch as low *mi*.
- Sing the piece through using solfège and hand signs or numbers with full ensemble.

4. Work on vowels.

Have students:

- Review the techniques for blended, unified vowel sound.
- Apply these techniques to "Welcome Now in Peace," one phrase at a time. (Notice that it is important to blend vowels regardless of the language that is being sung.)
- Sing the piece, focusing on blending vowels.

VOCAL DEVELOPMENT

To encourage vocal development, have students:

- Demonstrate good vocal tone by singing tall vowels and alter (or modify) the vowel sounds when necessary.
- Energize the ascending chords with increased breath support and a crescendo. Propel the sound with the rhythm.
- Energize sustained tones by increasing the breath support and dynamic level.
- Sustain phrases by staggering the breathing and moving forward through the eight-bar phrases.
- Increase intensity on repeated notes to feel forward movement of the melodic lines.
- Emphasize the two-note phrases by "leaning into" the first note and tapering off on the second note. Demonstrate this by moving the arm with the palm up in a circular motion away from the body, ending with the palm down to sense the feeling of loud to soft. Actually sing the loud-soft motion.
- Listen for diphthongs (two vowel sounds when one vowel is written) in words such as *now*. Sing or sustain the first vowel sound and barely sing the second vowel sound with the next syllable.
- Identify melodic (linear) and harmonic (vertical) intervals between the parts and tune them carefully. Note when the voices move from parts to unison singing to adjust the dynamic attack.

MUSIC LITERACY

To help students expand their music literacy, have them:

- Conduct and speak the rhythms of the piece precisely.
- Breathe on the rest of the pickup entrance in order to perform it precisely.
- Compose their own short melodies using the pitches of the F major chord, D minor chord, or both.
- Add the low *so* and high *do* if they wish.
- Use these melodies as warm-up exercises.

*Omit lower 3rd of R. H. if desired.

Assessment

Informal Assessment

During this lesson, students showed the ability to:

- Identify and use blended, uniform vowels in the Vocal Warm-Ups.
- Identify pitches and sight-sing in D minor in the Vocal Warm-Ups.
- Distinguish between F major and D minor chord tones in the Sight-Singing exercise.
- Sing in D minor with blended, uniform vowels in "Welcome Now in Peace."

Student Self-Assessment

Have students:

- Evaluate their performance with the How Did You Do? section on page 31.
- Answer the questions individually. Discuss them in pairs or small groups and/or write their responses on a sheet of paper.

Individual Performance Assessment

To further demonstrate accomplishment, have each student:

- In a double duet, sing measures 2–11 into a tape recorder in an isolated space, demonstrating blended, uniform vowels.
- Using Blackline Master 8, *Assessing Major and Minor Chords,* identify major and minor chords visually and aurally.

CURRICULUM CONNECTIONS

Dramatic Reading

Have students:

- Choose a dramatic poem from English class or a famous speech from history.
- Discuss and identify how the work with vowels in this lesson might relate to these pieces of literature.
- Practice and recite their piece, focusing on good vowel production and clear diction.

Extension

Phrasing and Interweaving Voices

Have students:

- Read through the piece, deciding where the phrases begin and end.
- Notice the interweaving of voices in each phrase.
- Decide where the high point of each phrase is, and then sing each phrase, building toward the high point and releasing the energy by the end of the phrase.
- Sing the piece through, focusing on phrase building and interweaving of voices.
- Find other examples of phrases that can be built and sung this way in pieces already learned.

Creating a Dance

Have students:

- Create a dance using the following elements as guidelines:
—Formation: circle or broken circle
—Hand formation: hands held up, arms forming a "w," or hold handkerchiefs or tambourines between each of dancers
—Possible steps: forward, back, step-touch, grapevine (side, cross front, side, cross back)
—Keep one movement for at least a phrase, or perhaps a section.
- Explain how the dance matches the music.

*optional meno mosso (♩ = 58) with
poco a poco accel. at measure 45

National Standards

The following National Standards are addressed through the Extension and bottom-page activities:

1. Singing, alone and with others, a varied repertoire of music. **(a, c)**
3. Improvising melodies, variations, and accompaniments. **(b)**
4. Composing and arranging music within specified guidelines. **(a, b)**
5. Reading and notating music. **(a, b)**
6. Listening to, analyzing, and describing music. **(a, b, c)**
8. Understanding relationships between music, the other arts, and disciplines outside the arts. **(a, c)**
9. Understanding music in relation to history and culture. **(a, b, d, e)**

The Klezmer Tradition

The accompaniment of this piece is written in klezmer instrumental style, which began in Eastern Europe and has become one style associated with Jewish music of today. Have students:

- Research the klezmer style, using written sources, recordings, and local community resources.
- Identify characteristics of the style.
- If there is a local klezmer band, invite them to perform for the ensemble or accompany this piece in performance.
- Write a clarinet part in klezmer style to go with this piece.

Silent the Forests

COMPOSER: Eugene Butler

TEXT: Torquato Tasso
(1544–1595)

Focus

OVERVIEW
Breath control; half steps and altered tones; chromatic passages.

OBJECTIVES
After completing this lesson, students should be able to:
- Sing softly with control.
- Identify and define half steps and altered tones.
- Sing descending chromatic passages.

CHORAL MUSIC TERMS
Define the Choral Music Terms for students, giving pronunciation, and answering any questions that may arise.

Warming Up

Vocal Warm-Ups
These Vocal Warm-Ups are designed to prepare students to:
- "Wake up" the diaphragm.
- Use diaphragmatic breathing.
- Sing softly with control.
- Perform staccato and legato articulation.

Have students:
- Read through the set of Vocal Warm-Up directions.
- Sing, following your demonstration.

Silent the Forests

COMPOSER: *Eugene Butler*
TEXT: *Torquato Tasso (1544-1595)*

CHORAL MUSIC TERMS
altered tones
chromatic
flat (♭)
half steps
natural (♮)
sharp (♯)

VOICING
SSA

PERFORMANCE STYLE
Slowly
Accompanied by piano

FOCUS
- Sing softly with control.
- Identify half steps and altered tones.
- Sing descending chromatic passages.

Warming Up

 Vocal Warm-Up 1
Practice your breathing. Place your hands on your waist with your elbows pointed outward. Now bark like a) a Pekingese, b) a fox terrier, and c) a Great Dane. Describe the difference in each sound. Did you notice your hands moving at your waist as your diaphragm supported the sound?

 Vocal Warm-Up 2
Sing this exercise using staccato articulation, supported from the diaphragm. Can you sing it softly, and still use support and control? Move up by a half step on each repeat.

Ho ho ho ho ho.

 Sight-Singing 1
Read and sing each of these exercises alone using solfège and hand signs or numbers, then divide into four groups and sing them together.

TEACHER'S RESOURCE BINDER
Blackline Master 9, *Altered Tones*
Blackline Master 10, *Altered Tones and Chromatic Passages*

National Standards
1. Singing, alone and with others, a varied repertoire of music. **(a, c, f)**
5. Reading and notating music. **(a, b)**
6. Listening to, analyzing, and describing music. **(a, b)**
7. Evaluating music and music performances. **(a)**
8. Understanding relationships between music, the other arts, and disciplines outside the arts. **(c)**

Sight-Singing 2

First look at the alto line, and notice the altered tones and descending chromatic line. Sing *si* for D♯ and *fi* for C♯. First, all sight-sing each part separately. Then divide into three voice parts and sing them together. Tune each pitch carefully before moving on.

Singing: "Silent the Forests"

Think of the difference between quiet and silent. Is a forest ever silent? Is the sea ever waveless? Are winds ever completely at peace? When are words quiet? When are they silent?

Read the text of "Silent the Forests." What is the author trying to say?

Now turn to the music for "Silent the Forests" on page 40.

HOW DID YOU DO?

? ?

When you sing softly, there is a mystery that helps convey quiet—even silent— thoughts. Think about your preparation and performance of "Silent the Forests."

1. Describe how you control your breath when you sing softly. Sing your line from measures 3–6 in "Silent the Forests" to demonstrate.

2. Explain what it means if a tone is "altered?" Point to some altered tones in "Silent the Forests."

3. Tell what a sharp, a flat, and a natural do to a note.

4. Define a chromatic passage. Sing the line with the chromatic passage in the Sight-Singing 2 exercise.

5. Do you think the music enhances the text of "Silent the Forests"? Why or why not? Be specific about your reasons, and give examples.

Lesson 6: Silent the Forests **39**

Sight-Singing

The Sight-Singing exercises are designed to prepare students to:
- Sing the following intervals in tune: *do-fa, so-do, so₁-do,* and *so-mi*.
- Sight-sing and sing in two parts.
- Identify altered tones and chromatic passages.
- Tune in three parts.

Have students:
- Read through the directions for both Sight-Singing exercises.
- Read through each voice part rhythmically, using rhythm syllables.
- Sight-sing through each part separately using solfège and hand signs or numbers.
- Sing all parts together.

Singing: "Silent the Forests"

Analyze the text for meaning. Have students:
- Read the text on page 39.
- Answer the questions.
- Read the text of the song.
- Discuss the meaning. (The forest, sea, and caves have secrets that are not told by their natural sounds. Love is like those secrets that cannot be, or are not yet, expressed in sound.)

TEACHING STRATEGY
Diaphragmatic Breathing

Have students:
- Remember that the diaphragm muscle is the major muscle of inhalation. In deep breathing, the diaphragm muscle descends approximately four inches.
- While lying on the back with legs drawn up toward the body, note the rise and fall of the abdomen during natural breathing.
- Use imagery to accomplish deep breathing, such as blowing up an inner tube or a balloon, or sipping in a thick milk shake.
- While pressing on the diaphragmatic muscle, take a surprise breath and feel the movement of the diaphragm.

Suggested Teaching Sequence

1. Review Vocal Warm-Ups.

Have students:

- Review the Vocal Warm-Ups on page 38.
- Feel the diaphragmatic breathing at the waist.
- Describe the difference between the three barks, from low to high, and identify the need to use diaphragmatic breathing for all three.
- Use diaphragmatic breathing to sing the Warm-Up 2 exercise with staccato and legato articulation.

2. Review Sight-Singing.

Have students:

- Review the Sight-Singing exercises on pages 38 and 39, using solfège and hand signs or numbers.
- Using Blackline Master 9, *Altered Tones,* learn about sharps, flats, naturals, and chromatic passages.
- Identify the alto line of Sight-Singing exercise 2 as a chromatic passage.
- Sing the exercise, listening carefully to the altered tones.
- Look at their voice part in "Silent the Forests" for altered tones.

3. Sight-sing "Silent the Forests" using solfège and hand signs or numbers.

Have students:

- Divide into voice sections (SSA) and read each part rhythmically, using rhythm syllables.
- Still in sections, sing with solfège and hand signs or numbers, identifying and working on problem areas.
- Sing the piece through using solfège and hand signs or numbers with full ensemble.
- Divide into sections and recite the text rhythmically for each voice part.
- Sing the piece through with text as a full ensemble.

Silent the Forests

Eugene Butler

Torquato Tasso

SSA Women's Voices Accompanied

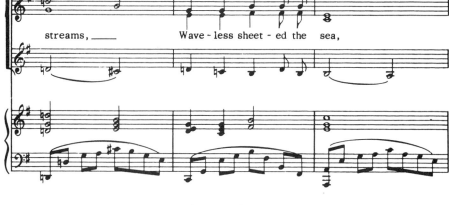

 TEACHING STRATEGY

Connecting Tones

Have students:

- Sing the first four measures of "Silent the Forests."
- Practice connecting one tone to the next by making slight dynamic increases on each tone.
- Determine if this technique helped them to keep their tone energized.

 MUSIC LITERACY

To help students expand their music literacy, have them:

- Conduct and speak the rhythms precisely.
- Breathe on the rest of the pickup entrance in order to perform it precisely.

VOCAL DEVELOPMENT

Have students:

- Demonstrate good vocal tone by singing tall vowels and alter (or modify) the vowel sounds when necessary.
- Energize the ascending chords with increased breath support.
- Energize sustained tones by increasing the breath support and dynamic level.
- Sustain phrases by staggering the

breathing through the eight-bar phrases.

- Increase intensity on repeated notes to feel forward movement.
- Emphasize the two-note phrases by "leaning into" the first note and tapering off on the second note.
- Listen for the diphthong in *now.*
- Identify melodic and harmonic intervals between the parts and tune them.

4. Sing softly with control.

Have students:

- Review diaphragmatic breathing. (See the Teaching Strategy on page 39.)
- Look through "Silent the Forests" for dynamic markings.
- Sing the piece, using diaphragmatic breathing and a supported tone, especially in the soft parts of the piece.

Assessment

Informal Assessment

During this lesson, students showed the ability to:

- Identify and use diaphragmatic breathing in the Vocal Warm-Up exercises.
- Identify altered tones and chromatic passages in the Sight-Singing 2 exercise.
- Sing altered tones, chromatic passages, and soft dynamics with breath support in "Silent the Forests."

Student Self-Assessment

Have students:

- Evaluate their performance with the How Did You Do? section on page 39.
- Answer the questions individually. Discuss them in pairs or small groups and/or write their responses on a sheet of paper.

Individual Performance Assessment

To further demonstrate accomplishment, have each student:

- In a trio, sing measures 3–6 into a tape recorder in an isolated space, demonstrating breath support while singing softly.
- Sing the alto line of the Sight-Singing 2 exercise into a tape recorder, checking the accuracy of singing a chromatic descending line.
- Using Blackline Master 10, *Altered Tones and Chromatic Passages,* visually and aurally identify and define sharps, flats, naturals, and chromatic passages.

41

Extension

Composing a Chromatic Piece

Have students:

- Write and sing several chromatic ascending and descending passages.
- Decide where the tonal center of their melody will be, and then use some connecting melodies between these chromatic passages.
- Experiment and revise until they find something that they like.
- Use their melody as a sight-singing exercise for the ensemble.

Visually Creating Mood

Have students:

- Discuss the mood of "Silent the Forest."
- Using either visual art, photography, or lighting, create a pattern that enhances the mood through fluid, warm, and soft tones and lines.
- Use these visual enhancements in the performance, either as a light show, or with slides projected above the ensemble on a screen.

Music and Text

Have students:

- Discuss the mood of the text and particular words or phrases they found meaningful.
- Identify the musical style and characteristics chosen by the composer for this piece.
- Discuss which musical elements are effective in setting this text and what they would change if they were the composer.

The Role of Conductor

A piece in a slow, fairly constant tempo is an excellent opportunity for students to begin conducting the ensemble. Have students:

- Learn the conducting pattern for 4/4 meter.
- Practice conducting as they sing.
- Volunteer to conduct a small group or an ensemble.

National Standards

The following National Standards are addressed through the Extension and bottom-page activities:

1. Singing, alone and with others, a varied repertoire of music. (**a, c**)
4. Composing and arranging music within specified guidelines. (**a**)
5. Reading and notating music. (**a, b**)
6. Listening to, analyzing, and describing music. (**a, b, c**)
7. Evaluating music and music performances. (**a, c**)
8. Understanding relationships between music, the other arts, and disciplines outside the arts. (**a, c**)
9. Understanding music in relation to history and culture. (**c**)

My Beloved

COMPOSER: *Johannes Brahms (1833–1897)*
ENGLISH TEXT: *Douglas McEwen*
EDITED BY: *Douglas McEwen*

CHORAL MUSIC TERMS
form
peak
phrase
section
3/4 meter

VOICING
| Two-part chorus

PERFORMANCE STYLE
| Slow
| Accompanied by piano

FOCUS
- Read and sing in 3/4 meter.
- Identify parts of a phrase.
- Shape phrases correctly while singing.
- Identify sections and form of a piece.

Warming Up

Vocal Warm-Up
Sing this exercise using solfège and hand signs or numbers. Move up or down a half step as you repeat. Clearly articulate the dotted rhythm in the first measure. Notice the 3/4 meter. The 3 tells you there are 3 beats in a measure, and the 4 tells you that a quarter note gets one beat.

Sight-Singing
First, read this exercise with your eyes. Notice the musical features—the key and meter signatures, same and different sections, and steps and skips. The breath marks show phrases. Where is the peak of each phrase? You will need to build energy toward the peak, then release to the end of the phrase. Now sight-sing using solfège and hand signs or numbers.

TEACHER'S RESOURCE BINDER
Blackline Master 11, *Translation and Pronunciation Guide for "My Beloved"*
Blackline Master 12, *Sight-Reading in 3/4 Meter and Identifying Form*

National Standards

1. Singing, alone and with others, a varied repertoire of music. **(a, c, f)**
5. Reading and notating music. **(a, b)**
6. Listening to, analyzing, and describing music. **(a, b, c)**
7. Evaluating music and music performances. **(a, b)**
8. Understanding relationships between music, the other arts, and disciplines outside the arts. **(c)**

My Beloved

COMPOSER: Johannes Brahms (1833–1897)
ENGLISH TEXT: Douglas McEwen
EDITED BY: Douglas McEwen

Focus

OVERVIEW
3/4 meter; phrases; form.

OBJECTIVES
After completing this lesson, students should be able to:
- Read and sing in 3/4 meter.
- Identify parts of a phrase.
- Sing, shaping phrases correctly.
- Identify sections and form of a piece.

CHORAL MUSIC TERMS
Define the Choral Music Terms for students, giving pronunciation, and answering any questions that may arise.

Warming Up

Vocal Warm-Up
This Vocal Warm-Up is designed to prepare students to:
- Relax and warm the voice.
- Sing in 3/4 meter using solfège and hand signs or numbers.
- Articulate the dotted quarter-eighth rhythm.
- Identify and describe 3/4 meter.

Have students:
- Read through the Vocal Warm-Up directions.
- Sing, following your demonstration.

Sight-Singing

The Sight-Singing exercise on page 43 is designed to prepare students to:

- Sight-sing in 3/4 meter using solfège and hand signs or numbers.
- Read and sing in the major diatonic scale.
- Identify and analyze phrases.
- Identify and describe form.

Have students:

- Read through the Sight-Singing exercise directions.
- Read through each voice part rhythmically, using rhythm syllables.
- Sight-sing through each part separately using solfège and hand signs or numbers.
- Sing all parts together.

Singing: "My Beloved"

Compare a musical phrase, sentence, and section to parallels in language arts. Have students:

- Read the text on page 44.
- Define a phrase as a thought.
- Discuss the parallels of music and language structures: phrase = phrase; sentence = sentence; section = paragraph.

Singing: "My Beloved"

Music's structure can be compared to our spoken language. Can you tell the meaning of the word *phrase* in language?

A musical phrase is a musical thought, containing a beginning, peak, and end. It is like a phrase in language. Musical phrases are combined into sentences. The sentences are grouped into sections, which loosely resemble paragraphs.

Now turn to the music for "My Beloved" on page 45.

HOW DID YOU DO?

Shaping phrases helps communicate the meaning of both music and text. Think about your preparation and performance of "My Beloved."

1. Describe 3/4 meter by telling what each number means. Now sing the Sight-Singing exercise to show that you can feel and sing 3/4 meter.

2. How do you shape a phrase? Sing the first phrase of "My Beloved" to demonstrate your skill.

3. What is the form of "My Beloved"? How do you know? What clues are in the music? Does form have anything to do with phrases?

4. Make a tape recording of your ensemble's performance of "My Beloved." After listening to a playback, describe and critique in writing how well the ensemble performed phrases. Make a recommendation to the group about what they should continue doing and what they could improve.

Composer Johannes Brahms

Johannes Brahms (1833–1897) occupied a position in the last half of the nineteenth century that is analogous to Mendelssohn's in the first half. Like Mendelssohn, he was content with the old forms, and he knew more about them than anybody in his period. Consequently, the tradition of the symphony as handed down by Beethoven, Mendelssohn, and Schumann came to an end. Brahms, like Bach, summed up an epoch. Never again would the symphonic form, the liturgical form of the requiem set to music, or the simple German folk and love songs be the same. Brahms harmonies and innovative settings of the old forms would forever alter the mold.

My Beloved

#13 from "Neue Liebeslieder"
(New Love songs)

Johannes Brahms, op. 65
Edited by Douglas McEwen
English text by Douglas McEwen

Two-part Chorus of Women's Voices
with Piano Four-hand Accompaniment

My Beloved **45**

"My Beloved"

"My Beloved" is the thirteenth piece in a set of love songs written by Johannes Brahms titled "Neue Liebeslieder." It was completed in 1876 and followed his first set of love songs titled "Liebeslieder Waltzes," written in 1871.

Suggested Teaching Sequence

1. Review Vocal Warm-Up.
Have students:
- Review the Vocal Warm-Up on page 43.
- Clearly articulate the dotted rhythm. Practice clapping first if necessary.
- Describe what the numbers in 3/4 meter mean to a classmate, repeating until it is learned.
- Sing the exercise again, swaying on the strong beats to feel the meter.

2. Review Sight-Singing.
Have students:
- Review the Sight-Singing exercises on page 43, using solfège and hand signs or numbers.
- Identify the beginning, peak, and end of each phrase.
- Practice building toward the peak, then releasing to the end of the phrase.
- Sing the exercise, using dynamic shaping of the phrase.
- Identify the sections of the exercise, and describe the form. (The sections are measures 1–8, 9–16, and 17–24; the form, with the repeats, is A ‖: B A :‖.)

3. Sight-sing "My Beloved" using solfège and hand signs or numbers.
Have students:
- Divide into voice sections and read each part rhythmically, using rhythm syllables.
- Still in sections, sing with solfège and hand signs or numbers, identifying and working on problem areas. Notice the altered tones.
- Sing the piece through using solfège and hand signs or numbers with full ensemble.

4. Learn the German pronunciation.

Have students:

- Using Blackline Master 11, *Translation and Pronunciation Guide for "My Beloved,"* echo each phrase of the A section.
- Speak the text in rhythm.
- Sing the text in German.
- Repeat for the B section.
- Sing "My Beloved," using correct German pronunciation.

5. Shape phrases.

Have students:

- Practice shaping phrases with dynamics as learned in the Sight-Singing exercise on page 43.
- Look through "My Beloved," identifying phrases and peaks of each phrase.
- Sing the piece, shaping the phrases using dynamics.

6. Identify form.

Have students:

- Identify the large sections of "My Beloved." (measures 3–10, 11–18, 19–28, 29–36)
- Identify the form of the piece as A ‖: B A :‖. (The same as the Sight-Singing form.)

 MUSIC LITERACY

Tell students that the form of a piece is shown in alphabetical order, with each new section being named by the next letter. The first section is always A, and any identical section will also be called A. If a section is nearly identical, it will become A' (A prime). The second section will be called B, the next C, and so on. Common forms are AB (verse-refrain), ABA (ternary), and ABACA (rondo).

These forms are frequently modified by the composer and may have introductions, interludes, and codas as well.

To help students expand their music literacy, have them:

- List the characteristics of the A and B sections of "My Beloved."
- Compare the lists, discussing any contrast between the two sections.

To encourage vocal development, have students:

- Demonstrate good vocal tone by singing tall vowels with the German or English text, following principles of good diction for either language.
- Energize sustained tones by increasing the breath support and dynamic level.
- Sustain phrases by staggering the breathing and moving forward through the phrases.
- Increase intensity on repeated notes to feel forward movement of the melodic lines.
- Emphasize the two-note phrases by "leaning into" the first note and tapering off on the second note. Demonstrate this by moving the arm with the palm up in a circular motion away from the body ending with the palm down to sense the feeling of loud to soft. Actually sing the loud-soft motion.
- Demonstrate the correct singing of the *r* consonant after a vowel when singing in English. It should be almost silent, as in *dear, heart, part, turn, ardent, art, your, burn, forbear, near, world,* and *yearn.*
- Listen for diphthongs (two vowel sounds when one vowel is written) in words such as *I*. Sing or sustain the first vowel sound and barely sing the second vowel sound with the next syllable.
- Identify melodic (linear) and harmonic (vertical) intervals between the parts and tune them carefully.
- Note the accidentals. Ask: How do they change the tonality?

 TEACHING STRATEGY
3/4 Meter and Dotted Rhythms

If students are not familiar with either the meter or dotted quarter-eighth rhythm, have them:

- Clap a rhythm challenge in 3/4 meter that you write on the board until they

are comfortable with the elements found in "My Beloved."

- Learn the conducting pattern for 3/4 meter and conduct as they sing to feel the meter more securely.

Assessment

Informal Assessment

During this lesson, students showed the ability to:

- Sing in 3/4 meter in the Vocal Warm-Up exercise.
- Identify and shape phrases in the Sight-Singing exercise.
- Identify sections and form in the Sight-Singing exercise.
- Sing in 3/4 meter, shaping phrases in "My Beloved."
- Identify form in "My Beloved."

Student Self-Assessment

Have students:

- Evaluate their performance with the How Did You Do? section on page 44.
- Answer the questions individually. Discuss them in pairs or small groups and/or write their responses on a sheet of paper.

Individual Performance Assessment

To further demonstrate accomplishment, have each student:

- Using Blackline Master 12, *Sight-Reading in 3/4 Meter and Identifying Form,* first analyze and write the form, and then read and clap the rhythm into a tape recorder.
- In a duet or quartet, sing measures 3–10 to a duo or quartet of peers, demonstrating shaping of phrases using dynamics, and receiving feedback from peers on shaping the phrases. Switch roles.

MUSIC LITERACY

To help students expand their music literacy, have them:

- Conduct and speak the rhythms of "My Beloved" precisely.
- Breathe on the rest shown before the pickup entrance in order to perform it precisely.

Extension

Composing Contrasting Sections
Have students:
- Write a rhythm that is eight measures long in 3/4 meter.
- List the characteristics of their rhythms on paper.
- Write contrasts for each characteristic in a parallel column.
- Compose a B section that contrasts with the first section.
- Share the composition with another classmate or group, getting feedback.
- Revise and confer several times until the piece seems to satisfy the composer and listeners.
- Arrange the rhythm for body percussion, found sounds, environmental sounds, unpitched percussion instruments, or MIDI percussion sounds.

Music and Text
The unification of music and text is the composer's job, and many choices are available. Have students:
- Discuss the mood of "My Beloved" and particular words or phrases they found meaningful.
- Identify the musical style and characteristics chosen by the composer for this piece, including 3/4 meter, slow tempo, pedal point in the bass of the A sections, simple rhythms, soft dynamic level, use of harmonic thirds, and sweet harmonies in the A section, altered tones in the B section, and so on.
- Discuss which musical elements are effective in setting this text, and what they would change if they were the composer.
- Compare this discussion to a similar one about "Silent the Forests" in Lesson 6. Compare and contrast the styles and strategies that the two composers used to communicate their messages.

National Standards
The following National Standards are addressed through the Extension and bottom-page activities:
1. Singing, alone and with others, a varied repertoire of music. **(a, c)**
4. Composing and arranging music within specified guidelines. **(a, b)**
5. Reading and notating music. **(a, b)**
6. Listening to, analyzing, and describing music. **(a, b, c, d, f)**
7. Evaluating music and music performances. **(a, c)**
9. Understanding music in relation to history and culture. **(a, c, d)**

COMPOSER: Johann Hermann Schein (1586-1630)

EDITED BY: Don Malin

Focus

OVERVIEW
Bright vocal tone quality; part independence; German pronunciation.

OBJECTIVES
After completing this lesson, students should be able to:
• Sing with a bright vocal tone quality.
• Sing a part independently with two other parts.
• Sing with correct German pronunciation.

CHORAL MUSIC TERMS
Define the Choral Music Terms for students, giving pronunciation, and answering any questions that may arise.

Warming Up

Vocal Warm-Up
This Vocal Warm-Up is designed to prepare students to:
• Sing lightly in the high register.
• Hear chord intervals sung as arpeggios.
• Hear the difference between darker and brighter vowels.
Have students:
• Read through the Vocal Warm-Up directions.
• Sing, following your demonstration.

Fresh Is the Maytime

COMPOSER: *Johann Hermann Schein* (1586–1630)

EDITED BY: *Don Malin*

CHORAL MUSIC TERMS
bright vocal tone quality
chords
harmony
part independence

VOICING
SSA

PERFORMANCE STYLE
Joyful
A cappella

FOCUS
• Sing with a bright vocal tone quality.
• Sing a part independently with two other parts.
• Sing with correct German pronunciation.

Warming Up

Vocal Warm-Up
Sing this exercise using first *loo*, then *nee*. Which syllable allows you to get the tone high in your head? Work for a light, bright vocal tone quality. Move up by a half step on each repeat.

Sight-Singing
Notice that the tonal center is G, or *so*. This gives the piece a modal feeling, typical of Renaissance music. First, all sight-sing each part separately, then divide into two voice parts and sing them together. Listen to both voice parts and tune the harmonies as you sing.

TEACHER'S RESOURCE BINDER
Blackline Master 13, *Translation and Pronunciation Guide for "Fresh Is the Maytime"*
Blackline Master 14, *Chord Inversions*

National Standards
1. Singing, alone and with others, a varied repertoire of music. **(a, c, f)**
5. Reading and notating music. **(a, b)**
6. Listening to, analyzing, and describing music. **(a, b, c)**
7. Evaluating music and music performances. **(a, b, c)**
8. Understanding relationships between music, the other arts, and disciplines outside the arts. **(a, c)**

Singing: "Fresh Is the Maytime"

A painter can decide to use bright or dark colors to convey a mood or style. As a singer, you can choose bright or dark vowels, depending upon the piece you sing. Sing these tones, using the vowels indicated:

mee meh moh moo

Which sound is bright? Which sound is dark? What mouth position causes each. Find the vowels in measures 1–12 of "Fresh Is the Maytime" on page 52. Brighten vowels by using the *ee* or *ih* mouth position.

Now sing the music for "Fresh Is the Maytime."

Sight-Singing

This Sight-Singing exercise is designed to prepare students to:
- Sing in two independent parts.
- Sing intervals of a third.
- Sing with *so* as a tonal center.
- Tune harmonies.

Have students:
- Read through the Sight-Singing exercise directions.
- Read through each voice part rhythmically, using rhythm syllables.
- Sight-sing through each part separately using solfège and hand signs or numbers.
- Sing all parts together.

Singing: "Fresh Is the Maytime"

Define and practice bright vocal tone quality. Have students:
- Read the text on page 51.
- Sing the tones with the indicated vowels.
- Describe the sounds in terms of brightness.
- Analyze the positions of the mouth—very rounded lips create dark sounds; an *ee* position brightens up vowel sounds.
- Write the vowels for every word from measures 1–12 of "Fresh Is the Maytime."
- Speak the vowels, keeping the *ee* or *ih* position of the mouth (forward placement) and bouncy articulation.
- Add the consonants crisply, keeping the bright quality.

HOW DID YOU DO?

? ? ? ?

In the seventeenth century, the month of May was a time to be joyful, celebrating the end of winter and the beginning of spring. Think about your preparation and performance of "Fresh Is the Maytime."

1. How did you learn to create a bright vocal tone color? Demonstrate by singing measures 1–12 of your voice part to "Fresh Is the Maytime."

2. How well can you sing your part independently when other parts are being sung? Choose a section of "Fresh Is the Maytime" and sing it with two classmates, showing your skill at holding your own voice part while others sing theirs.

3. How is your German pronunciation? Speak measures 1–12 in rhythm to show your skill.

4. Write a critique of your learning and performance in this lesson. Assess your vocal tone color, part independence, and German pronunciation. Tell what you have learned, how you have improved, and what you need to work on.

5. State whether you think your ensemble's performance evoked feelings or emotions in the audience. Were they the feelings and emotions the composer intended? How do you know?

Lesson 8: Fresh Is the Maytime **51**

 Composer Johann Schein

Johann Schein was one of J.S. Bach's predecessors at St. Thomas School and Church in Leipzig, Germany. He produced a considerable body of sacred and secular choral music, mostly for mixed voices.

 "Fresh Is the Maytime"

In the seventeenth century, the beginning of spring was reason for much celebration after a long, cold winter. The joys of Maytime are described in this short dance-song from Schein's "Waldliederlein."

Suggested Teaching Sequence

1. Review Vocal Warm-Up.
Stretch the upper register. Sing with a bright vocal tone quality. Have students:
- Review the Vocal Warm-Up on page 50.
- Review the *ee* sound for a bright vocal tone quality.

2. Review Sight-Singing.
Sing with solfège and hand signs or numbers independently in two parts. Have students:
- Review the Sight-Singing exercise on page 50, using solfège and hand signs or numbers.
- Sing both lines together, tuning each interval quickly and accurately.
- Work for part independence.

3. Sight-sing "Fresh Is the Maytime" using solfège and hand signs or numbers.
Have students:
- Divide into voice sections (SSA) and read each part rhythmically, using rhythm syllables.
- Still in sections, sing with solfège and hand signs or numbers, identifying and working on problem areas.
- Sing the piece through using solfège and hand signs or numbers with full ensemble.

4. Sing with a bright vocal tone quality.
Have students:
- Review the guidelines for forming bright vowels as practiced in the Vocal Warm-Up on page 50.
- Review ways to add crisp consonants.
- First speak, then sing the piece with a bright vocal tone quality.

Fresh Is the Maytime
Der Kühle Maien

Johann Hermann Schein (1586–1630)
Edited by Don Malin
English Translation by Don Malin

SSA, Unaccompanied

52 *Choral Connections   Level 3 Treble Voices*

MUSIC LITERACY
Cadences
To help students expand their music literacy, have them:
- Notice the three pitches at the end of each section of "Fresh Is the Maytime."
- Discuss the tension and release that give the feel of an ending.
- Identify this as a cadence, which comes just at the end of each phrase.
- Identify all four cadences in this piece as identical.

Dame Night-in - gale's Sweet song pre - vails Re - sound - ing through green-wood fair.
Frau Nach-ti - gall lässt ih - ren Schall im grü - nen Wald an - hö - ren.

Dame Night-in - gale's Sweet song pre - vails Re - sound - ing through green-wood fair.
Frau Nach-ti - gall lässt ih - ren Schall im grü - nen Wald an - hö - ren.

Dame Night-in - gale's Sweet song pre - vails Re - sound - ing through green-wood fair.
Frau Nach-ti - gall lässt ih - ren Schall im grü - nen Wald an - hö - ren.

Birds all re - joice As with one voice Wood mu - sic is ev - 'ry - where.
All Vö - ge - lein mit stim - men ein, die Wald - mu - sik ver - meh - ren.

Birds all re - joice As with one voice Wood mu - sic is ev - 'ry - where.
All Vö - ge - lein mit stim - men ein, die Wald - mu - sik ver - meh - ren.

Birds all re - joice As with one voice Wood mu - sic is ev - 'ry - where.
All Vö - ge - lein mit stim - men ein, die Wald - mu - sik ver - meh - ren.

Fresh Is the Maytime **53**

5. Learn the German pronunciation.

Have students:
- With Blackline Master 13, *Translation and Pronunciation Guide for "Fresh Is the Maytime,"* pronounce each word using the guide or echoing.
- Speak the text in rhythm.
- Sing the text in German.

VOCAL DEVELOPMENT

To encourage vocal development, have students:
- Demonstrate good vocal tone by singing tall vowels, following principles of good diction.
- Sing in the upper register with a light, floating sound.
- Feel the meter in one beat, noting the rhythmic change before each cadence.
- Feel the arch contour of each musical phrase as it begins, builds, then tapers off. The dynamics should reflect the melodic contour.
- Sustain phrases by staggering the breathing and moving forward through the phrases.
- Increase intensity on repeated notes to feel forward movement of the melodic lines.
- Demonstrate how the *r* consonant after a vowel should be almost silent, as in *shepherds, flowers, fair, birds, where, hearts,* and *honor.*
- Listen for diphthongs in *May, bright, delight, prime, resounding, rejoice, voice, joyous,* and *day.*
- Identify intervals and chords between the parts and tune them carefully.
- Note the accidentals.

TEACHING STRATEGY

Feeling 3/4 Meter in One

In this piece, each measure of 3/4 meter is felt as one beat, with three subdivisions. Have students:
- Look at the tempo marking for the dotted half note at the beginning of the piece.
- Listen to a setting of 56 on a metronome, and tap the three subdivisions.
- Explain how this meter works.

Form

Have students:
- Describe the sections. (measures 1–12, 13–26, 27–38, and 39–end)
- Identify which sections are the same.
- Identify the form as ABAB.

Style

Have students;
- Find the dynamic and tempo markings.
- Sing, following these markings.

Assessment

Informal Assessment

During this lesson, students showed the ability to:

- Use a bright vocal tone quality in the Vocal Warm-Up exercise.
- Sing a part independently with another part in the Sight-Singing exercise.
- Sing a part independently with two other parts in "Fresh Is the Maytime."
- Sing with a bright vocal tone quality in "Fresh Is the Maytime."
- Sing "Fresh Is the Maytime," using correct German pronunciation.

Student Self-Assessment

Have students:

- Evaluate their performance with the How Did You Do? section on page 51.
- Answer the questions individually. Discuss them in pairs or small groups and/or write their responses on a sheet of paper.

Individual Performance Assessment

To further demonstrate accomplishment, have each student:

- Into a tape recorder in an isolated place, perform the following three examples:
—Speak measures 1–12, demonstrating German pronunciation.
—Sing the appropriate voice part of measures 1–12, demonstrating bright vocal tone quality.
—With two classmates, sing measures 1–12 in three parts, demonstrating vocal independence.

CONNECTING THE ARTS
Creating a Maytime Dance

Have students:

- Create a dance showing the ABAB form. They might consider the following possibilities:
— begin by moving spontaneously while hearing the piece.
— formation could be a circle or concentric circles of partners.
— move in, out, or around the circle.
— swaying on strong beats or tiptoeing motions on every subdivision.
— a maypole dance, with weaving of two colors (like a grand right and left).
— use joyful, energetic, upward movements.
— use arms and hands.
— keep the movement simple and folk-like.
— contrasting motions for A and B.
- Perform the dance with the piece.

National Standards

The following National Standards are addressed through the Extension and bottom-page activities:

1. Singing, alone and with others, a varied repertoire of music. **(a, c)**
4. Composing and arranging music within specified guidelines. **(b)**
5. Reading and notating music. **(a, b)**
6. Listening to, analyzing, and describing music. **(a, b, c, f)**
8. Understanding relationships between music, the other arts, and disciplines outside the arts. **(a)**
9. Understanding music in relation to history and culture. **(a, d)**

Extension

Understanding Chord Inversions

Have students:

- Using Blackline Master 14, *Chord Inversions,* first listen to a G major chord in root position, first, and second inversion.
- Discuss what is the same and different about these three sounds. (same pitches, different relationships and positions of pitches)
- Construct chords in root position, first, and second inversions.
- Look at triads from measures 2–12 of "Fresh Is the Maytime" (piano rehearsal score), finding chords and identifying the position they are written in.

Listening to Madrigals

Have students:

- Research secular music of the Renaissance period.
- Listen to the choral and instrumental music of the Renaissance period.
- List characteristics of "Fresh Is the Maytime" in a column.
- List characteristics of Renaissance secular vocal music in a parallel column.
- Compare the two to determine how this piece either fits or does not fit the characteristics of the period.
- Identify current secular music styles they know that have similar characteristics to this piece. Consider text or musical characteristics.

Arranging the Piece for Different Voices or Instruments

Have students:

- Recruit some bases to sing the alto part an octave lower, since this was the composer's original voicing.
  or
- Arrange the voice parts for such instruments as recorders (two sopranos and an alto), strings, or winds.
- Expand the piece to add an instrumental verse.

Who Has Seen the Wind?

COMPOSER: Robert E. Kreutz

TEXT: Christina Rossetti
(1830–1894)

Focus

OVERVIEW

Sizzle rhythms; changing meters; strophic form.

OBJECTIVES

After completing this lesson, students should be able to:

- Read and sizzle rhythms in changing meters.
- Identify characteristics and sing in strophic form.

CHORAL MUSIC TERMS

Define the Choral Music Terms for students, giving pronunciation, and answering any questions that may arise.

Warming Up

Rhythm Drill

This Rhythm Drill is designed to prepare students to:

- Sizzle rhythms with sustained note values.
- Read and perform changing meters.
- Experience the rhythms they will sing in "Who Has Seen the Wind?"

Have students:

- Read through the Rhythm Drill directions.
- Perform the drill.

56

Who Has Seen the Wind?

COMPOSER: *Robert E. Kreutz*

TEXT: *Christina Rossetti* (1830–1894)

CHORAL MUSIC TERMS

changing meter

meter

rhythm

sizzle rhythms

strophic form

stony beat

VOICING

SA

PERFORMANCE STYLE

With quiet flow
Accompanied by piano

FOCUS

- Read and sizzle rhythms in changing meters.
- Identify characteristics and sing in strophic form.

Warming Up

Rhythm Drill

Read and "sizzle" this rhythm, using a *tsss* sound. Be very accurate, and sustain the long tones for their full value. Have a classmate tap the steady beat audibly as you read.

Vocal Warm-Up

Sing this Warm-Up using solfège and hand signs or numbers. Tune each interval accurately as you sing. Notice the steps, skips, and leaps as the intervals get farther apart.

TEACHER'S RESOURCE BINDER

National Standards

In this lesson, students should develop the following skills and concepts:

1. Singing, alone and with others, a varied repertoire of music. **(a, c, f)**
4. Composing and arranging music within specified guidelines. **(a)**
5. Reading and notating music. **(a, b)**
6. Listening to, analyzing, and describing music. **(a, b, c)**
7. Evaluating music and music performances. **(a, b, c)**
8. Understanding relationships between music, the other arts, and disciplines outside the arts. **(a, c)**

Sight-Singing

Clap the rhythm of each line of this exercise as a classmate taps the steady beat. Keep the quarter note constant, noticing the different meters. Now sight-sing the exercise using solfège and hand signs or numbers.

Singing: "Who Has Seen the Wind?"

Beats can be grouped in many ways, but you are probably used to groups of two, three, or four beats in a measure. Walk the beat, and clap the strong beat (beat 1) for sets of two, then three, then four. When your group beats in fives, they are usually felt as 2+3 or 3+2. When you walk, count to five, but clap on beats 1 and 3. Start again and clap on beats 1 and 4.

Now you are ready to read a piece with beats in sets of three, four, five, and six. See if you can figure out why the composer would shift meters like this!

Now turn to the music for "Who Has Seen the Wind?" on page 58.

HOW DID YOU DO?

Were you steady enough to withstand the shifting meters? Think about your preparation and performance of "Who Has Seen the Wind?"
1. How well can you read rhythms when the meter keeps changing? Demonstrate by "sizzling" measures 3–13 of "Who Has Seen the Wind?"
2. Describe the characteristics of strophic form. Is "Who Has Seen the Wind?" strophic? Give specific examples that match the description.

3. If you were evaluating an ensemble singing "Who Has Seen the Wind?" what criteria would you use to determine whether or not it was a good performance? How would you assess your ensemble's performance?

Lesson 9: Who Has Seen the Wind? **57**

Robert E. Kreutz

Robert Kreutz received his bachelor of music degree from the American Conservatory of Music in Chicago, Illnois, and his master of arts degree from the University of Denver. In 1976 he won the 41st International Eucharistic Congress Hymn Competition. His published vocal, orchestral, and instrumental works number close to 300.

"Who Has Seen the Wind?"

This piece is based on the poem by Christina Rosetti of the same title that describes that mystical aspect of a gentle wind. A flowing rhythm in the piano accompaniment helps set the quiet, peaceful mood.

Vocal Warm-Up
This Vocal Warm-Up is designed to prepare students to:
- Read and sing the major scale intervals using solfège and hand signs or numbers.
- Tune intervals.
- Identify steps, skips, and leaps.

Have students:
- Read through the Vocal Warm-Up directions.
- Sing, following your demonstration.

Sight-Singing
This Sight-Singing exercise is designed to prepare students to:
- Read and clap rhythms in changing meters.
- Identify the constant quarter note in changing meters.
- Sight-sing using solfège and hand signs or numbers.
- Sing independently in three parts.

Have students:
- Read through the Sight-Singing exercise directions.
- Read through each voice part rhythmically, clapping the rhythm.
- Sight-sing through each part separately using solfège and hand signs or numbers.
- Sing all parts together.

Singing: "Who Has Seen the Wind?"

Feel the strong beats in different meters. Have students:
- Read the text on page 57.
- Walk the steady beat, and then clap the strong beat in sets of two.
- Continue with the directions, stepping the beat and clapping the strong beat for each pattern until it is natural before going on.
- Clap both variations of 5/4.
- Try stepping the beat and alternating between meters; for example, two measures of 4/4, then two measures of 5/4, and so on.

Robert E. Kreutz
Christina Rossetti

Suggested Teaching Sequence

1. Review Rhythm Drill.
Read and sizzle rhythms in changing meters. Have students:
- Review the Rhythm Drill on page 56.
- Feel the diaphragmatic push at the beginning of each sizzle.
- Work for rhythmic precision.
- Look at "Who Has Seen the Wind?" to find this rhythm. (the piece begins this way)
- Sizzle the rhythm of the whole piece.

2. Review Vocal Warm-Up.
Sing steps, skips, and leaps. Read and sing intervals of the major scale. Have students:
- Review the Vocal Warm-Up on page 56.
- Listen and tune each pitch carefully.
- Identify the steps, skips, and leaps they are singing, and then find steps, skips, and leaps in their voice part of "Who Has Seen the Wind?"

3. Review Sight-Singing.
Clap rhythms in changing meters, keeping the quarter note constant. Sight-sing in three parts using solfège and hand signs or numbers. Have students:
- Review the Sight-Singing exercise on page 57, first clapping, then singing with solfège and hand signs or numbers.
- Sing all three lines together, tuning each interval quickly and accurately.
- Work for part independence.

SA, Accompanied

58 *Choral Connections   Level 3 Treble Voices*

TEACHING STRATEGY

Reading Changing Meters

The only way to get comfortable with changing meters is to encounter them daily. Have students:
- Compose short rhythms for each other to read, using at least two meters.
- Use different constants; for example, try 2/8, 3/8, 4/8, 5/8, and 6/8, with the eighth note as the steady beat.
- Make up changing meter dances that have accents or stamps on the strong beats of each measure, so students feel the change with their whole body.

4. Sight-sing "Who Has Seen the Wind?" using solfège and hand signs or numbers.

Have students:

- Divide into voice sections (SA) and read each part rhythmically, using rhythm syllables.
- Still in sections, sing with solfège and hand signs or numbers, identifying and working on problem areas.
- Sing the piece through using solfège and hand signs or numbers with full ensemble.
- Divide into sections and recite the text rhythmically for each voice part.
- Sing the piece through with text as a full ensemble.

5. Identify strophic form.

Have students:

- Discuss the form of "Who Has Seen the Wind?" discovering that there are two large sections in this piece that are similar but in different keys.
- Identify strophic form as the same melody for each verse.
- Identify this piece as being in strophic form.
- Sing the piece once again.

TEACHING STRATEGY

Singing High Pitches in Tune

Have students:

- Reach high pitches by vocalizing gradually up to and past the pitch.
- Always use the *awh* vowel sound on high pitches. Add the resonance of the *oo* vowel on the high pitches for tone quality and to sing in tune.
- "Zero in" on the precise pitch after phonating above it on an *awh* or *oo*

sound. Feel the sensation of the vocal tract when reaching the exact pitch.

- Modify the vowel sound of the word to be sung to achieve the best tone quality and intonation.
- Use full breath support to sing the tops of the high pitches.
- When singing descending lines, think or gesture with upward motions.

VOCAL DEVELOPMENT

To encourage vocal development, have students:

- Demonstrate good vocal tone by singing tall vowels and alter (or modify) the vowel sounds when necessary.
- Enjoy the resonance of the *oo* vowel sound on such words as *who, you,* and *through.*
- Energize sustained tones by increasing the breath support and dynamic level.
- Sustain phrases by staggering the breathing and moving forward through the phrases.
- Increase intensity on repeated notes to feel forward movement of the melodic lines.
- Demonstrate the correct singing of the *r* consonant after a vowel. It should be almost silent, as in *neither* and *nor.*
- Listen for diphthongs (two vowel sounds when one vowel is written) in such words as *bow* and *by.* Sing or sustain the first vowel sound and barely sing the second vowel sound with the next syllable.
- Identify intervals between the parts and tune them carefully. Note when the voices move from parts to unison singing to adjust the dynamic attack.

TEACHING STRATEGY
Strophic Form

Have students:

- Review pieces they have already performed to find other examples of strophic form; for example: "My Beloved" (Lesson 7) and "Welcome Now in Peace" (Lesson 5).

Assessment

Informal Assessment

During this lesson, students showed the ability to:

- Read and sizzle rhythms in changing meters in the Rhythm Drill.
- Sing and identify steps, skips, and leaps in the Vocal Warm-Up exercise.
- Sing a part independently with two other parts in the Sight-Singing exercise.
- Sing a part independently with two other parts in "Who Has Seen the Wind?"
- Sing changing meters in "Who Has Seen the Wind?"
- Identify the strophic form of "Who Has Seen the Wind?"

Student Self-Assessment

Have students:

- Evaluate their performance with the How Did You Do? section on page 57.
- Answer the questions individually. Discuss them in pairs or small groups and/or write their responses on a sheet of paper.

Individual Performance Assessment

To further demonstrate accomplishment, have each student:

- Compose a rhythm using 2/4, 3/4, 4/4, and 5/4 measures, and then sizzle the composed rhythm into a tape recorder in an isolated space.
- Write a description of strophic form, giving reasons why "Who Has Seen the Wind?" is, or is not, in strophic form.

 MUSIC LITERACY

To help students expand their music literacy, have them:

- Conduct the mixed meters found in "Who Has Seen the Wind?" while speaking the rhythm or text.

Extension

Identifying the Period

Have students:

- Predict what period this piece was composed in.
- Look for clues in the music, both musical and factual, about the poet and composer.
- Discuss what characteristics were good clues to the style and period.
- Listen to other examples of music, and classify them as from the same period or a different one.

Composing in Strophic Form

Have students:

- Remember that strophic form is the same melody for each verse.
- Using a poem by Rossetti or another poet for text, create a melody for the first stanza.
- Use the same melody for each stanza, making modifications to fit the rhythm of the words or any changes of mood.
- Sing the melody with text, deciding where it needs a little variety to keep it interesting.
- Use creative solutions to the issue of boredom without changing so much that it is no longer strophic.
- Share their pieces as an introduction to "Who Has Seen the Wind?" at a concert, or just with each other.

National Standards

The following National Standards are addressed through the Extension and bottom-page activities:

1. Singing, alone and with others, a varied repertoire of music. **(a, c)**
4. Composing and arranging music within specified guidelines. **(a)**
5. Reading and notating music. **(a, b)**
6. Listening to, analyzing, and describing music. **(a, b, c, f)**

7. Evaluating music and music performances. **(a)**
8. Understanding relationships between music, the other arts, and disciplines outside the arts. **(a, e)**
9. Understanding music in relation to history and culture. **(a, d)**

Mixed Meter and the Wind

Have students:

- Discuss reasons the composer chose mixed meter for this particular text. (Perhaps because the wind is so unpredictable, not metered, or does not blow with a steady pattern.)
- Discuss whether they enjoyed the challenge of changing meters.
- Suggest other ways a composer might deal with this text other than changing meters.
- Discuss how a choreographer, visual artist, or dramatist might work with this text to interpret the mood and message of the poet.
- Optional: Plan and execute a multiarts interpretation of the poem, integrating across the arts and using either this setting of the music or creating their own.

I Never Saw a Moor

COMPOSER: Michael Larkin

TEXT BY: Emily Dickinson
(1830–1886)

Focus

OVERVIEW
Stepwise melodies; major tonality; sight-singing; musical characteristics which enhance mood.

OBJECTIVES
After completing this lesson, students should be able to:
• Identify and sight-sing stepwise melodies.
• Sight-sing in major tonality.
• Identify musical characteristics that enhance the mood of a poem.

CHORAL MUSIC TERMS
Define the Choral Music Terms for students, giving pronunciation, and answering any questions that may arise.

Warming Up

Vocal Warm-Up
This Vocal Warm-Up is designed to prepare students to:
• Sing vowels with a rounded mouth to avoid spreading vowel sounds.
• Focus the tone in the "mask of the face."
• Sing scalewise, stepwise patterns.
• Sing the major scale.
Have students:
• Read through the Vocal Warm-Up directions.
• Sing, following your demonstration.

64

LESSON 10

I Never Saw a Moor

COMPOSER: *Michael Larkin*

TEXT: *Emily Dickinson* (1830-1886)

CHORAL MUSIC TERMS
major tonality
melodic leaps
mood
musical characteristics
stepwise melodic motion

VOICING
SSA

PERFORMANCE STYLE
Moderately, flowing
Accompanied by keyboard

FOCUS
• Identify and sight-sing stepwise melodies.
• Sight-sing in major tonality.
• Identify musical characteristics that enhance the mood of a poem.

Warming Up

Vocal Warm-Up
Sing this warm-up using the syllables provided. Bend forward at the waist as you sing up the scale, and return to upright position as you descend the scale. Give good, full resonance to the "m" of each syllable, and keep the tone focused in the mask of the face. Keep your mouth rounded to avoid spreading the vowel sounds. Move up by half steps on each repeat.

Mi — me — ma — mo — moo.

Sight-Singing
Sight-sing all three parts together in ensemble, using solfège and hand signs or numbers. Listen carefully as you tune to the other voice lines, comparing their rhythmic movement to yours. Can you read this straight through the first time? Where are the steps and leaps in your voice part?

64 *Choral Connections   Level 3 Treble Voices*

TEACHER'S RESOURCE BINDER
Blackline Master 15, *Sight-Singing in Stepwise Movement*

National Standards
1. Singing, alone and with others, a varied repertoire of music. **(a, c, f)**

4. Composing and arranging music within specified guidelines. **(a)**
5. Reading and notating music. **(a, b)**
6. Listening to, analyzing, and describing music. **(a, b, c)**
7. Evaluating music and music performances. **(a, b, c)**
8. Understanding relationships between music, the other arts, and disciplines outside the arts. **(c)**

Singing: "I Never Saw a Moor"

If you watch a child stepping and leaping, you will notice that the steps are much more in control, but the leaps are far more exciting. Your voice can move in steps and leaps with the same effect. Sing a scale up and down using solfège and hand signs or numbers. Sing the tonic chord up and down (*do, mi, so, do', so, mi,* and *do*). With half the ensemble singing the scale, the others will sing the triad. Then switch roles.

Now turn to the music for "I Never Saw a Moor" on page 66.

HOW DID YOU DO?

? ? ?

Step by step, you have learned the concepts and skills necessary to sing "I Never Saw a Moor." Think about your preparation and performance of "I Never Saw a Moor."

1. Define the musical characteristics of a stepwise melody, and how you recognize it in notation.

2. Sing a major scale up and down to show your understanding of major tonality.

3. Describe the stepwise melodic movement in your voice line of "I Never Saw a Moor."

4. Decide what three performance characteristics are most important to this piece. What would be a satisfactory, good, or excellent performance for each of these characteristics? Make a tape of your ensemble's performance. Listen to a playback; then rate each of these characteristics according to your list.

Emily Dickinson

During her life, Emily Dickinson was unknown to the literary world, because she chose to live a secluded life, secretly writing over 1,000 poems. After her death in 1886, her sister Lavinia published three volumes of Emily's poems. However reclusive she was, Emily's poetry demonstrated an intense understanding of human nature. Her influence on American poets could hardly have been predicted by her obscurity while alive.

Sight-Singing

This Sight-Singing exercise is designed to prepare students to:
- Sight-sing independent lines with divided beats.
- Sight-sing with increasing accuracy.
- Identify melodic steps and leaps.

Have students:
- Read through the Sight-Singing exercise directions.
- Read through each voice part rhythmically, using rhythm syllables.
- Sight-sing through each part separately using solfège and hand signs or numbers.
- Sing all parts together, tuning to other parts.

Singing: "I Never Saw a Moor"

Identify steps and leaps. Have students:
- Read the text on page 65.
- Sing a scale up and down.
- Sing the tonic chord up and down.
- In two groups sing both together, fitting the stepwise scale tones in between the skips and leaps of the chord tones.
- Identify the scale tones as stepwise, and the chord tones as skips or leaps.
- Look at the voice part to visually identify steps and skips in the melody they will be learning.

Suggested Teaching Sequence

1. Review Vocal Warm-Up.

Sing scalewise, stepwise motion. Practice round vowel sounds. Have students:

- Review the Vocal Warm-Up on page 64.
- Review the correct mouth position for vowels.
- Add the movement to help produce a free sound on the high pitches.

2. Review Sight-Singing.

Sight-sing in three parts using solfège and hand signs or numbers. Identify melodic steps and leaps. Have students:

- Sight-sing all three parts in the exercise together as best they can.
- Identify sight-singing as an effort to be as accurate as possible the first time through.
- Identify melodic steps and leaps in their voice part.
- Practice reading and singing the exercise once each day, tracking improvement.

3. Sight-sing "I Never Saw a Moor" using solfège and hand signs or numbers.

Have students:

- Divide into voice sections (SSA) and read each part rhythmically, using rhythm syllables.
- Still in sections, sing with solfège and hand signs or numbers, identifying and working on problem areas.
- Sing the piece through using solfège and hand signs or numbers with full ensemble.
- Divide into sections and recite the text rhythmically for each voice part.
- Sing the piece through with text as a full ensemble.

I Never Saw a Moor

Music by Michael Larkin
Text by Emily Dickinson

SSA, Accompanied

 MUSIC LITERACY

To help students expand their music literacy, have them:

- Clap and speak the rhythm.
- Conduct and speak the text in rhythm.
- Examine a previously performed piece in this book for stepwise melodic passages in their own voice part.
- Compare the length of the passages with those in this piece.

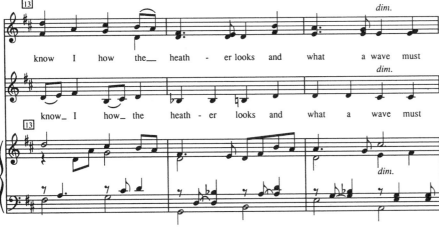

4. Add interpretive elements to enhance the mood of the piece.

Have students:

- Read the text, identifying the mood as wistful, yet optimistic and confident.
- Look through the notation for dynamic, tempo, and style indications.
- Review shaping phrases through legato articulation to connect tones and building/releasing tension through the phrase.
- Rehearse and sing the piece, using these guidelines for interpretation.
- Make a list of the interpretive characteristics that they used to enhance the mood of the text.

TEACHING STRATEGY

Steps and Leaps

Once students understand how to recognize steps and leaps, they can begin approximating the distance from one pitch to the other. With practice, they become more and more accurate. Have students:

- Draw a five line staff and number the lines and spaces from the bottom up.
- Each suggest two locations for noteheads.
- Write the noteheads, and then tell whether it is a step or leap, and whether it is upward or downward.
- Listen to the interval, then sing it on *loo* three times.
- Repeat this activity frequently, until students are volunteering to sing the interval themselves.

CURRICULUM CONNECTIONS
Creative Writing

Emily Dickinson's poem relates her knowledge of places and things she had never physically experienced, but yet she somehow understood.

Have students:

- Think of something, or some place, they have never seen yet know how it looks or feels.

- Write a short essay or poem, using Emily Dickinson's poem as a point of departure, but then telling what their own sense of this thing or place is, using the senses of touch, taste, smell, sight, hearing, and inner awareness.

VOCAL DEVELOPMENT

To encourage vocal development, have students:

- Demonstrate good vocal tone by singing tall vowels and alter (or modify) the vowel sounds when necessary.
- Energize sustained tones by increasing the breath support and dynamic level.
- Sustain phrases by staggering the breathing and moving forward through the phrases.
- Enrich the intensity on repeated notes in the harmony parts to propel the forward movement of the melodic lines.
- Emphasize the two-note phrases by "leaning into" the first note and tapering off on the second note. Demonstrate this by moving the arm with the palm up in a circular motion away from the body, ending with the palm down to sense the feeling of loud to soft. Actually sing the loud-soft motion.
- Plan the dynamics. "Sneak" into a phrase, grow to the most important note/word of the phrase (usually the longest or highest note of the phrase), and taper off at the end of the phrase.
- Demonstrate the correct singing of the *r* consonant after a vowel. It should be almost silent, as in *never, nor, heather, certain,* and *chart.*
- Identify intervals and chords between the parts and tune them carefully.

TEACHING STRATEGY

Constructing a Rubric for Assessment

Have students:

- Choose three criteria for the rubric to be used for "I Never Saw a Moor."
- Discuss performance characteristics that would constitute an adequate, good, and excellent performance.
- Make a grid with the criteria across the top, and the categories of achievement (adequate, good, and excellent) down the right column.
- Fill in the characteristics appropriate to each box.
- Listen to a performance of the piece and use the rubric to assess the quality of performance.

Assessment

Informal Assessment

During this lesson, students showed the ability to:

- Sing scalewise, stepwise melody in the Vocal Warm-Up exercise.
- Identify melodic steps and leaps in the Sight-Singing exercise.
- Identify the purpose of sight-singing in the Sight-Singing exercise.
- Identify and perform interpretive musical characteristics that enhance the mood of the text in "I Never Saw a Moor."

Student Self-Assessment

Have students:

- Evaluate their performance with the How Did You Do? section on page 65.
- Answer the questions individually. Discuss them in pairs or small groups and/or write their responses on a sheet of paper.

Individual Performance Assessment

To further demonstrate accomplishment, have each student:

- Sight-sing one or more exercises from Blackline Master 15, *Sight-Singing in Stepwise Movement,* to demonstrate accomplishment in reading stepwise melodic patterns.
- Compose a 16-beat melody in D major with only stepwise melodic movement, using basic rhythms and meter.
- Sight-sing a classmate's composed melody, demonstrating pitch and rhythmic accuracy.
- Construct a rubric for assessing the performance of "I Never Saw a Moor" that takes into account the expressive musical characteristics that enhance the mood of the text.

TEACHING STRATEGY
Constructive Criticism

Introduction of assessment rubrics should be handled carefully to prepare students for constructive criticism. Have students:

- Discuss the purposes of assessment, such as grades, as a method of identifying strengths and weaknesses.
- Identify the rubric as a tool for showing both strengths and weaknesses.
- Discuss the pros and cons of receiving constructive criticism, such as gaining an objective point of view, but getting hurt feelings.
- Discuss the responsibility of the person filling out the rubric to be objective and honest and make concrete suggestions for improvement.

Extension

Sight-Singing from Hand Signs

Have students:
- Watch your hand signs using the diatonic major scale, and sing from your signs.
- Divide into two groups, each group following one hand.
- In two groups, follow two different students who listen carefully to both groups and improvise melodies that will harmonize.
- Repeat this activity in three groups.

Steps and Leaps

Have students:
- Explore steps and leaps in movement.
- Create patterns of steps and leaps that can be repeated like an ostinato.
- Accompany themselves with vocal steps and leaps to match the movement patterns.
- In small groups, share their individual patterns, then combine them to create a movement composition with vocal accompaniment.

Multiarts Interpretation of a Poem

Have students:
- Discuss the mood of the poem "I Never Saw a Moor," and decide whether the composer enhanced the text with his musical choices.
- Suggest other ways a composer might set this text.
- Discuss how a choreographer, visual artist, sculptor, photographer, or dramatist might work with this text to interpret the mood and message of the poet.
- Optional: Plan and execute a multiarts interpretation of the poem, integrating across the arts and using this setting of the music or creating their own.

National Standards

The following National Standards are addressed through the Extension and bottom-page activities:

1. Singing, alone and with others, a varied repertoire of music. **(a, c)**
3. Improvising melodies, variations, and accompaniments. **(b)**
5. Reading and notating music. **(a, b)**
6. Listening to, analyzing, and describing music. **(a, b, c, f)**
7. Evaluating music and music performances. **(a, b, c)**
8. Understanding relationships between music, the other arts, and disciplines outside the arts. **(a, c, e)**
9. Understanding music in relation to history and culture. **(a, c, d)**

LESSON 11

Arruru

Spanish Carol
ARRANGERS: Ruth E. Dwyer and Thomas Gerber

CHORAL MUSIC TERMS
harmony
legato articulation
staccato articulation
thirds

VOICING
Two-part chorus

PERFORMANCE STYLE
Rocking
Accompanied by piano

FOCUS
- Sing a harmony part in thirds.
- Use staccato and legato articulation.
- Identify some characteristics of Spanish music.

Warming Up

Vocal Warm-Up
Sing this warm-up using the word "Arruru." Sing the first measure legato, and the second measure staccato. Use your diaphragm to perform the staccato articulation. Sway as you sing, and roll the "r"s. Move up by half steps on each repetition.

Ah - roo - roo, roo-hoo-hoo-hoo - hoo.

Sight-Singing
Sight-sing this exercise twice using solfège and hand signs or numbers, switching parts the second time through. Notice the harmony in thirds, a common harmonization in Spanish folk music.

TEACHER'S RESOURCE BINDER

National Standards

1. Singing, alone and with others, a varied repertoire of music. **(a, c, f)**
5. Reading and notating music. **(a, b)**
6. Listening to, analyzing, and describing music. **(a, b, c)**
7. Evaluating music and music performances. **(a, b, c)**
8. Understanding relationships between music, the other arts, and disciplines outside the arts. **(c)**
9. Understanding music in relation to history and culture. **(a)**

Arruru

Spanish Carol
ARRANGERS: Ruth Dwyer and Thomas Gerber

Focus

OVERVIEW
Harmony in thirds; staccato and legato articulation; characteristics of Spanish music.

OBJECTIVES
After completing this lesson, students should be able to:
- Sing a harmony part in thirds.
- Use staccato and legato articulation.
- Identify some characteristics of Spanish music.

CHORAL MUSIC TERMS
Define the Choral Music Terms for students, giving pronunciation, and answering any questions that may arise.

Warming Up

Vocal Warm-Up
This Vocal Warm-Up is designed to prepare students to:
- Read and sing in 6/8 meter.
- Use staccato and legato articulation.
- Use the tonic triad tones as reference points.
- Roll the "r"s.
Have students:
- Read through the Vocal Warm-Up directions.
- Sing, following your demonstration.

Sight-Singing

The Sight-Singing exercise on page 71 is designed to prepare students to:
- Sight-sing two parts in thirds on one staff, using solfège and hand signs or numbers.
- Read rhythms in 6/8 meter.
- Sing one of two parts independently.

Have students:
- Read through the Sight-Singing exercise directions.
- Read through each voice part rhythmically, using rhythm syllables.
- Sight-sing through each part separately using solfège and hand signs or numbers.
- Sing all parts together; then sing again, switching parts.

Singing: "Arruru"

Identify characteristics of Spanish folk music. Have students:
- Read the text on page 72.
- Describe and list the characteristics they anticipate being part of Spanish music.
- Listen to "Arruru," and then compare the characteristics to the above list.
- Identify the characteristics of Spanish music that are part of "Arruru." For example: stepwise melody with narrow range; harmony in thirds; swaying 6/8 rhythm with unexpected accents; guitarlike accompaniment; verse-refrain form; Spanish language.

Singing: "Arruru"

You have probably heard Spanish folk music at some time, and remember what it sounds like. Describe some of the musical characteristics that you imagine when you think of Spanish folk music.

One characteristic of Spanish folk music is that the accompaniment is often performed on a guitar. Look through the notation of the accompaniment to find places where the piano might be imitating the sound of a guitar.

Now turn to the music for "Arruru" on page 73.

HOW DID YOU DO? ? ? ?

Spanish folk music has a highly distinctive style. Think about your preparation and performance of "Arruru."

1. Can you sing harmony in thirds? Sing measures 8–11 of "Arruru" with a classmate to demonstrate your skill.
2. Describe the difference between staccato and legato articulation, and tell how you used these in "Arruru."

3. Listen to a tape of your ensemble's performance of "Arruru" and discuss the characteristics of Spanish folk music that are present in this song.

TEACHING STRATEGY

6/8 Meter

If students are not familiar with reading 6/8 meter, have them:
- Review Skill Master 6, *Rhythm Challenge in 6/8 Time,* in the TRB, until it is familiar.
- Construct rhythmic reading exercises for the ensemble using 6/8 building blocks: ♩., ♩, ♩♪, and ♪♩ and ♫ .

Diction

Have students:
- Review what they know about forming vowels.
- Sing the piece with just vowels.
- Add the consonants crisply and clearly, without getting in the way of the vowels.
- Sing the piece with clear diction.

Arruru

Spanish Carol
Arranged by Ruth E. Dwyer and
Thomas Gerber

Two-part Chorus with Piano

Arruru **73**

MUSIC LITERACY

To help students expand their music literacy, have them:
- Clap and speak the rhythm of "Arruru."
- Conduct and speak the text in rhythm.
- Identify the main Spanish cultures that influence the United States. (Spain, Mexico, Central and South America, the islands in the Caribbean)
- Research types of Spanish music and

the cultures from which they come, identifying influences on the music.
- Find recorded examples of the music they are researching.
- Explore availability of Spanish performers in your community.
- Share information, playing recordings whenever possible, and compare and contrast Spanish musical styles.

Suggested Teaching Sequence

1. Review Vocal Warm-Up.
Have students:
- Review the Vocal Warm-Up on page 71.
- Use legato articulation on the first measure and staccato on the second.
- Feel the diaphragm move with the staccato articulation.
- Sing the exercise, swaying on the strong beats.
- Identify the rocking effect of 6/8 meter.
- Practice rolling the "r"s.

2. Review Sight-Singing.
Have students:
- Review the Sight-Singing exercise on page 71.
- Sight-sing both lines, switching parts on the repeat.
- Identify the stepwise melodic movement and the harmony in thirds.
- Look at the notation for "Arruru," finding the harmony in thirds.

3. Sight-sing "Arruru" using solfège and hand signs or numbers.
Have students:
- Divide into voice sections and read each part using rhythm syllables.
- Still in sections, sing with solfège and hand signs or numbers, identifying and working on problem areas.
- Sing the piece through using solfège and hand signs or numbers with full ensemble.
- Divide into sections and recite the text rhythmically for each voice part.
- Sing the piece through with text as a full ensemble.

4. Use staccato and legato articulation in "Arruru."
Have students:
- Review staccato and legato articulation.
- Determine where each would be appropriate in "Arruru."
- Sing "Arruru," using their articulation as planned.

5. Identify the Spanish characteristics of "Arruru."

Have students:

- Identify the combination of characteristics in "Arruru" that make it feel and sound like a Spanish folk song, including stepwise melodic movement, harmony in thirds, 6/8 meter at a swaying tempo, the rhythm, AB (verse-refrain) song form, the guitarlike accompaniment, and the Spanish words in the text.

VOCAL DEVELOPMENT

To encourage vocal development, have students:

- Demonstrate good vocal tone by singing tall vowels in Spanish and English and alter (or modify) the vowel sounds when necessary.
- Energize sustained tones, especially the *oo* vowel sound by increasing the breath support and dynamic level.
- Sustain phrases by staggering the breathing and moving forward through the phrases.
- Demonstrate the correct singing of the *r* consonant after a vowel in English. It should be almost silent, as in *shepherds, their, newborn,* and *winter's.*
- Identify the intervals of thirds between the parts and tune them carefully.
- Listen for diphthongs (two vowel sounds when one vowel is written) in English words, such as *I, way, sky, bright,* and *high.* Sing or sustain the first vowel sound and barely sing the second vowel sound with the next syllable.

CURRICULUM CONNECTIONS
Spanish Arts

Have students:

- Research the literature, art, drama, dance, and classical music of the same culture they are exploring musically in the Music Literacy activity on page 73.
- Add this information to their presentation about their Spanish culture.
- Draw appropriate parallels between the arts of the culture.

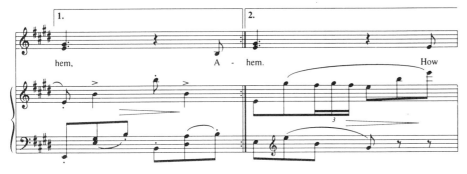

Assessment

Informal Assessment

During this lesson, students showed the ability to:

- Identify and sing staccato and legato articulation in the Vocal Warm-Up exercise.
- Read and sing in thirds in the Sight-Singing exercise.
- Sing using staccato and legato articulation in "Arruru."
- Identify characteristics of Spanish folk songs and sing them in "Arruru."

Student Self-Assessment

Have students:

- Evaluate their performance with the How Did You Do? section on page 72.
- Answer the questions individually. Discuss them in pairs or small groups and/or write their responses on a sheet of paper.

Individual Performance Assessment

To further demonstrate accomplishment, have each student:

- In a duet, sing measures 8–20 of "Arruru" into a tape recorder in an isolated space, demonstrating staccato and legato articulation and harmony in thirds.
- Write a program introduction for "Arruru," describing the characteristics of Spanish folk songs that are in this piece.

TEACHING STRATEGY

Phrasing

Have students:

- Review the staccato and legato articulation decided upon for performance of the piece.
- Look at the piece and determine where the phrases begin and end.
- Discuss how to combine the articulation and shaping of phrases. (The articulation should not stop students from building energy toward the peak of each phrase, then releasing energy to the end of the phrase.)
- Sing with articulation and shaping of phrases.

Extension

Conducting in 6/8

Have students:

- Sing the first verse of "Arruru," swaying with the beat.
- Look at the meter signature to see that it is 6/8, and analyze their movement to realize that they are moving in 2, rather than 6. (Because the beats go by so fast, they are felt as two sets of three subbeats.)
- Conduct in 2 as they sing.
- Sing as volunteers conduct the piece.

Create Movement for a Processional

Have students:

- Identify a processional as a movement of a group from one place to another in an organized fashion, usually to music.
- Try out different movements individually and in pairs, thinking about a processional as they sing the piece.
- Dividing into two groups, each group watches as the other improvises movement.
- Choose one movement for each section of the song (A and B), and choose a formation (single line, pairs, threes, or fours).
- Practice and refine the movements until a processional emerges.
- Perform the piece with the music, either at the beginning or to move from one segment to the next.

Guitar Accompaniment

If there is a guitarist in your community who plays acoustic guitar, work with the person to adapt the piano accompaniment to guitar, and use guitar accompaniment with this piece for a more authentic rendition. Have students:

- Locate a willing volunteer guitarist in the community.
- Work with the performer to adapt the accompaniment.

National Standards

The following National Standards are addressed through the Extension and bottom-page activities:

1. Singing, alone and with others, a varied repertoire of music. **(a, b)**
4. Composing and arranging music within specified guidelines. **(a, b)**
5. Reading and notating music. **(a, b)**
6. Listening to, analyzing, and describing music. **(a, b, c, e, f)**
7. Evaluating music and music performances. **(a, b, c)**
8. Understanding relationships between music, the other arts, and disciplines outside the arts. **(a, b, d)**
9. Understanding music in relation to history and culture. **(a, c, d)**

Peace Today Descends from Heaven

COMPOSER: *Alessandro Grandi (c. 1575–1630)*
TRANSLATED AND EDITED BY: *Dr. William Tortolano*

LESSON 12

Peace Today Descends from Heaven

COMPOSER: Alessandro Grandi
(c. 1575–1630)

TRANSLATED AND EDITED BY:
Dr. William Tortolano

CHORAL MUSIC TERMS
imitative
melismatic
syllabic
3/2 meter
2/2 meter

VOICING
SA

PERFORMANCE STYLE
Slowly
Accompanied by keyboard

FOCUS
- Read and perform in 2/2 and 3/2 meter.
- Identify and perform syllabic, melismatic, and imitative passages.

Focus

OVERVIEW
2/2 and 3/2 meter; syllabic, melismatic, and imitative treatment of text.

OBJECTIVES
After completing this lesson, students should be able to:
- Read and perform in 2/2 and 3/2 meter.
- Identify and perform syllabic, melismatic, and imitative passages.

CHORAL MUSIC TERMS
Define the Choral Music Terms for students, giving pronunciation, and answering any questions that may arise.

Warming Up

 Rhythm Drill
Clap these rhythms as someone taps the half-note pulse throughout. Notice the shift from beats in sets of two to beats in sets of three, and stress the strong beat at the beginning of each measure. What visual clue tells you to expect imitative style?

 Vocal Warm-Up
Sing this exercise using a sigh, maintaining good breath support.

Ah ___ ah. ___

Lesson 12: Peace Today Descends from Heaven **77**

Warming Up

Rhythm Drill
This Rhythm Drill is designed to prepare students to:
- Read and clap in 2/2 and 3/2 meter.
- Identify and clap imitative and syllabic style.
- Clap rhythms from the piece.
Have students:
- Read through the Rhythm Drill directions.
- Perform the drill.

TEACHER'S RESOURCE BINDER
Blackline Master 16, *Translation and Pronunciation Guide for "Peace Today Descends from Heaven"*

National Standards
1. Singing a varied repertoire of music. **(a, c, f)**
3. Improvising melodies, variations, and accompaniments. **(b)**
4. Composing and arranging music within specified guidelines. **(a)**
5. Reading and notating music. **(a, b)**
6. Listening to, analyzing, and describing music. **(a, b, c)**
7. Evaluating music and music performances. **(a, b)**
8. Understanding relationships between music and other disciplines. **(c)**
9. Understanding music in relation to history and culture. **(a)**

Vocal Warm-Up

The Vocal Warm-Up on page 77 is designed to prepare students to:

- Relax and warm up the body.
- Practice correct breathing for singing.
- Sing octave leaps and descending scale passages in tune.

Have students:

- Read through the Vocal Warm-Up directions.
- Sing, following your demonstration.

Sight-Singing

This Sight-Singing exercise is designed to prepare students to:

- Clap rhythms in 2/2 and 3/2 meters.
- Sight-sing pitches in F major.

Have students:

- Read through the Sight-Singing exercise directions.
- Read through each voice part rhythmically, clapping the rhythm.
- Sight-sing through each part separately using solfège and hand signs or numbers.
- Sing all parts together.

Singing: "Peace Today Descends from Heaven"

Have students:

- Read the text on page 78.
- Individually or in small groups, try out each of the suggested text treatments, using a familiar tone set, for example, F major.
- Identify syllabic as one pitch per syllable, melismatic as many pitches per syllable, and imitative as one part imitating the other (exactly or approximately).
- Look at the notation for "Peace Today Descends from Heaven" for examples of these three treatments of text. (syllabic = measures 9–12; imitative = measures 9–12; melismatic = 35–37; some sections have more than one treatment.)

Sight-Singing

Clap the rhythm first, then sight-sing this exercise using solfège and hand signs or numbers. Watch for the changing meter as you read.

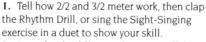

Singing: "Peace Today Descends from Heaven"

A composer can use text in many ways. Read this text out loud:

Now, today, peace descends from heaven. Alleluia!

Be a composer for the text in these ways:

- Sing one pitch for each syllable of the text.
- Sing each syllable for more than one pitch, stretching it out into a long thread. (When you do this, you create a *melismatic passage*.)
- With a partner, read the text with the same rhythm, but different pitches that create harmony.
- Next, wait while your partner imitates each word or group of words that you sing, before you go on.

Can you tell which of these is syllabic, melismatic, and imitative?

Now turn to the music for "Peace Today Descends from Heaven" on page 79.

HOW DID YOU DO?

You needed to use known information in new ways to learn this piece. Think about your preparation and performance of "Peace Today Descends from Heaven."

1. Tell how 2/2 and 3/2 meter work, then clap the Rhythm Drill, or sing the Sight-Singing exercise in a duet to show your skill.

2. Describe the difference between syllabic, melismatic, and imitative treatment of text. As you sing "Peace Today Descends from Heaven," signal by holding up one finger for syllabic, two fingers for melismatic and three fingers for imitative passages.

3. Compare "Peace Today Descends from Heaven" to other pieces you have sung in this book. How is it musically the same? How is it musically different?

4. Which characteristics of this piece do you prefer, and which would you change? List the factors you think led the composer to write the music as he did, (cultural, historical, musical, and/or textual factors).

TEACHING STRATEGY

2/2 and 3/2 Meter

These meters may throw students off simply because they might assume that the quarter note should get one beat. Help familiarize everyone with the half-note pulse. Place eight "beat bars" (horizontal line each of the same length), on the board, prefaced by a 2/2 meter signature. Have students:

- Pat once for each beat bar as you point.
- Place a half note above each beat bar,

and then clap once on each beat as you point.

- Substitute two quarter notes for some of the half notes and clap as you point.
- Substitute other rhythms from the piece into the rhythm, and then clap it.
- Continue to play with the rhythms in 2/2 meter until they become familiar.

Peace Today Descends from Heaven

Hodie, nobis de caelo

Alessandro Grandi
Translated and Edited by
Dr. William Tortolano

SA, Accompanied

Suggested Teaching Sequence

1. Review Rhythm Drill.
Read and clap in 2/2 and 3/2 meter. Have students:
- Review the Rhythm Drill on page 77.
- Clap each part as the other group taps the steady half-note pulse.
- Clap both parts together, working for accuracy, and feeling the strong pulse at the beginning of each measure.
- Identify the visual clue for imitative style. (The notation for Part II is the same as Part I, but one measure later.)

2. Review Vocal Warm-Up.
Warm up voice. Sing with good breath support. Have students:
- Review the Vocal Warm-Up on page 77.
- Use a sigh to sing the exercise.
- Identify the octave leap and stepwise downward scale.

3. Review Sight-Singing.

Read, clap, and sing in 2/2 and 3/2 meter. Have students:

- Review the Sight-Singing exercise on page 78.
- First clap the rhythm, over a steady half-note pulse if necessary. Secure the rhythm before adding pitch.
- Sight-sing using solfège and hand signs or numbers.
- Identify the phrases, and sing through the phrases to give musical structure to the sound. (One suggestion for phrasing is measures 1–5, 6–9, and 10–end. However, other interpretations are possible.)

4. Sight-sing "Peace Today Descends from Heaven" using solfège and hand signs or numbers.

Have students:

- Divide into voice sections (SA) and read each part rhythmically, using rhythm syllables.
- Clap the rhythm in full ensemble, listening for imitative sections.
- In sections, sing with solfège and hand signs or numbers, identifying and working on problem areas.
- Sing the piece through using solfège and hand signs or numbers with full ensemble.

CURRICULUM CONNECTIONS
Science

The concept of imitation is related to the scientific understanding of shadow and mirror image, which were of great interest to Renaissance scholars. Many of these scholars, such as Leonardo da Vinci, were also artists and musicians. It has been suggested that many scientific discoveries were intuitively represented by artists centuries before they were "discovered" by scientists.

Have students:

- Learn more about how imitative style in music and art might have informed the scientific discoveries relating to shadow (affected learning about time, space, and astronomy), and mirror image (affected studies of vision, led to camera images and studies of the nature of light).

5. Learn the Latin pronunciation.

Have students:

- Using Blackline Master 16, *Translation and Pronunciation Guide for "Peace Today Descends from Heaven,"* echo or read the pronunciation slowly.
- Speak the Latin text in rhythm.
- Sing the piece with correct Latin pronunciation.

6. Identify syllabic, melismatic, and imitative treatment of text in "Peace Today Descends from Heaven."

Have students:

- Review the definitions of syllabic, melismatic, and imitative.
- In three groups, each search the notation for all examples of either syllabic, melismatic, or imitative treatment of text.
- In full ensemble, perform the piece, each group standing when their treatment is occurring. (Sometimes there will be two groups standing.)

VOCAL DEVELOPMENT

To encourage vocal development, have students:

- Demonstrate good vocal tone by singing pure Latin vowels. Use a tall resonant space in the mouth and throat with a large *oo* vowel sound.
- Sing with a consistent tall mouth shape on the word *Alleluia*, articulating the consonants with the tongue and lips.
- Energize sustained tones by increasing the breath support and dynamic level.
- Sustain phrases by staggering the breathing and moving forward through the phrases to resting points.
- Increase intensity on repeated notes to feel forward movement of the melodic lines.
- Demonstrate the correct singing of the *r* consonant after a vowel when singing in English. It should be almost silent, as in *earth* and *there.*
- Listen for diphthongs in words when singing in English, as in *now, today, joy, shines, light,* and *rejoice.* Sing or sustain the first vowel sound and barely sing the second vowel sound with the next syllable.
- Analyze the imitative writing between the parts. Note the number of beats between entrances.

TEACHING STRATEGY
Exploring Syllabic, Melismatic, and Imitative Treatment of Text

The strategy used to help students discover and identify syllabic, melismatic, and imitative text treatment allows students to use their own knowledge to construct meaning. This exploration is sometimes a bit noisy, but allows the students to take control of their own learning, and is highly motivating and engaging.

Have students:

- Choose a proverb or short line of text from the newspaper.
- Compose short pieces using one treatment or combinations of these three treatments of the text.

 MUSIC LITERACY

To help students expand their music literacy, have them:

- Conduct the changing meters, feeling the half-note unit of measure.
- Recognize that when the meter is challenging, it is necessary to work to get the rhythm accurate. At the same time, the piece only works musically if the musical phrases are shaped.

- Identify the musical phrases, using the text to help when there are differences of opinion.
- Review strategies for shaping phrases.
- Sing the piece, focusing on shaping phrases.

Assessment

Informal Assessment
During this lesson, students showed the ability to:
- Clap rhythms in 2/2 and 3/2 meter in the Rhythm Drill.
- Sight-sing in changing meters in the Sight-Singing exercise.
- Read and sing in 2/2 and 3/2 meter in "Peace Today Descends from Heaven."
- Identify and sing using syllabic, melismatic, and imitative treatment of text in "Peace Today Descends from Heaven."

Student Self-Assessment
Have students:
- Evaluate their performance with the How Did You Do? section on page 78.
- Answer the questions individually. Discuss them in pairs or small groups and/or write their responses on a sheet of paper.

Individual Performance Assessment
To further demonstrate accomplishment, have each student:
- Compose and then perform a rhythmic piece with four measures in 2/2 and four measures in 3/2.
- Listen to a tape of the ensemble performance, signaling 1 for syllabic, 2 for melismatic, and 3 for imitative passages.
- In a duet, sing from measures 1–19 into a tape recorder in an isolated space, demonstrating the ability to perform in 2/2 and 3/2 meter, using syllabic, melismatic, and imitative treatment of text.

Extension

Conducting in 2/2 and 3/2

Have students:

- Learn the conducting patterns for 2 and 3.
- Sing the piece, with half the group conducting in 2 during the 2/2 meter, and the other half conducting in 3 during the 3/2 meter.
- Switch parts.
- Sing, conducting the whole piece.
- Sing as an ensemble, with volunteers conducting the group.

Evaluating a Composition

"Peace Today Descends from Heaven" was written during the Renaissance period, and has many characteristics typical of sacred Renaissance music. In every period, good, average, and poor quality music is written. Ask: How do you know if this is a good one?

Have students:

- Discuss what criteria might be used to determine the quality of a piece, regardless of style or period.
- Discuss the characteristics of this piece that warrant ratings of good, average, or poor, taking into consideration the cultural and historical context in which it was written.
- Write a critique of the piece for the school newspaper, evaluating the piece in terms of its aesthetic qualities, and explaining how it evokes feelings and emotions.

National Standards

The following National Standards are addressed through the Extension and bottom-page activities:

1. Singing, alone and with others, a varied repertoire of music. **(a, c)**
4. Composing and arranging music within specified guidelines. **(a)**
5. Reading and notating music. **(a, b)**
6. Listening to, analyzing, and describing music. **(a, b, c, e, f)**
7. Evaluating music and music performances. **(c)**
8. Understanding relationships between music, the other arts, and disciplines outside the arts. **(a, b, c)**
9. Understanding music in relation to history and culture. **(a, c, d)**

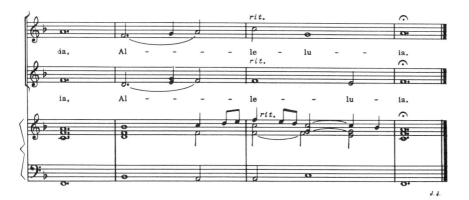

Descending and Ascending

Have students:

- Think about the word *descend* from the title of this piece, and how it might be represented musically. (descending patterns)
- Explore the notation for examples of descending patterns (text has peace descending, light shining down), and also the text for clearly ascending inferences. (create, resurrect, redemption, rejoice)
- Discuss the treatment of the word *Alleluia*. (melismatic, with upward and downward movement depending upon what the text around it suggests)
- Consider how these images might be represented in visual art, taking into consideration characteristics of the Renaissance art style—flat, with little use of shadow or depth.
- Create a painting or drawing that explores these elements visually and represents syllabic, melismatic, and imitative treatment of subject matter.

Os Justi

COMPOSER: Eleanor Daley
TEXT: Psalm 37:30–31

Focus

OVERVIEW
Dark tone quality; correct diction.

OBJECTIVES
After completing this lesson, students should be able to:
• Sing with a dark tone quality.
• Sing with correct diction.

CHORAL MUSIC TERMS
Define the Choral Music Terms for students, giving pronunciation, and answering any questions that may arise.

Warming Up

Vocal Warm-Up
This Vocal Warm-Up is designed to prepare students to:
• Sing downward patterns.
• Mix vocal registers from high to low.
• Think upward during descending lines, helping to mix registers.
Have students:
• Read through the Vocal Warm-Up directions.
• Sing, following your demonstration.

LESSON 13
Os Justi
COMPOSER: *Eleanor Daley*
TEXT: *Psalm 37:30–31*

| CHORAL MUSIC TERMS |
| consonants |
| dark tone quality |
| diction |
| vowels |

VOICING
SSAA

PERFORMANCE STYLE
Slowly in two
A cappella

FOCUS
• Sing with a dark tone quality.
• Sing with correct diction.

Warming Up

 Vocal Warm-Up
Sigh as though you have finished a difficult chore. Then start high and begin sighing downward, making an upward motion with your hands. Now use the same sighing breath to sing this Warm-Up. Move up or down by half steps on each repeat.

Sight-Singing
Sight-sing each part separately, using solfège and hand signs or numbers. Now sing both parts together. Switch parts. Sing this exercise using first a light tone quality, then a darker one.

TEACHER'S RESOURCE BINDER
Blackline Master 17, *Translation and Pronunciation Guide for "Os Justi"*
Blackline Master 18, *Diction Guide*

 National Standards
1. Singing a varied repertoire of music. **(a, b, c)**
3. Improvising melodies. **(b)**
4. Composing and arranging music. **(a)**
5. Reading and notating music. **(a, b)**
6. Listening to, analyzing, and describing music. **(a, b, c)**
7. Evaluating music and performances. **(a)**
8. Understanding relationships between music, the other arts, and disciplines outside the arts. **(c)**
9. Understanding music in relation to history and culture. **(c)**

Singing: "Os Justi"

A performer can choose tone quality to match the mood and message of a composition. Sing:

"The mouth of the righteous speaketh wisdom"

on one pitch. First form a round mouth, and sing the words, focusing on the vowels. Next, form a round mouth, then drop the jaw as much as possible as you sing.

Describe the difference between these two tone qualities, and when each would be appropriate to use.

Now turn to the music for "Os Justi" on page 88.

HOW DID YOU DO?

The composer writes the piece, but the performer interprets it, deciding how to bring the message to the audience. Think about your preparation and performance of "Os Justi."

1. Describe how to create a dark tone quality as you sing, then sing from the beginning of "Os Justi" to A, demonstrating this tone quality.

2. Tell a neighbor what you need to think about to have good diction, demonstrating with examples from "Os Justi."

3. Write a "diction manual" for an imaginary newcomer to your ensemble, informing them what is expected to create good diction.

VOCAL DEVELOPMENT

Have students:
- Demonstrate good vocal tone by singing with a large *oo* vowel sound.
- Sing with a consistent tall mouth shape on the word *Alleluia,* articulating the consonants with the tongue and lips.
- Sustain phrases by staggering the breathing through the phrases.
- Increase intensity on repeated notes to feel forward movement of the lines.
- Emphasize the two-note phrases by "leaning into" the first note and tapering off on the second note.
- Identify melodic (linear) and harmonic (vertical) intervals between the parts and tune them carefully.

Sight-Singing

This Sight-Singing exercise is designed to prepare students to:
- Sight-sing in minor tonality.
- Sing a descant harmony part with a melody.
- Sing using a bright and dark tone quality.
- Read the dotted quarter-eighth rhythm.

Have students:
- Read through the Sight-Singing exercise directions.
- Read through each voice part rhythmically, using rhythm syllables.
- Sight-sing through each part separately using solfège and hand signs or numbers.
- Sing all parts together; switch parts.

Singing: "Os Justi"

Identify and practice light and dark tone quality. Have students:
- Read the text on page 87.
- Try both tone qualities suggested.
- Describe the two qualities, determining that the first produces a brighter quality, and the second a darker quality.
- Read the word *sapientiam* in measures 3 and 4 of "Os Justi," using the correct rhythm and dark tone quality.

TEACHING STRATEGY

Dark Tone Quality

Have students:
- Think of mental images that will help keep the position of the mouth correct for producing a dark tone quality, for example: yawning while singing, or keeping the mouth cavernous.

Suggested Teaching Sequence

1. Review Vocal Warm-Up.

Have students:

- Review the Vocal Warm-Ups on page 86.
- Use the sighing movement, and feel the mixing of registers.
- Move up or down by half steps.

2. Review Sight-Singing.

Have students:

- Review the Sight-Singing exercise on page 86.
- Sing in two parts, tuning each interval and with bright, then dark, tone quality.
- Read the first four measures of "Os Justi," using the dark tone quality.

3. Sight-sing "Os Justi" using solfège and hand signs or numbers.

Have students:

- Divide into voice sections (SSAA) and read each part rhythmically, clapping the rhythm in full ensemble.
- Still in sections, sing with solfège and hand signs or numbers, identifying and working on problem areas.
- Sing the piece through using solfège and hand signs or numbers with full ensemble.

4. Learn the Latin pronunciation.

Have students:

- Using Blackline Master 17, *Translation and Pronunciation Guide for "Os Justi,"* echo or read the pronunciation slowly.
- Speak the Latin in rhythm.
- Sing with correct Latin.

5. Work on correct diction.

Have students:

- Using Blackline Master 18, *Diction Guide,* read the guidelines for correct diction.
- Sing "Os Justi," attending to correct diction throughout.

88

To El's Angels

Os Justi

Eleanor Daley
Psalm 37:30–31

SSAA, A cappella

Translation: The mouth of the righteous speaketh wisdom, and his tongue talketh of judgement. The law of God is in his heart; none of his steps shall slide. (Psalm 37:30-31)

TEACHING STRATEGY
Phrasing and Interpretation

Have students:

- Identify the phrases in the piece by reading the text and finding natural pauses in the music.
- Look through the notation for dynamic markings.
- Discuss shaping phrases using dynamics and techniques for building or releasing of energy and/or tension.
- Sing, shaping the phrases and following the dynamic markings.
- Discuss how this performance was different than before this aspect was added.

Os Justi **89**

During this lesson, students showed the ability to:

- Experiment with and use bright and dark tone quality.
- Read and sing in two parts in minor tonality, using solfège and hand signs or numbers in the Sight-Singing exercise.
- Use bright and dark tone quality in the Sight-Singing exercise.
- Sing using dark tone quality and correct diction in "Os Justi."

Student Self-Assessment
Have students:

- Evaluate their performance with the How Did You Do? section on page 87.
- Answer the questions individually. Discuss them in pairs or small groups and/or write their responses on a sheet of paper.

Individual Performance Assessment
To further demonstrate accomplishment, have each student:

- In an isolated space, tape record a phrase of her voice part, demonstrating dark tone quality and correct diction.
- Write program notes for this piece, telling the audience what to listen for regarding dark tone quality and correct diction.

Extension

Quartets
Have students:

- Volunteer to form quartets, and sing "Os Justi" with one singer on a part.
- Critique their own performance.
- Listen as classmates identify which parts they performed especially well.

National Standards

The following National Standards are addressed through the Extension and bottom-page activities:

1. Singing, alone and with others, a varied repertoire of music. **(a, b, c, f)**
4. Composing and arranging music within specified guidelines. **(b, d)**
5. Reading and notating music. **(a, b)**
6. Listening to, analyzing, and describing music. **(a, b, c, e)**
7. Evaluating music and music performances. **(a, b, c)**
8. Understanding relationships between music, the other arts, and disciplines outside the arts. **(a, c)**
9. Understanding music in relation to history and culture. **(a, c, d)**

Dance on My Heart

COMPOSER: Allen Koepke

TEXT: Allen Koepke

Focus

OVERVIEW

Syncopated rhythms; two keys; mixed meters.

OBJECTIVES

After completing this lesson, students should be able to:
- Read rhythms in mixed meter.
- Identify and perform syncopated rhythms.
- Read and sing in two keys.

CHORAL MUSIC TERMS

Define the Choral Music Terms for students, giving pronunciation, and answering any questions that may arise.

Warming Up

Rhythm Drill

This Rhythm Drill is designed to prepare students to:
- Read and clap mixed meter, from 4/4 to 7/8 meter.
- Identify and clap syncopated rhythms.

Have students:
- Read through the Rhythm Drill directions.
- Perform the drill.

Vocal Warm-Up

This Vocal Warm-Up is designed to prepare students to:
- Sing using solfège and hand signs or numbers.
- Form vowels correctly.
- Sing with vocal flexibility.

Have students:
- Read through the Vocal Warm-Up directions.
- Sing, following your demonstration.

Dance on My Heart

COMPOSER: *Allen Koepke*

TEXT: *Allen Koepke*

CHORAL MUSIC TERMS
key signatures
mixed meter
rhythm
syncopated rhythms

VOICING
SSA

PERFORMANCE STYLE
Sprightly
Accompanied by piano

FOCUS
- Read rhythms in mixed meter.
- Identify and perform syncopated rhythms.
- Read and sing in two keys.

Warming Up

 Rhythm Drill

Read and clap this rhythm over a steady eighth-note pulse. You will not need the pulse until you get to the 7/8 measure—then you will be glad it is there! Point out the syncopated rhythms.

Vocal Warm-Up

Sing this exercise using solfège and hand signs or numbers. Move up or down by half steps on the repeats. Now sing the exercise to practice forming vowels correctly, using *mah, meh, mee, moh,* and *moo.*

mi do mi fa so
3   1   3   4   5

TEACHER'S RESOURCE BINDER

 National Standards

1. Singing a varied repertoire of music. **(a, b, c)**
5. Reading and notating music. **(a, b)**
6. Listening to, analyzing, and describing music. **(a, b, c)**
7. Evaluating music and music performances. **(a, b)**
8. Understanding relationships between music and other disciplines. **(c)**
9. Understanding music in relation to history and culture. **(c)**

Sight-Singing

First, speak and clap the rhythms. Then sight-sing both exercises slowly, tuning each chord. Sing them more and more quickly, keeping the tuning accurate. How are these two exercises different?

Singing: "Dance on My Heart"

A musical score is like a map. It won't help you much until you know how to read it. Look at "Dance on My Heart." Read the text, following the directions very carefully. Can you find your way through this word map without getting lost?

Tell the story in your own words, verse by verse.

Now turn to the music for "Dance on My Heart" on page 92.

Now turn to the music for "Dance on My Heart" on page 92.

HOW DID YOU DO?

??

By now, even a complicated map shouldn't stop you from singing from the heart. Think about your preparation and performance of "Dance on My Heart."

1. Tell how you negotiate changing from 4/4 to 7/8 meter, then clap the Rhythm Drill to show your skill.

2. Describe how syncopated rhythms work, then point some out in the notation of "Dance on My Heart."

3. Tell which two keys are used in "Dance on My Heart." How are they the same? How are they different? Sing the two Sight-Singing exercises to show your ability to sing in these two keys.

4. Write an imaginary radio critique of your ensemble's performance of "Dance on My Heart," comparing it to similar or exemplary models. Record the report, with yourself as the reporter for a local radio station.

Lesson 14: Dance on My Heart **91**

Composer Allen Koepke

For the past 30 years, Allen Koepke has been active as a choral conductor and composer in Iowa. He is a graduate of Luther College, Decorah, Iowa, with an M.A. from the University of Northern Iowa.

"Dance on My Heart"

"Dance on My Heart" is a fusion of madrigal and contemporary styles. The piece should be performed with the spirit of a light-hearted madrigal. Careful diction is a must so that the audience can enjoy the story. The 7/8 measures should be felt as 3/8 plus 4/8, with the downbeats on one and four receiving their own natural accents.

Sight-Singing

This Sight-Singing exercise is designed to prepare students to:
• Tune chords in three parts.
• Sight-sing in F and D major.
• Compare two keys for similarities and differences.
• Sing and hear harmonies they will encounter in "Dance on My Heart."

Have students:
• Read through the Sight-Singing exercise directions.
• Read through each voice part rhythmically, using rhythm syllables.
• Sight-sing through each part separately using solfège and hand signs or numbers.
• Sing all parts together.

Singing: "Dance On My Heart"

Following the notation map to read the story. Have students:
• Read the text on page 91.
• Read through the text of the song, following the written directions along the way.
• Tell the story, verse by verse.

Suggested Teaching Sequence

1. Review Rhythm Drill.
Read and clap mixed meters. Have students:
- Review the Rhythm Drill on page 90.
- Clap the rhythms over a steady eighth-note pulse.
- Discuss how many pulses there will be for each quarter note in 4/4 meter. (2)
- Discuss how to feel 7/8 meter as sets of 3, 2, and 2 in various arrangements. (322, 223, 232)
- Identify syncopation as moving the accent off the normally accented beat, and point to where this occurs in the Rhythm Drill. (one example: over the bar line from measures 2 and 3)
- Look at the notation for "Dance on My Heart," locating the meter changes and examples of syncopation that occur across the bar line.

2. Review Vocal Warm-Up.
Sing using solfège and hand signs or numbers. Form vowels correctly. Have students:
- Review the Vocal Warm-Up on page 90.
- Use a different vowel each day, checking for a unified vowel sound from the ensemble.

3. Review Sight-Singing.
Sight-sing in three parts and two different keys. Tune chords. Have students:
- Review the Sight-Singing exercise on page 91.
- Sing in three parts, tuning each interval.
- Compare the two keys, F major and D major, noticing that they have many overlapping pitches, but those pitches have different syllable names in each key.

Dance on My Heart

Allen Koepke

SSA, Accompanied

© Copyright 1992 by Santa Barbara Music Publishing / For all countries

92 *Choral Connections   Level 3 Treble Voices*

TEACHING STRATEGY

Mixed Meter
If students are not familiar with the 4/4 and 7/8 meters, have them:
- Practice until they are familiar with the rhythms and meters.
- Conduct in both meters, using a 4/4 pattern for 4/4 meter, and a 3 pattern for 7/8, conducting on the 1st, 4th, and 6th eighth notes in each measure.

Syncopation
Have students:
- Think of other places than over the bar line that syncopation could occur to put accents off the strong beats.
- Watch as you show them some other possibilities for syncopation, including the familiar.

4. Sight-sing "Dance on My Heart" using solfège and hand signs or numbers.

Have students:

- In voice sections (SSA), read the rhythm from measures 3–20, clapping and using rhythm syllables or text.
- Speak and clap the rhythm in full ensemble, from measures 3–20.
- In sections, sight-sing measures 3–20 using solfège and hand signs, numbers, or text.
- Sing measures 3–20 in full ensemble, using solfège and hand signs, numbers, or text, identifying and working on problem areas.
- Repeat this sequence with each large section of the piece.
- Sing the piece through with full ensemble.

5. Follow the composer's performance markings and specifications.

Have students:

- Look through the notation for all composer markings, identifying each and looking up the ones they don't know. (Sprightly = 126, and is just a little over two beats per second with crisp diction; *dal segno* indicates the point of return—see measures 3 and 36; *coda* is the extension and closing from measure 37, and a *bit slower* at measure 28; *a tempo* is a return to speed at measure 33.)
- Practice each of these until it is correct and familiar.
- Practice adding dynamics, following markings.
- Sing using composer's performance suggestions.

VOCAL DEVELOPMENT

To encourage vocal development, have students:

- Demonstrate good vocal tone by singing tall vowels and alter (or modify) the vowel sounds when necessary, as in *hand, affection, one, love,* and *danced.*
- Enjoy the resonance of the *oo* vowel sound on words such as *who, you,* and *through.*
- Energize sustained tones by increasing the breath support and dynamic level.
- Sustain phrases by staggering the breathing and moving forward through the phrases.
- Increase intensity on repeated notes to feel the forward movement of the melodic lines.
- Demonstrate the correct singing of the *r* consonant after a vowel. It should be almost silent, as in *fair, your, far, other, braver, marry,* and *heart.*
- Listen for diphthongs (two vowel sounds when one vowel is written) in words such as *I.* Sing or sustain the first vowel sound and barely sing the second vowel sound with the next syllable.
- Identify intervals and chords between the parts and tune them carefully.

I'm a-dor-ing-ly sweet." (to m. 11, v. 2)
you'll be sat-is-fied." (to m. 20-21, v. 3)
say you'll be my wife." (to m. 20-21, v. 5)

3."Well" she re-plied, "I'd make my se-lec-tion, and you'd re-ceive my
5. "Sir," she re-plied, "you are my se-lec-tion, and you'll re-ceive my

love and af-fec-tion if you danced on my heart,
love and af-fec-tion for you dance on my heart,

CURRICULUM CONNECTIONS

Mime and Creative Dance

Have students:

- Discuss possibilities for movement interpretation to go with "Dance on My Heart," considering both mime and creative dance.
- Discuss the advantages and disadvantages of each for this piece.
- In two groups, create two different movement settings for the piece.

- Share, revise, and refine them, and then prepare them to be performed.
- Compare the creative process in dance (choreography and performance) to music (composition and performance), citing similarities and differences in the creative, preparation, and performance process.

Assessment

Informal Assessment

During this lesson, students showed the ability to:

- Read and clap mixed meters including 4/4 and 7/8 in the Rhythm Drill.
- Identify and perform syncopation in the Rhythm Drill.
- Sight-sing in three parts and in two keys, using solfège and hand signs or numbers in the Sight-Singing exercise.
- Sing mixed meter with syncopation and in two keys in "Dance on My Heart."

Student Self-Assessment

Have students:

- Evaluate their performance with the How Did You Do? section on page 91.
- Answer the questions individually. Discuss them in pairs or small groups and/or write their responses on a sheet of paper.

Individual Performance Assessment

To further demonstrate accomplishment, have each student:

- In a small group, speak the text of measures 11–19 with accurate rhythm.
- Sing "Dance on My Heart," signaling when she sings syncopated rhythm over a bar line.
- Individually read her voice part of the Sight-Singing exercise, measures to be chosen by you, using the correct solfège and hand signs or numbers for the key indicated.

TEACHING STRATEGY

Quarter Note Triplet

Have students:

- Find examples of the quarter note triplet in the notation for "Dance on My Heart." (measures 17, 18, 25, 27, 29, and 31)
- In pairs or small groups, write a definition of this rhythm in their own words.
- Compare their definition to the following: A triplet is a group of three notes performed in the time of two of the same kind. It is shown by a bracketed "3" above or below the notes.
- Practice performing the triplets, making sure they are three equal durations and take the time of two quarter notes.

Extension

Trios

Have students:
- Volunteer to form trios, and sing "Dance on My Heart" with one singer on a part.
- Critique their own performance.
- Listen as classmates identify which parts they performed especially well.

Telling the Story with Music

Have students:
- Choose a poem that tells a story in verses; for example: "The Raven," by Edgar Allan Poe; "O Captain, My Captain," by Walt Whitman; "Rock and Roll Band" or "The Toad and the Kangaroo," by Shel Silverstein; or write their own story poem.
- Read the poem until a rhythm emerges. It may be that there is more than one rhythm such as a verse and refrain, or an A and B rhythm that alternate, as in "Dance on My Heart."
- Determine the mood and select a key that reflects that mood.
- Write a melody to fit the rhythm. There may be a change in key if there is a change in mood.
- Share the first draft with classmates, getting suggestions for improvements.
- Revise and refine.

Historical Perspective

Have students:
- Predict when this piece was created based on the text and musical characteristics.
- Make a list of the predictions with supporting evidence.
- Research when the piece was written, and compare to their predictions. (The composer is contemporary and resides in Iowa.)
- Speculate on the composer's use of madrigal characteristics and the choice of text.

National Standards

The following National Standards are addressed through the Extension and bottom-page activities:

1. Singing, alone and with others, a varied repertoire of music. (**a, b, c, f**)
4. Composing and arranging music within specified guidelines. (**a, d**)
5. Reading and notating music. (**a, b**)
6. Listening to, analyzing, and describing music. (**a, b, c, e**)
7. Evaluating music and music performances. (**a, b, c**)
8. Understanding relationships between music, the other arts, and disciplines outside the arts. (**a, c, e**)
9. Understanding music in relation to history and culture. (**a, c, d, e**)

Making Historical Connections

Renaissance Period

Focus

OVERVIEW

Understanding the development of choral music during the Renaissance period.

OBJECTIVES

After completing this lesson, students should be able to:

• Describe characteristics of architecture, fine art, and music during the Renaissance period.

• Identify several musical forms of the Renaissance period.

• Define *a cappella, madrigal, motet,* and *polyphony.*

• Identify some of the key musical composers of the Renaissance.

CHORAL MUSIC TERMS

Define the Choral Music Terms for students, giving pronunciation, and answering any questions that may arise.

Introducing the Lesson

Introduce the Renaissance through visual art.

Analyze the artwork and basilica on pages 98 and 101 of the text. Have students:

• Study the painting and basilica, describing features in as much detail as possible.

• Discuss the information about each illustration provided at the bottom of pages 99 and 101 in your Teacher's Wraparound Edition.

The Adoration of the Magi **by Sandro Botticelli (1445–1510) reflects the Renaissance interest in religious subjects. Framing the central figures within the strong geometric pillars emphasized those subjects over others. Similar organizational principles are apparent in the Renaissance composers' ability to create intricate polyphonic works.**

c. 1481. Sandro Botticelli. *The Adoration of the Magi.* (Detail.) Tempera on wood. 70 x 104 cm (27⅛ x 41"). National Gallery of Art, Washington, D.C. Andrew W. Mellon Collection.

TEACHER'S RESOURCE BINDER

Fine Art Transparency 1, *The Adoration of the Magi,* by Botticelli

Optional Listening Selections:

Music: An Appreciation, 6th edition

"As Vesta Was Descending": CD 1, Track 77

Ricercar in the Twelfth Mode: CD 1, Track 79

National Standards

This lesson addresses the following National Standards:

6. Listening to, analyzing, and describing music. **(a)**

8. Understanding relationships between music, the other arts, and disciplines outside the arts. **(a, b, c, d, e)**

9. Understanding music in relation to history and culture. **(a, c, d)**

Renaissance Period
c. 1430–1600

After completing this lesson, you should be able to:

- *Describe some of the major developments of the Renaissance period.*
- *Explain the difference between sacred music and secular music.*
- *Discuss the major musical forms of the Renaissance period.*
- *Identify at least three major composers of the Renaissance period.*

In the history of Western Europe, the period from around 1430 until 1600 is called the Renaissance. This name comes from a French word meaning "rebirth," and the period was in many ways a time of rebirth or renewal. The scholars and artists of the Renaissance made a conscious effort to reestablish the standards of intellectual and cultural greatness they saw in the accomplishments of the ancient Greeks and Romans. Although the great figures of the Renaissance may have been looking back to earlier cultures, they were not moving back; instead, they were moving radically ahead into modern times.

A Time of Discovery

The Renaissance was a time of discovery in many fields. Modern science and scientific methods began to develop. Scholars no longer simply accepted what they read. Rather, they realized that careful observation and experimentation could help them draw new conclusions about the world around them. The results of this approach were a series of important advancements in science, mathematics, and technology. Better clocks and navigating instruments became available; scientists began to develop better lenses for instruments such as telescopes and microscopes. Astronomers established that the Earth and other planets revolved around the sun, and the positions of many stars were accurately calculated.

In part because of the technological advances of the period, the Renaissance was an era of increasing exploration and trade. For the first time, European sailing ships reached the southern coast of Africa, the Americas, and India. In 1519, the first successful round-the-world voyage was undertaken. These journeys brought a new, expanding sense of the world and an influx of new ideas—as well as new opportunities for trade—to the people of Renaissance Europe.

One technological advancement of the Renaissance had an impact on many aspects of life: the invention of the printing press with movable type, usually credited to Johann Gutenberg. Until this development, books had been copied by hand. The development of the printing press meant that books could be produced much more quickly and easily, and much less expensively. More and more people had access to books and the ideas they communicated, and thus prepared themselves to take advantage of this opportunity by learning to read both words and music. Books—of facts, of new ideas, and of music—were no longer the property of only the privileged.

COMPOSERS

John Dunstable (c. 1390–1453)
Guillaume Dufay (1400–1474)
Josquin Desprez (c. 1440–1521)
Heinrich Isaac (c. 1450–1517)
Clement Janequin (c. 1485–1560)
Adrian Willaert (1490–1562)
Christopher Tye (c. 1500–c. 1572)
Thomas Tallis (1505–1585)
Andrea Gabrieli (1520–1586)
Giovanni Pierluigi da Palestrina (c. 1525–1594)
Orlando di Lasso (1532–1594)
William Byrd (1543–1623)
Thomas Morley (c. 1557–c. 1602)
Michael Praetorius (c. 1571–1621)
Thomas Weelkes (1575–1623)

ARTISTS

Donatello (1386–1466)
Sandro Botticelli (1445–1510)
Leonardo da Vinci (1452–1519)
Albrecht Dürer (1471–1528)
Michelangelo (1475–1564)
Raphael (1483–1520)
Titian (c. 1488–1576)

AUTHORS

Sir Thomas More (1478–1536)
Martin Luther (1483–1546)
Miguel de Cervantes (1547–1616)
Sir Walter Raleigh (c. 1552–1618)
Sir Philip Sidney (1554–1586)
William Shakespeare (1564–1616)

CHORAL MUSIC TERMS

a cappella
Gregorian chant
madrigal
mass
motet
polyphony
sacred music
secular music

Renaissance Period **99**

Suggested Teaching Sequence

1. Examine the Renaissance period.

Have students:

- Read the text on pages 99–103.
- Share what they know about the composers, artists, and authors listed on this page.
- Read, discuss, and answer the review questions individually, in pairs, or in small groups.
- Discuss their answers with the whole group, clarifying misunderstandings.

2. Examine the Renaissance in historical perspective.

Have students:

- Turn to the time line on pages 100–103 and read the citations.
- Discuss why these people and events are considered important to the Renaissance period.
- Compare each of these events to what they know occurred before and after the Renaissance.
- Write a statement of one or two sentences in length that describes the Renaissance, based on one of the events in the time line. (The Renaissance spirit prospered as a result of the invention of the printing press. Because of the press, more people were exposed to new ideas and could write down their ideas.)

The Adoration of the Magi

During the Renaissance, there was a renewed focus back to the ancient culture of the Roman empire and the classical spirit. In visual art this was represented by a shift from sacred symbolism to realistic art. Perspective was explored as a result of interest in geometry, and the flat canvas now represented three-dimensional perspective from one point of view outside the plane of the art. The human form was celebrated, and the ideal was a realistic representation. *The Adoration of the Magi* illustrates some of the characteristic changes in Renaissance art, including the humanizing of figures, the use of light and shadow, the use of perspective, and the idealization of the Roman classical form, indicated by the columns and ruins.

Gutenberg press; beginning of modern printing   Copenhagen becomes Danish capital   First printed music appears

▼ c. 1435   ▼ 1445   ▼ 1465

• •

▼ 1441   ▼ 1453

Eton College and King's College,   Ottoman Turks capture Constantinople, marking end
Cambridge, founded   of Byzantine Empire

3. Define the musical aspects of the Renaissance period.

Have students:

• Review the changes in music during the Renaissance period.

• Define *a cappella, madrigal, motet,* and *polyphony,* telling how they reflected the development of choral music during the Renaissance.

• Describe the contributions of Renaissance composers such as John Dunstable, Josquin Desprez, Adrian Willaert, and Martin Luther.

• Identify musicians who contributed to the popularity of the madrigal. (Clement Jonequin, Heinrick Isaac, Thomas Tallis, William Byrd, Thomas Morley, and Thomas Weelkes)

During the Renaissance, the Catholic church gradually lost some of the influence it had exerted as a center of learning, a formidable political power, and an important force in the daily lives of nearly all Europeans. Rejecting the absolute laws set down by the Church, though not necessarily rejecting any faith in God, Renaissance scholars accepted humanism, a belief in the dignity and value of individual human beings. In addition, the first Protestant churches were established, in opposition to the rule of the Catholic hierarchy.

A Renaissance of the Visual Arts

The developments and discoveries of the Renaissance were reflected in the arts of the period. The works of painters and sculptors became more lifelike and realistic. Painters gave new depth to their work by using perspective and by manipulating light and shadow; they also began using oil paints, which allowed them to revise and refine their work. Sculptors created more individualized human figures, and sculpture began to be considered a true art, rather than a craft.

Many paintings and sculptures of the Renaissance depicted religious subjects, especially scenes from the Bible. However, artists increasingly crafted works with non-religious subjects, often taken from Greek and Roman mythology.

Careful observation and an intense interest in the natural world helped Renaissance artists develop more realistic and individualized paintings and sculptures. Some of the most notable artists worked in several media and delved deeply into science as well. Leonardo da Vinci, one of the foremost painters and sculptors of the Renaissance, was also an architect, a scientist, an engineer, and a musician.

The Influence of the Catholic Church on Music

In the centuries preceding the Renaissance—a time usually called the Middle Ages—most composed music was for the Catholic church and performed as part of religious services. The most important musical form of the period was the **Gregorian chant,** *a melody sung in unison by male voices.* The chants were sung **a cappella,** *without instrumental accompaniment.* All the chants were composed in Latin, the language of all Church services at that time, and were based on sacred texts, often from the Book of Psalms in the Old Testament.

Although the earliest Gregorian chants consisted of a single melodic line, a second melodic line was added to most chants during the Middle Ages. This was the beginning of **polyphony,** *the simultaneous performance of two or more melodic lines.* In polyphonic music, each part begins at a different place, and each part is independent and important. The use of various kinds of polyphony has continued through the centuries; in fact, polyphony is a significant feature in some modern jazz compositions.

da Vinci sketches an early helicopter design

1483

Columbus lands in West Indies/Americas

1492

1473-1480
Sistine Chapel built

1488
Diaz sails around the Cape of Good Hope

1498
da Gama sails around Africa
and lands in India

Informal Assessment
In this lesson, students showed
the ability to:
- Identify characteristics of the
  Renaissance period and
  music of the Renaissance.
- Compare music in the
  Renaissance period to
  today's world.
- Define *a cappella, madrigal,
  motet,* and *polyphony,*
  telling how they reflected
  Renaissance choral music.

Student Self-Assessment
Have students:
- Return to page 103 and
  answer the Check Your
  Understanding questions.
- Write a paragraph describing
  how much they understand
  about the development of
  music during the Renaissance period.

Individual Performance
Assessment
To further demonstrate accomplishment, have each student:
- Learn more about one aspect
  of the music during the
  Renaissance period.
- Share information with the
  class in a creative way, such
  as in a poster, demonstration,
  CD or video design contest,
  and so on.

**The artists and architects of the Renaissance rediscovered Classical antiquity
and were inspired by what they found. In 1547, Michelangelo (1475-1564)
became chief architect for the replacement of the original basilica of Old St.
Peter's. Architect Giacomo della Porta finished the dome 26 years after
Michelangelo's death.**

1546–64. Michelangelo. Exterior view, St. Peter's. St. Peter's Basilica, Vatican State, Rome, Italy. (Dome completed
by Giacomo della Porta, 1590.)

Sacred Music of the Renaissance

During the Renaissance, the Catholic church continued to exert a strong influence
on daily life and on the arts. Much of the important music composed during the Renaissance was **sacred music**, *music used in religious services.*

The two most important forms of sacred Renaissance music were the **mass**—*a long
musical composition that includes the five major sections of the Catholic worship service*—*and the*
motet—*a shorter choral work, set to Latin texts and used in religious services, but not part of the regular mass.* In the early years of the Renaissance, one of the most influential composers

Renaissance Period **101**

St. Peter's Basilica

When Michelangelo assumed responsibility
for the design and construction of the basilica at Old St. Peter's, he applied his belief
that architecture, like the human body,
should be symmetrical. He established this
sense of balance and unity in the dome of the

basilica. Although della Porta later altered
Michelangelo's plans, when the dome is
viewed from the west (apse) end, one sees
how it unifies the building from the base to
the summit. Such unity harkens back to the
classical symmetry of Roman architecture.

Extension

Notation

Musical notation had its beginnings in the churches during the Middle Ages. Notation continued to develop throughout the Renaissance, spurred by the invention of the printing press. Have students:

• Research the development of musical notation from the Middle Ages through the Renaissance period, including how and when the following became used: one line staff, five line staff, *do* clef, treble clef, bass clef, key signatures, rhythmic stem notation, note heads (diamond, triangle, circular), meter signatures, bar lines, dynamics, and markings for tempo.

Networking with Your Community

Renaissance music is performed today by madrigal groups and small chamber choirs or orchestras. Many use early instruments to achieve an authentic representation of the sound. Renaissance dancing is also an area of interest for local groups. Have students check with their local arts council and neighboring universities to discover groups who might be willing to perform for the students, and discuss the unique pleasures and challenges of performing Renaissance music and dance.

Sistine Chapel ceiling painted by Michelangelo
1508

Cortez conquers Mexico
1519

Women seen for the first time on Italian stages
1529

Council of Trent meets to discuss Reformation and Counter Reformation
1545

1517
Protestant Reformation begins in Germany with Luther's 95 Theses

1531
Henry VIII declared head of the Church of England

1519
Magellan begins voyage around the world

of both masses and motets was John Dunstable. Dunstable developed a new harmonic structure of polyphony; his music helped establish the Renaissance as the "golden age of polyphony."

Later in the period, Josquin Desprez began to change the sound of Renaissance choral music. He believed that music should be structured to make the words of the text understandable, and he also thought that all the voices in a choral setting could be equal in importance. Desprez is considered one of the founders of Renaissance music, because he introduced three new musical concepts:

1. Homophonic harmonies, produced by chords that support a melody;
2. Motive imitation, short repeating melodies between voice parts;
3. A more natural cadence, or sense of conclusion.

During the Renaissance, instruments were added to accompany and echo the voices used in sacred music. Adrian Willaert was one of the first composers to combine voices, pipe organs, and other instruments. He also began to use dynamics and was among the first to compose for two imitative voices.

The first music for Protestant religious services was written during this period. Here, sacred music was sung not in Latin but in the languages of the worshipers. One of the most important leaders of the Protestant Reformation, Martin Luther, wrote German hymns that are still sung in Protestant churches today.

The Evolution of Secular Music

Secular music, *any music that is not sacred*, changed in quality and quantity during the Renaissance period. Secular music became increasingly important as the center of musical activity began to shift from churches to castles and towns. Many court and town musicians traveled throughout Europe, so new styles and musical ideas spread relatively rapidly.

The **madrigal**, *a secular form of music written in several imitative parts*, became popular during the Renaissance. Madrigals were composed by such musicians as Clement Janequin, Heinrich Isaac, Thomas Tallis, William Byrd, Thomas Morley, and Thomas Weelkes, to be sung by everyday people. Whole collections of songs in the madrigal form were printed in part books. A family might purchase a set of part books (one for soprano, one for alto, and so on); then family members and friends would gather around these part books and sing.

Most madrigals were composed for three or more voices. Typically, a madrigal was based on a secular poem and incorporated the expression of strong emotions, usually about love. The polyphony within madrigals was often quite challenging, even though the songs were intended primarily for home entertainment. Europeans of the noble and emerging middle classes placed an increased importance on the education of the individual; reading music and singing were considered essential aspects of that education.

Elizabeth I crowned Queen of England
(died 1603)

1558

Portuguese colonize Angola
and found São Paulo

1574

William Shakespeare begins play writing

c. 1590

1564

First violins made by Andrea Amati

1584

Sir Walter Raleigh discovers Virginia

1599

Globe Theatre built in London

Check Your Understanding

Recall

1. What were the most important differences between the music of the Middle Ages and the music of the Renaissance?

2. What is a cappella music?

3. What is polyphony?

4. What is the difference between a mass and a motet?

5. What is the difference between sacred music and secular music?

6. How are motets and madrigals alike? How are they different?

Thinking It Through

1. The word *polyphony* comes from two roots: poly, meaning *many*, and phony, meaning *sounds*. Explain the relationship between these roots and polyphonic music.

2. If you listened to a piece of unidentified music, what clues could help you decide whether it was a Renaissance composition?

Enrichment Projects

The Renaissance is an exciting theme for a unit of study. Have students research possible approaches to the period by making a chart with columns for "What We Know," "What We'd Like to Know," and "How We Can Find Out." Using the information in this textbook, and quick research in encyclopedias, on-line services, or other resources, fill out the columns, and then determine what projects each individual or group will work on. These projects can take many forms, ranging from reviewing a performance to performing a madrigal.

One popular and exciting all-school event is the creation of a Renaissance fair, including food preparation, costumes, music, games (chess, log wrestling), and so on. Each student should be encouraged to choose some task where learning and rigor will be required. Students should also be aware of all other projects going on, and link ideas together whenever possible.

Native American, Asian, and African Cultures and the Renaissance

Have students:

* Explore the music that was being performed and created in other cultures from 1430 to 1600, using the following questions as guides: Was there music occurring in the culture during this time period? What was the music like? Was there any influence from European Renaissance music? If so, how did these music types change each other, if at all?

ANSWERS TO RECALL QUESTIONS

1. During the Middle Ages, most music was composed in Latin for religious services and vocal parts were equal.

2. Without instrumental accompaniment.

3. The simultaneous performance of two or more melodic lines.

4. The mass is a long musical composition that includes the five major sections of the Catholic worship service; the motet is a shorter choral work, set to Latin texts and used in religious services, but not part of the regular mass.

5. Sacred music is used in religious services; secular music is any music that is not sacred.

6. Both are short choral works. Madrigals are secular while motets are sacred.

RENAISSANCE CONNECTIONS

Listening to...
Renaissance Music

This feature is designed to expand students' appreciation of choral and instrumental music of the Renaissance period.

CHORAL SELECTION: "As Vesta Was Descending" by Weelkes

Have students:

• Read the information on this page to learn more about "As Vesta Was Descending."

• Watch as you follow a transparency of Blackline Master, Listening Map 1.

Using the Listening Map

Begin at the top left and follow the text. The key is at the bottom of the map.

Have students:

• Read the English text and the translation in contemporary jargon.

• Listen as you explain that each picture on the map represents the text painting on that line.

• Identify examples of text painting. See if students can identify how many times "Fair Oriana" is sung. (The score states 68 times.)

• Listen to the selection as you point to the transparency.

Listening to...
Renaissance Music

CHORAL SELECTION

Thomas Weelkes — "As Vesta Was Descending"

Thomas Weelkes (1575–1623), an organist and church composer, was one of England's best madrigalists. "As Vesta Was Descending" is found in a collection of madrigals called *The Triumphes of Oriana*, published in 1601. This is a six-voice madrigal that uses text painting.

In the song "As Vesta Was Descending," Vesta is portrayed as the Roman goddess of the hearth fire coming down the hill with her servants, "Diana's darlings." (Diana is the protector of servants.) At the same time, Oriana (Queen Elizabeth I) is climbing the hill with her shepherd followers. When Vesta's attendants see the Queen, they desert Vesta and hurry down the hill to join Oriana, whereupon everyone sings the Queen's praises.

INSTRUMENTAL SELECTION

Andrea Gabrieli — Ricercar in the Twelfth Mode

Andrea Gabrieli (c. 1520–1586) was the organist at St. Mark's Cathedral in Venice, Italy, from 1564 until his death. He composed instrumental as well as sacred and secular vocal music.

A *ricercar* is a polyphonic instrumental composition that uses imitation. "In the Twelfth Mode" means that it is based on a scale corresponding to C major.

TEACHER'S RESOURCE BINDER

Blackline Master, Listening Map 1
Blackline Master, Listening Map 2

Optional Listening Selections:
Music: An Appreciation, 6th edition
"As Vesta Was Descending": CD 1, Track 77
Ricercar in the Twelfth Mode: CD 1, Track 79

National Standards

This lesson addresses the following National Standard:

6. Listening to, analyzing, and describing music. **(a)**

RENAISSANCE CONNECTIONS

Introducing...
"I Go Before, My Charmer"

Thomas Morley

Setting the Stage

"I Go Before, My Charmer" is a canzonet, a song written for group singing during the Renaissance period. This madrigal has been written for two equal voices, and its imitative yet independent lines, and light, buoyant tempo provide the character so typical of Renaissance secular music. The meter changes, which seem a bit difficult today, were quite familiar to the Renaissance singer and also were typical of the period's music.

Meeting the Composer

Thomas Morley (c. 1557–1602)

Thomas Morley, best known for his madrigals and canzonets, was born in Norwich, England, and later became the organist of Norwich Cathedral. In 1588, he received his Bachelor of Music Degree from Oxford and became the organist of St. Paul's Cathedral.

Morley was also a printer, holding a monopoly on all music publications under a patent granted to him by the English government in 1598. In addition to publishing his own works, he acted as editor, arranger, translator, and music publisher of music by other composers.

Renaissance Connections **105**

INSTRUMENTAL SELECTION: Ricercar in the Twelfth Mode by Andrea Gabrieli
Have students:
- Read the information on page 104 to learn more about Ricercar in the Twelfth Mode.
- Watch as you point to a transparency of Blackline Master, Listening Map 2.

Using the Listening Map
Begin at the first jester hat at the top left. Each icon is one strong beat. Note the meter change from B to C. At the castle, point to the dot in the window and then to each dot on the wall. Point to the knight when the meter changes.
Have students:
- Understand that this ricercar is played by four recorders. (soprano, alto, tenor, and bass)
- Listen as you go over the motive and theme key at the bottom of the listening map. Explain that the icons represent the entrance of an imitative motive or theme in the different recorder voices.
- Listen as you play the listening selection and point to the transparency.

INTRODUCING. . . "I Go Before, My Charmer"
This feature is designed to introduce students to the Renaissance Lesson on the following pages.
Have students:
- Read Setting the Stage on this page to learn more about "I Go Before, My Charmer."
- Read Meeting the Composer to learn more about Thomas Morley.
- Turn the page and begin the Renaissance Lesson.

ASSESSMENT

Individual Performance Assessment
To further demonstrate understanding of Renaissance music, have each student:
- Listen again to "As Vesta Was Descending" and circle other examples of text painting.
- Try to identify all 68 times that "Fair Oriana" is sung.

- Listen again to Ricercar in the Twelfth Mode and circle where the motive is heard in the A section. For the B section, tap the strong beat. For the C section, notice the phrase marks when the theme is imitated.

I Go Before, My Charmer

COMPOSER: Thomas Morley
(c. 1557–1602)

Focus

OVERVIEW

Independent singing; imitative style; mixed meter (4/4 and 3/2).

OBJECTIVES

After completing this lesson, students should be able to:

- Sing one part independently with another part.
- Identify and sing in imitative style.
- Read and sing rhythms in mixed meter, with 4/4 and 3/2 meter.

CHORAL MUSIC TERMS

Define the Choral Music Terms for students, giving pronunciation, and answering any questions that may arise.

Warming Up

Rhythm Drill

This Rhythm Drill is designed to prepare students to:

- Speak and clap rhythms in 4/4 and 3/2 meters.
- Shift from 4/4 to 3/2 meter, identifying the change in pulse from quarter to half.
- Perform in imitative style.

Have students:

- Read through the Rhythm Drill directions.
- Perform the drill.

CHORAL MUSIC TERMS
canzonets
4/4 meter
imitative style
independent singing
madrigals
mixed meter
3/2 meter

I Go Before, My Charmer

COMPOSER: *Thomas Morley (c. 1557–1602)*
TEXT: *Unknown Authorship*

VOICING

Two-part voices

PERFORMANCE STYLE

Moderately
A cappella

FOCUS

- Sing one part independently with another part.
- Identify and sing in imitative style.
- Read and sing rhythms in mixed meter, with 4/4 and 3/2 meter.

Warming Up

 Rhythm Drill

Speak and clap this rhythm in two parts. Notice the imitative style. Can you describe how you will feel the pulse as you change from 4/4 to 3/2 meter? What will be equal?

 Vocal Warm-Up

Sing this warm-up using solfège and hand signs or numbers, then using vowels with a consonant in front (*mah, meh, mee, moh, moo*). On measure 1, bend at the waist and touch your toes. On measure 2, return gradually to an upright position. Repeat this movement each time these measures are repeated. Move up or down a half step as you repeat.

do re mi fa so
1 2 3 4 5

TEACHER'S RESOURCE BINDER

 National Standards

Through involvement with this lesson, students should develop the following skills and concepts:

1. Singing, alone and with others, a varied repertoire of music. **(a, c)**
5. Reading and notating music. **(a, b)**
6. Listening to, analyzing, and describing music. **(b, c)**
7. Evaluating music and music performances. **(a, b)**
8. Understanding relationships between music, the other arts, and disciplines outside the arts. **(c)**
9. Understanding music in relation to history and culture. **(a, c, d)**

Sight-Singing

Before singing, study this exercise and determine the form. Which phrases are the same? Sight-sing using solfège and hand signs or numbers. Can you sing accurately the first time through? Conduct in 4/4 as you sing.

Singing: "I Go Before, My Charmer"

What entertainment can you imagine if there were no movies, television or radio, and not even electricity for light!

As printed secular music became easily accessible, many canzonets and madrigals were written for public use. The texts were light and charming, and often had a romantic theme. During the Renaissance, a popular form of entertainment was to invite guests for dinner and then sing around the table after supper.

Read the text of "I Go Before, My Charmer" starting on page 108. Then tell the story in your own words.

Now sing "I Go Before, My Charmer."

HOW DID YOU DO?

You have probably built skills and understanding by now and found you had no dilemma in performing "I Go Before, My Charmer" successfully. Think about your preparation and performance of "I Go Before, My Charmer."
1. How well can you sing your voice part alone? How well can you sing it when the other part is being sung? Is it easier with the full ensemble, or would it be easier in a smaller group?

2. Describe the characteristics of imitative style, and point out where it can be heard and seen in "I Go Before, My Charmer."
3. Tell how you felt the shift from 4/4 to 3/2 meter. What remains the same? Clap the rhythm drill to show your skill at making this change.
4. Assess your ensemble's performance of "I Go Before, My Charmer." What will your criteria for assessment be?

I Go Before, My Charmer **107**

Vocal Warm-Up
This Vocal Warm-Up is designed to prepare students to:
• Sing with a relaxed vocal style.
• Sing with focused vowels.
Have students:
• Read through the Vocal Warm-Up directions.
• Sing, following your demonstration.

Sight-Singing
This Sight-Singing exercise is designed to prepare students to:
• Analyze the form of a piece as a Sight-Singing aid.
• Sight-sing accurately.
• Conduct in 4/4 meter.
Have students:
• Read through the Sight-Singing exercise directions.
• Read through each voice part rhythmically, using rhythm syllables.
• Sight-sing through each part separately using solfège and hand signs or numbers.
• Sing all parts together.

Singing: "I Go Before, My Charmer"

Determine the context and meaning of the text. Have students:
• Read the text on page 107.
• Tell the meaning of the text of "I Go Before, My Charmer" in their own words. (The girl walks ahead of her "charmer," or boyfriend, to the bower in a nearby passageway, where they secretly kiss and show affection to one another, implied by the "dally, dally" text.)

Suggested Teaching Sequence

1. Review Rhythm Drill.

Have students:

- Review the Rhythm Drill on page 106.
- Identify the imitative style, comparing it to a round. (It begins with imitation, but the parts end together.)
- Describe the common pulse between 4/4 and 3/2 changing from a quarter to a half note.
- Clap the rhythms until the change becomes familiar.

2. Review Vocal Warm-Up.

Have students:

- Review the Vocal Warm-Up on page 106, using suggested movement to relax the body.
- Each day sing with a different vowel, focusing and unifying the ensemble sound.

3. Review Sight-Singing.

Have students:

- Review the Sight-Singing exercise on page 107.
- Analyze the form of the exercise as AABA.
- Sing once through every day, tracking improved accuracy.
- Conduct in 4/4 while reading and singing.

4. Sight-sing "I Go Before, My Charmer" using solfège and hand signs or numbers.

Have students:

- Divide into voice sections and read each part rhythmically, clapping the rhythm in full ensemble and noticing that the parts are similar.
- Still in sections, sing with solfège and hand signs or numbers, identifying and working on problem areas.
- Sing the piece through using solfège and hand signs or numbers with full ensemble.
- Divide into sections and recite the text rhythmically for each voice part.
- Sing the piece through with text as a full ensemble.

108

I Go Before, My Charmer

Thomas Morley (1557–1602)
Text of unknown authorship
Edited by G. Wallace Woodworth

Canzonet for Unaccompanied Two-part Voices

© Copyright 1927 by E. C. Schirmer Music Company, Boston

108 *Choral Connections   Level 3 Treble Voices*

MUSIC LITERACY
Metric Flow and Pitch

There is a conflict between meter and pitch in this piece. The strong beats in 4/4 meter are 1 and 3, and should be emphasized naturally. There is also a natural inclination to sing higher pitches stronger than the lower pitch before them. The higher pitches sometimes fall on weak beats, inviting the performer to emphasize the weaker beats of the measures.

Have students:

- By section, identify pitch problems that will disturb the metric flow. (Sopranos—measures 6, 7, 10, 11, 12, 13, 15, and so on. Altos—measures 6, 10, 11, 12, 13, and so on.)
- Work on each measure individually, emphasizing the strong beats, and holding back on the weaker beats while maintaining pitch accuracy.

I Go Before, My Charmer **109**

Have students:

- Review the meaning of imitative style. (One part imitates the other, beginning later.)
- Sing the piece, raising a hand at the beginning of each imitative section.
- Discuss how to use dynamics to highlight imitative style by bringing out the theme, then drawing back a little when the second part imitates, weaving parts back and forth.
- Sing the piece using dynamics to enhance the imitative sections.

Assessment

Informal Assessment

During this lesson, students showed the ability to:

- Speak and clap rhythms in 4/4 and 3/2 meter in the Rhythm Drill.
- Identify and perform imitative style in the Rhythm Drill.
- Sight-sing and sing using solfège and hand signs or numbers in 4/4 meter in the Sight-Singing exercise.
- Sing independently in two parts with dynamic variation to highlight imitative style in "I Go Before, My Charmer."

Student Self-Assessment

Have students:

- Evaluate their performance with the How Did You Do? section on page 107.
- Answer the questions individually. Discuss them in pairs or small groups and/or write their responses.

(Continued on page 110)

Individual Performance Assessment

To further demonstrate accomplishment, have each student:

- In a quartet, sing the piece, demonstrating part independence.
- Compose an eight-measure rhythm exercise with four measures of 4/4 and four measures of 3/2, then clap it with metric and rhythmic accuracy.
- In a duet or double duo, sing measures 33–end into a cassette tape player in an isolated space, demonstrating the ability to change from 4/4 to 3/2 meter, and sing independently.

Extension

Practice with Mixed Meters

Have students:

- Review the rhythms in 4/4 and 3/2 to become familiar with the feel of each.
- Have them write four measure rhythms in either 4/4 or 3/2, then pair with someone who chose the other meter to create an eight-measure mixed meter piece.
- Use these pieces as warm-up exercises at the beginning of class.

Interpretation

Have students:

- Explore the notation for dynamics, tempo, and articulation markings.
- Perform the piece following the markings in the notation.

Small Ensembles

This piece was written for an intimate gathering, and is more easily performed by a small ensemble.

Have students:

- Form small ensembles of no more than 16, to work on refining diction, accuracy, and interpretation of this piece.
- Perform for one another, identifying the differences in interpretation.

E. C. SCHIRMER • BOSTON | Music Publishers

National Standards

The following National Standards are addressed through the Extension and bottom-page activities:

1. Singing, alone and with others, a varied repertoire of music. **(a, c)**
4. Composing and arranging music within specified guidelines. **(a)**
5. Reading and notating music. **(a, b)**
6. Listening to, analyzing, and describing music. **(a, b, c, e, f)**
7. Evaluating music and music performances. **(b)**
8. Understanding relationships between music, the other arts, and disciplines outside the arts. **(a, c)**
9. Understanding music in relation to history and culture. **(a, c, d)**

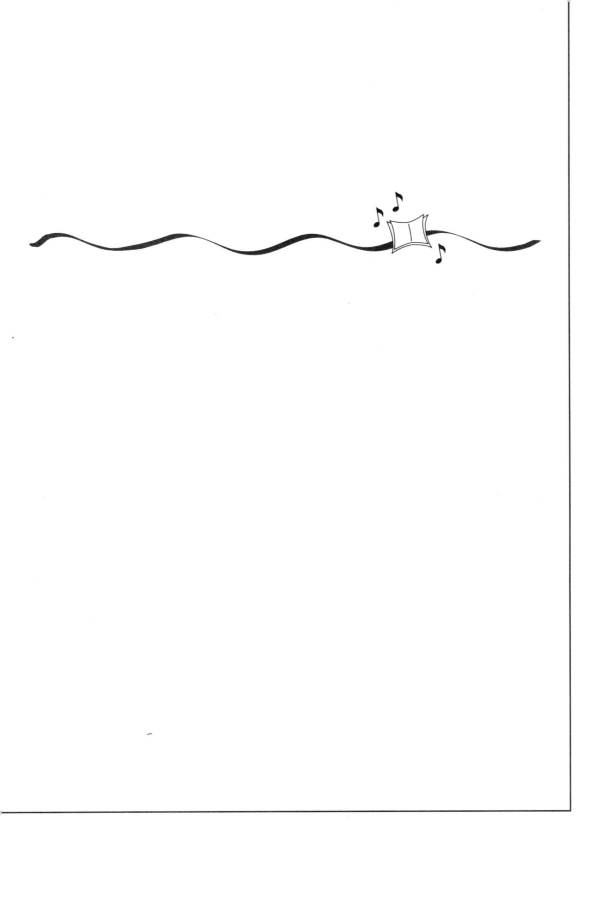

Baroque Period

Focus

OVERVIEW
Understanding the development of choral music during the Baroque period.

OBJECTIVES
After completing this lesson, students should be able to:
- Describe characteristics of architecture, fine art, and music during the Baroque period.
- Identify several musical forms of the Baroque period.
- Define *aria, cantata, chorale, concerto grosso, continuo, opera, oratorio,* and *recitative.* Explain how each of these terms is related to the Baroque period.
- Identify some of the key musical figures of the Baroque.

CHORAL MUSIC TERMS
Define the Choral Music Terms for students, giving pronunciation, and answering any questions that may arise.

Introducing the Lesson

Introduce the Baroque period through visual art.
Analyze the artwork and architecture on pages 112 and 114. Have students:
- Study the painting and architecture.
- Discuss the information about each illustration provided at the bottom of pages 113 and 114 in your Teacher's Wraparound Edition.

▲ Attention to detail, particularly in direct and reflected light in mirrors and doorways, characterizes this work of Diego Velázquez (1599–1660). The challenge to the viewer to find all the images in *Las Meninas* equals the challenge to comprehend the intricacies in a Bach fugue or concerto, representative musical works of the same period.

1645–52. Diego Velázquez. *Las Meninas.* Oil on canvas. 3.20 x 2.76 m (10'5" x 9'). Museo del Prado, Madrid, Spain.

112 *Choral Connections Level 3 Treble Voices*

TEACHER'S RESOURCE BINDER
Fine Art Transparency 2, *Las Meninas,* by Velázquez

Optional Listening Selections:
Music: An Appreciation, 6th edition
Chorale from Cantata No. 140: CD 2, Track 34
Suite No. 3 in D Major: CD 2, Track 22

National Standards

This historical lesson addresses the following National Standards:
6. Listening to, analyzing, and describing music. **(a)**
8. Understanding relationships between music, the other arts, and disciplines outside the arts. **(a, b, c, d, e)**
9. Understanding music in relation to history and culture. **(a, c, d)**

Baroque Period

After completing this lesson, you should be able to:

- Describe the general characteristics of Baroque visual arts.
- Discuss the most important differences between Renaissance music and Baroque music.
- Identify at least five new musical forms of the Baroque period.
- Identify at least four major composers of the Baroque period.

The artworks of the Renaissance reflect the ideas and ideals of the period. They are balanced and restrained; they communicate a sense of calm. The next period of European history—the Baroque period, which lasted from about 1600 until around 1750—was an age of reaction against the restraint and balance of the Renaissance. Baroque artists expressed the ideals of their own time by adding emotion, decoration, and opulence to their works.

A Time of Continued Development

The explorations and developments of the Renaissance continued into the Baroque period. European trade with distant lands increased, and European kingdoms sought to expand their power by establishing empires. The first European settlers left their homes and sailed to the Americas. People had a growing sense of possibility and excitement.

The study of science and mathematics continued to advance, and new technological developments were made. The basis of modern chemistry was established, and medical research, as well as medical practices, improved. The study of science became a more complex and consuming endeavor, one that no longer attracted the special interests of artists.

During the Baroque period, aristocrats—including emperors, kings, princes, and other nobles—seemed intent on displaying their wealth and power. Part of this display involved attracting great artists, including musicians, to their courts. Both the aristocracy and the Catholic church were generous patrons of the arts throughout the Baroque period. The artworks created during the Baroque period are typically large in scale and dramatic in effect. Painters and sculptors of the time built upon the forms established by Renaissance artists and added their own complex details and dramatic elaborations.

Baroque Music

Baroque music reflected the same style exhibited in the visual arts of the time; it was written on a grand scale, full of vitality and emotion. Compositions typically had a strong sense of movement, often including a **continuo**, *a continually moving bass line*. Usually the melody was highly ornamental. In many compositions, additional ornamentations were improvised, or invented on the spur of the moment during performances.

COMPOSERS

Claudio Monteverdi (1567–1643)
Arcangelo Corelli (1643–1713)
Henry Purcell (1659–1695)
Antonio Vivaldi (1678–1741)
Georg Philipp Telemann (1681–1767)
Johann Sebastian Bach (1685–1750)
George Frideric Handel (1685–1759)

ARTISTS

El Greco (1541–1614)
Michelangelo da Caravaggio (c.1565–1609)
Peter Paul Rubens (1577–1640)
Frans Hals (1580–1666)
Artemisia Gentileschi (c.1597– c.1651)
Gianlorenzo Bernini (1598–1680)
Diego Velazquez (1599–1660)
Rembrandt van Rijn (1606–1669)
Judith Leyser (1609–1660)

AUTHORS

John Donne (c.1573–1631)
Rene Descartes (1596–1650)
John Milton (1608–1674)
Molière (1622–1673)

CHORAL MUSIC TERMS

arias
cantata
chorale
concerto grosso
continuo
movements
opera
oratorio
recitative
suite

Baroque Period **113**

Las Meninas

The Baroque period was a time of opulence and ornamentation. Using similar forms as the Renaissance, Baroque artists decorated each element. The distinction between the aristocracy and the common people was highly defined during this period, with the wealthy involved in the arts for their own pleasure and in an effort to represent their status in society.

Las Meninas, by Velázquez, is representative of the visual art of the period. The wealthy are represented in their finery. Notice the elaboration and ornamentation of the artist's style.

Suggested Teaching Sequence

1. Examine the Baroque period.

Have students:

- Read the text on pages 113–115.
- Share what they know about the composers, artists, and authors listed on this page.
- Read, discuss, and answer the review questions individually, in pairs, or in groups.
- Discuss their answers with the whole group.

2. Examine the Baroque period in historical perspective.

Have students:

- Turn to the time line and read the citations.
- Discuss why these events and people are important to the Baroque period.
- Compare each of these events to what occurred before and after the Baroque period.
- Write a statement of one or two sentences in length that describes the Baroque period based on one of the events in the time line. (Louis XIV's building of Versailles was characteristic of the Baroque period, during which the rich taxed the general population in order to maintain their opulent lifestyle and impress one another.)
- Write one additional sentence which tells how this Baroque event is related to the student's world. (Today, many people complain that the middle class and poor are taxed to benefit the rich in much the same way.)

3. Define the musical aspects of the Baroque period.

Have students:

- Review the changes in music during the Baroque period.
- Define *aria, cantata, chorale, concerto grosso, continuo, opera, oratorio,* and *recitative.*

Galileo	Henry Hudson explores the Hudson River	Pilgrims land in America	Isaac Newton	Quakers arrive in Massachusetts
▼ 1564–1642	▼ 1609	▼ 1620	▼ 1642–1727	▼ 1656

▲ 1607	▲ 1618–1648	▲ 1636	▲ 1643–1715
Jamestown, Virginia, established settlement	Thirty Years' War	Harvard College founded	Reign of Louis XIV as King of France

▲ 1608
Telescope invented in Holland

Assessment

Informal Assessment

In this lesson, students showed the ability to:

- Identify characteristics of the Baroque period and music of the Baroque.
- Compare music in the Baroque period to today's world.
- Define *concerto grosso, chorale, cantata, oratorio,* and *opera;* explain how each of these terms is related to the Baroque period.

Student Self-Assessment

Have students:

- Return to page 115 and answer the Check Your Understanding questions.
- Write a paragraph describing how much they understand about the development of music during the Baroque period.

Individual Performance Assessment

To further demonstrate accomplishment, have each student:

- Learn more about one aspect of the music during the Baroque period.
- Share information with the class in a creative way, such as in a poster, demonstration, CD or video design contest, and so on.

Extension

Networking with Your Community

Baroque music is performed today frequently by chamber, vocal, and instrumental groups. Large orchestras have many Baroque pieces in their repertoire, and simply dismiss parts of the larger orchestra for the specific piece. Baroque music is likewise performed in many church concerts. Check with your local arts council, performing groups, and neighboring universities to discover locations and times of Baroque performances for students to attend.

During this period, instrumental music gained in importance, both in the church and as music commissioned for the entertainment of the courts of Europe. Vocal music also underwent changes. Instrumental accompaniments were increasingly added to both sacred and secular vocal works, and several new musical forms developed.

▲ The ornate interior decor is reflected endlessly in the Hall of Mirrors, designed by François de Cuvilliés (1696–1768). Musical embellishment and ornamentation of the Baroque period provide similar stylistic elements in compositions by Johann Sebastian Bach and his contemporaries.

1734–39. François de Cuvilliés. Hall of Mirrors, Amalienburg, Munich, Germany.

Instrumental Forms

As instrumental music grew more important, the musical instruments themselves were refined and their uses changed. The violin, previously a solo instrument, was added to ensemble groups. The harpsichord and the organ became the most important keyboard instruments.

Longer instrumental works were composed during the Baroque period. Often, these compositions consisted of several **movements**, *individual pieces that sound fairly complete within themselves but are part of a longer work.*

One of the new instrumental forms of the Baroque period was the **concerto grosso**. This *composition for a small chamber orchestra consists of several movements* and features a moving bass line and an elaborate melody. Most of the major Baroque composers wrote concerti grossi. Among the best known are *The Four Seasons* by Antonio Vivaldi and the set of six *Brandenburg Concertos* by Johann Sebastian Bach.

Another instrumental form that developed was the **suite**, *a set of musical movements, usually inspired by dances, of contrasting tempos and styles.* Suites and suite-related compositions were very popular during this time; the most famous suites were those composed by Bach.

Vocal and Mixed Forms

Vocal music became more varied and notably more dramatic during the Baroque period. Sacred music continued to be predominantly choral, but new instrumental accompaniment added greater variety and strength to many compositions. One of the new forms of the Baroque period was the **chorale**, or *hymn tune.* Chorales were

114 *Choral Connections Level 3 Treble Voices*

The Hall of Mirrors

Call students' attention to the opulence of the Hall of Mirrors. Have them notice how the mirrors tease the eye at every curve. The use of mirrors was new in the Baroque period, and allowed images to be produced in multiples. In a sense, they decorated the decoration.

Johann Sebastian Bach
1685–1750

First American newspaper
established, *Boston News Letter*
1704

Handel comes to England
1710

1682
LaSalle explores
the Mississippi

1685–1759
George Frideric Handel

1706–1790
Benjamin Franklin

1687
Publication of Newton's *Mathematical Principles*

composed for Lutheran services, using German texts. They were easy to sing and to remember, so all members of a church congregation could join in.

A related Baroque form was the **cantata**, *a collection of compositions with instrumental accompaniment consisting of several movements based on related secular or sacred text segments.* The fact that this form could be composed as either a sacred or a secular work itself marks a new development of the period. Music directors at important Protestant churches were required to compose cantatas for weekly services. Bach, who served as a music director in Leipzig for 25 years, composed nearly 300 sacred cantatas.

Another mixed form from the Baroque period is the **oratorio**, *a composition for solo voices, chorus, and orchestra, that was an extended dramatic work on a literary or religious theme presented without theatrical action.* Like a cantata, an oratorio was composed to be performed in a concert setting, without costumes and scenery. However, the oratorio was written on a larger scale and told a story, usually religious, with plot and resolution. The oratorio was typically performed by a small chorus, an orchestra, and four vocal soloists.

Of all the new musical forms that developed during the Baroque period, perhaps the most characteristic is the **opera**, *a combination of singing, instrumental music, dancing, and drama that tells a story.* Opera combined many art forms, including drama, dance, architecture, and visual art, with music. And, in the true sense of Baroque style, opera was emotional and lavish. The best known composers of Baroque opera were Claudio Monteverdi, who wrote *Orfeo*, the first important opera, in 1607, and Henry Purcell.

The highlights of most operas are the **arias**, *dramatic songs for solo voices with orchestral accompaniment.* Another important feature of an opera is the **recitative**, *a vocal line that imitates the rhythm of speech.*

Check Your Understanding

Recall

1. What is a continuo?

2. What is a concerto grosso? Which Baroque composers are particularly remembered for this kind of composition?

3. What is a cantata?

4. What is the difference between an oratorio and an opera?

5. How are an aria and a recitative alike? How are they different?

6. List at least three adjectives you would use to describe the music of the Baroque period.

Thinking It Through

1. Identify one Baroque composition you have listened to. What characteristics mark that composition as a Baroque work?

2. For whom was Baroque music written? Who were the intended performers and the intended audience?

Baroque Period **115**

ANSWERS TO RECALL QUESTIONS

1. A continually moving bass line.
2. A composition for a small chamber orchestra that consists of several movements and features a moving bass line and an elaborate melody. Antonio Vivaldi and Johann Sebastian Bach.
3. A collection of compositions with instrumental accompaniment consisting of several movements based on related secular or sacred text segments.

4. The opera includes theatrical action, while the oratorio does not.
5. Both are part of an opera. The aria is a song; the recitative is a vocal line that imitates speech.
6. Answers will vary, but should indicate that students recognize the elaborate, decorative style of the Baroque period.

Notation and Improvisation

In the character of the Baroque period, melodic lines and harmonies became more and more fancy, but not all the decorations were written down. During the Baroque period, one measure of good musicianship was the ability to improvise around the original melody, remaining stylistically and harmonically correct.
Have students:

• Take a well-known, simple melody.

• Sing it over and over, adding more and more ornamentation through passing tones, sustaining tones longer than written, adding chord tones between pitches, and adding grace notes and melismas.

• Avoid any judgmental behaviors for as long as possible, getting more and more frivolous, to get the feel of Baroque-style improvisation.

North America and the Baroque

What was going on in North America during the Baroque period?
Have students:

• Look at the time line and discover any citations that relate to North America.

• Research what music was being sung, played, and created in North America. Was there any contact between Europe and North America that affected music? Did the Baroque spirit foster any new musical inventions in North America?

• What non-European music was being performed and created in North America?

BAROQUE CONNECTIONS

Listening to...
Baroque Music

This feature is designed to expand students' appreciation of choral and instrumental music of the Baroque period.

CHORAL SELECTION:
Cantata No. 140, Seventh Movement (Chorale), by Bach
Have students:
- Read the information on this page to learn more about Bach's Cantata No. 140.
- Watch as you follow a transparency of Blackline Master, Listening Map 3.

Using the Listening Map
Start at the top left-hand side of the church and follow words to the A and B sections. Each chord bar represents one half note in 4/4. Have students:
- Identify the four voice parts and the instruments featured in the Chorale.
- Discover that all four parts move together in chords.
- Listen as you define a chorale as a hymn tune sung to a German religious text.
- Listen as you define a church cantata from Bach's time as a work composed for chorus, vocal soloists, organ, and small orchestra, whose religious text was meant to reinforce a religious sermon.
- Listen as you define a cadence as a harmonic progression that signals the end of a musical phrase or section. Cadences on the map are indicated with a fermata.
- Find the total number of phrases in section A (3) and in section B (5).
- Listen to the recording as you point to the transparency.

Listening to...
Baroque Music

CHORAL SELECTION

Bach—Cantata No. 140, Seventh Movement

The music of Johann Sebastian Bach (1685–1750) exemplifies the Baroque style of music. He was born at Eisenach, Germany, into a very musical family. He worked as a court organist and chamber musician to the Duke of Weimar. Bach fathered 20 children from two marriages, with four of his sons becoming well-known composers. Bach wrote roughly 295 cantatas as the music director of a Lutheran church One hundred ninety-five of these are still in existence today. Cantata No. 140 is one of Bach's most famous cantatas. The Seventh Movement brings back the chorale tune, set in a simple homophonic texture for four voices doubled by instruments.

INSTRUMENTAL SELECTION

Bach—Suite in No. 3 in D Major, Second Movement

The Baroque suite consists of a set of dance-inspired movements which are all in the same key and usually in two-part form, with the A and B sections repeated. Each movement has a different tempo, meter, and character, representing the music of different countries. The A section usually begins in the tonic key and modulates to the dominant, and the B section begins in the dominant key and returns to the tonic. Bach wrote four suites for orchestra. Suite No. 3 in D Major, "Air," is written for strings and continuo in the style of an Italian aria.

TEACHER'S RESOURCE BINDER
Blackline Master, Listening Map 3
Blackline Master, Listening Map 4

Optional Listening Selections:
Music: An Appreciation, 6th edition
Chorale from Cantata No. 140: CD 2, Track 34
Suite No. 3 in D Major: CD 2, Track 22

National Standards
This lesson addresses the following National Standard:
6. Listening to, analyzing, and describing music. **(a)**

Introducing ...

"O Death, None Could Conquer Thee"

Johann Sebastian Bach

Setting the Stage

Some believe that Johann Sebastian Bach was the greatest composer that ever lived. The Baroque period ended with his death, yet the period lives on because of the legacy he left for all to study and enjoy today. Bach's influence can even be seen in contemporary music—especially jazz. The prominent feature of jazz is improvisation. Bach was the greatest of all improvisors. For example, take a close look at the left-hand bass line of the accompaniment in "O Death, None Could Conquer Thee." This is "notated improvisation" at its best: a typical walking bass line of the Baroque.

Take another look at this piece of music. Its typical Baroque style is exemplified in its steady tempo and stately setting. This would be a good song to use for improvising, if it were not for its sad text. However, just for fun try to improvise on the rhythm the way you will do in the warm-up exercise. Certainly Bach would approve!

Meeting the Composer

Johann Sebastian Bach (1685–1750)

Johann Sebastian Bach was born into a family that had produced musicians for several generations. However, his parents died when he was ten. Young Bach went to live with his brother, Johann Christoph, who gave him musical training. So thorough was his training that he became a masterful organist, and the output of music he composed staggers the imagination.

Baroque Connections **117**

INSTRUMENTAL SELECTION: Suite No. 3 in D Major by Bach
Have students:
• Read the information on page 116 to learn more about Bach's Suite No. 3 in D Major.
• Watch as you follow a transparency of Blackline Master, Listening Map 4.

Using the Listening Map
Start at the top left of the map and follow left to right. The dove in the A theme and the butterfly in the B theme represent the melody in the violins. The dots (rabbit in A and frog in B) represent the cello-basso continuo. Point to the melody line on the first hearing of each section and the continuo on the repeats. Have students:
• Look at the listening map and discuss what the map reveals about melodic contour (legato and curved lines of the bird and butterfly), continuo (marcato, on the beat, and with many upward and downward skips), and form (AABB).
• Discover how the musical phrases are shown on the map. (Each bird or butterfly introduces a new phrase, and there is a definite break at the end of phrase lines.) Note that all the phrases are not the same length, a characteristic of Baroque music.
• Find repeat signs and first and second endings on the map.
• Listen to the recording as you point to the transparency.

INTRODUCING... "O Death, None Could Conquer Thee"
This feature is designed to introduce students to the Baroque Lesson on the following pages. Have students:
• Read Setting the Stage on this page to learn more about "O Death, None Could Conquer Thee."
• Read Meeting the Composer to learn more about Johann Sebastian Bach.
• Turn the page and begin the Baroque Lesson.

ASSESSMENT

Individual Performance Assessment
To further demonstrate understanding of Baroque music, have each student:
• Signal when the cadences are heard while listening to Cantata No. 140 without looking at the map.
• Define a chorale and a cantata to a partner.

• On the worksheet for the instrumental selection, draw the shape of the melody line on the first playing of the A section, and the shape of the continuo on the repeat of the A section, while listening to Bach's Suite without the listening map.

O Death, None Could Conquer Thee

COMPOSER: Johann Sebastian Bach (1685–1750)

ARRANGER: Lee Kjelson

Focus

OVERVIEW

Minor key; independent singing; imitative; woven parts; German text; musical enhancement of text.

OBJECTIVES

After completing this lesson, students should be able to:
- Read and sing in a minor key.
- Sing imitative and interweaving lines independently.
- Sing using correct German pronunciation.
- Identify musical enhancement of text.

CHORAL MUSIC TERMS

Define the Choral Music Terms for students, giving pronunciation, and answering any questions that may arise.

Warming Up

Vocal Warm-Up

This Vocal Warm-Up is designed to prepare students to:
- Sing in a minor tonality.
- Use a skeleton melody for rhythmic improvisation.
- Sing with a free, fluid tone.

Have students:
- Read through the Vocal Warm-Up directions.
- Sing, following your demonstration.

BAROQUE LESSON

O Death, None Could Conquer Thee

COMPOSER: *Johann Sebastian Bach* (1685–1750)

ARRANGER: *Lee Kjelson*

CHORAL MUSIC TERMS
enhancement of text
imitative style
independent singing
interweaving lines
minor key

VOICING
Two-part chorus

PERFORMANCE STYLE
Sustained
Accompanied by piano

FOCUS
- Read and sing in a minor key.
- Sing imitative and interweaving lines independently.
- Sing using correct German pronunciation.
- Identify musical enhancement of text.

Warming Up

Vocal Warm-Up

Sing this warm-up using solfège syllables or numbers. Move up or down a half step on each repeat.

Each time you sing the Warm-Up, try to spontaneously vary the rhythm, creating a rhythmic improvisation on the pitches. Keep the basic pitches the same, but add some imaginative rhythm. The example below will give you an idea, but once it is written down, it's no longer an improvisation.

TEACHER'S RESOURCE BINDER

Blackline Master 19, *Translation and Pronunciation Guide for "O Death, None Could Conquer Thee"*

National Standards

1. Singing, alone and with others, a varied repertoire of music. **(a, c)**
3. Improvising melodies. **(b)**
5. Reading and notating music. **(a, b)**
6. Listening to, analyzing, and describing music. **(a, b, c)**
7. Evaluating music and music performances. **(a, b, c)**
8. Understanding relationships between music, the other arts, and disciplines outside the arts. **(c)**
9. Understanding music in relation to history and culture. **(a, c, d)**

Sight-Singing

Sight-sing this exercise in two parts. Notice how the lines weave together, using imitation and independent rhythms. Look for ways to get clues from the other voice part for your pitches after rests.

Singing: "O Death, None Could Conquer Thee"

What would you say to death? Read the text of "O Death, None Could Conquer Thee." What did the composer say to death? Why would such a text be chosen? What musical characteristics would you choose to set this text to if you were the composer? When might it be performed?

Now turn to the music for "O Death, None Could Conquer Thee" on page 120.

| **HOW DID YOU DO?** ? . ? . ? | Even a mournful text can be hauntingly beautiful when well sung. Think about your preparation and performance of "O Death, None Could Conquer Thee." **1.** Sing the Vocal Warm-up to show your ability to sing in a minor key. **2.** Describe how the composer used imitative and interweaving lines in "O Death, None Could Conquer Thee." How well can you sing your part independently when the other part is being sung? | **3.** How well do you sing in German? What do you do well? What could be better? **4.** How did Bach musically enhance the text of "O Death, None Could Conquer Thee?" What musical characteristics did he employ? Would you use the same ones if you were the composer? What would you do differently? |

Sight-Singing

This Sight-Singing exercise is designed to prepare students to:
- Identify and sing imitative entrances.
- Read and sing in E minor.
- Sing with part independence.
- Listen to another part as they sing, finding aural clues for accurate pitches after rests.

Have students:
- Read through the Sight-Singing exercise directions.
- Read through each voice part rhythmically, using rhythm syllables.
- Sight-sing through each part separately using solfège and hand signs or numbers.
- Sing all parts together.

Singing: "O Death, None Could Conquer Thee"

Determine the mood, meaning, and context for the text. Have students:
- Read the text on page 119.
- Discuss what they would say to death. (Avoid judging any answers.)
- Read the text, and discuss what the composer's message to death is. (Death is the conqueror of all humans and takes each too soon.)
- Identify reasons for choosing this text, musical characteristics possible for setting it, and performance opportunities. (probably part of a church service or funeral ceremony, the music would most likely be somber and reverent, using minor mode, close harmonies, descending passages, pensive melismas)

Suggested Teaching Sequence

1. Review Vocal Warm-Up.

Sing in minor mode. Improvise rhythmically. Have students:

- Review the Vocal Warm-Up on page 118.
- Look at and analyze the improvisation model to understand the process of rhythmic improvisation while keeping the melody the same.
- Increasingly add rhythmic improvisation as they sing.
- Look at and listen to the piano accompaniment for "O Death, None Could Conquer Thee," imagining how it might have begun as a basic chordal outline, improvised by Bach, and eventually notated.

2. Review Sight-Singing.

Read and sing in two parts in an imitative, weaving passage. Find clues for accurate pitches. Have students:

- Review the Sight-Singing exercise on page 119.
- Notice the weaving, imitative nature of the two lines, and the need for independent performance.
- Discuss ways of getting clues from both their own previous pitches, and the other line, for pitch accuracy. (For example: The soprano line in measure 3 begins on the pitch the altos have just sung.)
- Look through the notation of "O Death, None Could Conquer Thee," finding similar imitative, weaving lines between soprano and alto. (measures 3, 15, 38)
- Clap and speak the rhythm of the piece, noticing imitative rhythms and text throughout.

O Death, None Could Conquer Thee

(Den Tod, Niemand Zwingen Kunnt')

Two-part Chorus SA or TB (with Piano Accompaniment)

J. S. Bach
Arr. Lee R. Kjelson

TEACHING STRATEGY

Reading and Singing in Minor

If students are not familiar with singing in minor, have them:

- Read and sing exercises in minor modes that you put on the board until they become familiar with the sound and intervallic relationships.

- Write warm-up exercises using stepwise and chord tone patterns in minor.
- Use these warm-ups at the beginning of each class.

3. Sight-sing "O Death, None Could Conquer Thee" using solfège and hand signs or numbers.

Have students:

- Divide into voice sections and read each part rhythmically, using rhythm syllables.
- Clap and speak the rhythm in full ensemble.
- In sections, read through the piece using solfège and hand signs or numbers, identifying and working on problem areas.
- Identify the key as E minor, and discuss names of altered tones on page 1 (A♯ is *fi*, C♯ is *li*)
- Sing the piece through using solfège and hand signs or numbers with full ensemble, building part independence.
- Sing the piece in full ensemble.

4. Learn the German pronunciation.

Have students:

- Using Blackline Master 19, *Translation and Pronunciation Guide for "O Death, None Could Conquer Thee,"* echo or read the words slowly.
- Speak the text in German in rhythm.
- Sing the piece in German, using correct pronunciation.

Dealing with the Topic of Death

In today's world, the topic of death is not foreign to teens, and should be approached with a careful ear. As students discuss the text and context of "O Death, None Could Conquer Thee," listen carefully for those responses that might be a sign of students who are at risk. With a trained counselor, discuss possible techniques for handling students' reactions. This piece can be an extremely important outlet for students if handled with sensitivity and care.

5. Identify musical elements that enhance the meaning and mood of the text.

Have students:

- Review the mood and meaning of the text, including possible contexts and the historical period in which it was written. (Baroque)

- In groups, analyze the musical elements that enhance the text, including minor tonality, downward sighing motion, soft hushed quality with sudden loud bursts of fear, continuous motion toward the conclusion in the accompaniment, contrasting measures 27–43 which ascend in a hopeful section and eventually return to the resigned lower pitches, and augmented sighing motif toward the end.

- Discuss how effective the piece is in communicating its message, and whether they would consider it adequate, good, or excellent as an example of the way music enhances text. (Cultural and historical context should be part of this discussion.)

MUSIC LITERACY
The "Sigh Motif"

Have students:

- Identify a musical motif as a shortened expression, sometimes contained within a phrase, but occasionally standing alone as an independent entity—a small cell of expression.

- Identify a "sigh" as a sound moving from high to low, expressing longing, pain, or sorrow.

- Devise a definition for a sigh motif— a short melodic segment moving from high to low, often paired with longing, pain, or sorrow in the text.

- Find examples of the sigh motif in the notation of "O Death, None Could Conquer Thee," beginning with the first series of imitative motifs.

Bel.Oct.2131

O Death, None Could Conquer Thee **123**

TEACHING STRATEGY

Interpretation

Have students:

- Explore the notation for dynamics, tempo, and articulation markings.
- Perform the piece following the markings in the notation.

Baroque Characteristics

Have students:

- Describe the musical characteristics of "O Death, None Could Conquer Thee."
- Recall characteristics of Baroque music.
- Construct a Venn diagram, demonstrating the overlapping characteristics of the two that define the piece as an example of Baroque music.

Assessment

Informal Assessment

During this lesson, students showed the ability to:

- Read and sing in E minor in the Vocal Warm-Up exercise.
- Sight-sing, using solfège and hand signs or numbers, two imitative, weaving parts in the Sight-Singing exercise.
- Sing independently in two parts, in minor tonality, and in imitative style in "O Death, None Could Conquer Thee."
- Sing in German with correct pronunciation in "O Death, None Could Conquer Thee."
- Identify musical characteristics that enhance the text in "O Death, None Could Conquer Thee."

Student Self-Assessment

Have students:

- Evaluate their performance with the How Did You Do? section on page 119.
- Answer the questions individually. Discuss them in pairs or small groups and/or write their responses on a sheet of paper.

Individual Performance Assessment

To further demonstrate accomplishment, have each student:

- Sing the piece in a quartet, demonstrating part independence.
- Sing the Sight-Singing exercise in a quartet, demonstrating the ability to sing in E minor.
- Write a short essay describing the musical characteristics of "O Death, None Could Conquer Thee" and their relationship to the text, context, and period of the piece.
- Into a cassette tape player in an isolated space, speak her voice part from measures 15–26, demonstrating correct German pronunciation.

123

Extension

The Power of Accompaniment

Have students:

- Sing the piece a cappella.
- Sing the piece through with accompaniment.
- Discuss what the accompaniment adds to the piece, and whether it is important or not.

Comparing Your Performance to Another

Have students:

- Listen to a different Bach vocal piece.
- Identify any characteristics of Baroque music, and critique the performance, telling what was especially good and what could have been better.
- Compare their performance of "O Death, None Could Conquer Thee" to the recorded performance, describing what was similar and what was different.
- Determine any changes to be made in their performance, and then sing "O Death, None Could Conquer Thee" again.

National Standards

The following National Standards are addressed through the Extension and bottom-page activities:

1. Singing, alone and with others, a varied repertoire of music. (**a, c**)
3. Improvising melodies, variations, and accompaniments. (**b, c, e**)
4. Composing and arranging music within specified guidelines. (**a**)
5. Reading and notating music. (**a, b**)
6. Listening to, analyzing, and describing music. (**a, b, c, e, f**)
7. Evaluating music and music performances. (**a, b, c**)
8. Understanding relationships between music, the other arts, and disciplines outside the arts. (**a, c**)
9. Understanding music in relation to history and culture. (**a, c, d**)

Vocal Improvisation

Bach's legacy, and the legacy of the Baroque period, was one of embellishment and improvisation over a rhythmic, melodic, or harmonic skeleton. Have students:

- Choose or compose a very simple rhythm, melody, or harmonic sequence.
- Clap or sing the pattern until it is spontaneous and assimilated.
- Begin repeating the pattern with small changes or embellishments.
- Continue repeating the pattern, becoming more adventuresome, but returning every once in a while to the original idea.
- Choose different styles in which to improvise with the same materials.
- Focus on the process and freedom of improvisation within a set structure, rather than the product.
- Eventually consider how these improvisations might be structured so they can be shared, perhaps through a rondo form (ABACADA etc.), which returns to the original after several individual or small group improvisations.

Composing in the Baroque Style

In groups or individually, have students:

- Analyze the composition by Bach, writing down the most important characteristics.
- Choose or write a text modeled after the Bach text.
- Compose a short piece that follows the characteristics found in the Bach piece.
- Revise, practice, and perform their piece.

VOCAL DEVELOPMENT
Pitch-Matching Clues from the Other Part

To encourage vocal development, have students:

- Sight-sing pitch challenges that you write on the board, with one group beginning, then switching parts each time you signal. (say "change" or snap your fingers)

- Discuss how well they sang their first pitch in tune, getting the pitch from the "other part."
- Listen more and more carefully in order to become more accurate with their entry pitches.

Classical Period

Focus

OVERVIEW
Understanding the development of choral and instrumental music during the Classical period.

OBJECTIVES
After completing this lesson, students should be able to:

- Describe characteristics of architecture, fine art, and music during the Classical period.
- Identify several musical forms of the Classical period.
- Define *chamber music, sonata-allegro form,* and *symphony;* explain how each of these terms is related to the Classical period.
- Identify some of the key musical figures of the Classical period.

CHORAL MUSIC TERMS
Define the Choral Music Terms for students, giving pronunciation, and answering any questions that may arise.

Introducing the Lesson

Introduce the Classical period through visual art.
Analyze the artwork and building on pages 126 and 128. Have students:

- Study the painting and library, describing features in as much detail as possible.
- Discuss the information about each artwork provided at the bottom of pages 127 and 128 in your Teacher's Wraparound Edition.

 Anne Louis Girodet-Trioson (1767–1824), through this portrait of *Jean-Baptiste Bellay, Deputy of Santo Domingo,* expressed the interest of Europeans in revolution for the rights of the individual. As visual artists worked with such themes, composers were also influenced by similar revolutionary thought. The *Eroica Symphony in E-Flat* by Beethoven is one of many examples of music inspired by revolution.

1797. Anne Louis Girodet-Trioson. *Jean-Baptiste Bellay, Deputy of Santo Domingo.* (Detail.) Oil on canvas. 160 x 114 cm (63 x 45"). Musée National du Château de Versailles.

126 *Choral Connections   Level 3 Treble Voices*

TEACHER'S RESOURCE BINDER
Fine Art Transparency 3, *Jean-Baptiste Bellay, Deputy of Santo Domingo,* by Anne Louis Girodet-Trioson

Optional Listening Selections:
Music: An Appreciation, 6th edition
"Là Ci Darem la Mano": CD 3, Track 61
Symphony No. 94 in G Major *(Surprise):* CD 3, Track 35

National Standards
This historical lesson addresses the following National Standards:

6. Listening to, analyzing, and describing music. **(a, b, c)**
7. Evaluating music. **(a)**
8. Understanding relationships between music, the other arts, and disciplines outside the arts. **(a, b, c, d, e)**
9. Understanding music in relation to history and culture. **(a, c, d, e)**

Classical Period

After completing this lesson, you should be able to:

- Discuss the major changes that took place during the Classical period.
- Identify the ideals of the Classical arts.
- Discuss the most important musical forms of the Classical period.
- Identify the two most important Classical composers.

The emotion and drama of the Baroque period were followed by the clarity and simplicity of the Classical period. The word *Classical* has many meanings. It refers to the works and ideas of ancient Greece and Rome. It also refers to the period of European art and music that lasted from about 1750 until around 1820. During this time, artists "looked back" to the standards of balance and unity they saw in ancient Greek and Roman artworks.

The Age of Enlightenment

The Classical period is often called the Age of Enlightenment. It was a time when people put their faith in reason and thought, not in tradition and emotion. It was also a time of great faith in "progress." Members of the growing middle classes believed that their rights could and would be established and that the power and privilege of the aristocracy would be curtailed.

The attitudes of the Classical period were reflected in the major political events of the era. The American colonists revolted against their British rulers and established an independent United States. Thirteen years after the signing of the Declaration of Independence, the French Revolution began; this uprising established a new government and a new societal structure in France.

During the Classical period, the Catholic church's support of the arts declined sharply. However, noble and wealthy individuals and families commissioned artworks of all kinds in increasing numbers. In spite of this patronage, some important visual artists created works that poked subtle fun at the activities and attitudes of the aristocracy.

The paintings, sculpture, and architecture of this period are usually referred to as Neoclassical. (The prefix *neo-* adds the meaning "new"; this term distinguishes Neoclassical artworks from the Classical artworks created in ancient Greece and Rome.) Neoclassical works stress the balance and grandeur that artists saw in the ancient Classical works. Painters such as Jacques Louis David used ancient Roman settings and emphasized firm lines and clear structures. The simpler and grand styles developed in painting, sculpture, and architecture were both an evocation of Classical balance and a reaction against the emotional excesses of late Baroque art.

COMPOSERS

Franz Joseph Haydn (1732–1809)
Wolfgang Amadeus Mozart (1756–1791)
Luigi Cherubini (1760–1842)
Ludwig van Beethoven (1770–1827)
Vincento Bellini (1801–1835)

ARTISTS

Antoine Watteau (1684–1721)
Francois Boucher (1703–1770)
Jean-Honoré Fragonard (1732–1806)
Francisco Gôya (1746–1828)
Jacques Louis David (1748–1825)
Anne Louis Girodet-Trioson (1767–1824)

AUTHORS

Jonathan Swift (1667–1745)
Samuel Richardson (1689–1761)
Voltaire (1694–1778)
Henry Fielding (1707–1754)
Wolfgang Goethe (1749–1832)
Friedrich von Schiller (1759–1805)
Jane Austen (1775–1817)

CHORAL MUSIC TERMS

chamber music

sonata form

string quartets

symphony

Classical Period **127**

Jean-Baptiste Bellay, Deputy of Santo Domingo

The Classical period was highlighted by a return to the ideal of Greek and Roman simplicity and balance. Likewise, social development seemed to swing like a pendulum along a continuum from excess to control. When the Baroque period was at its most opulent, there began to be an upsurge of indignant rebellion from the common people, leading to a return to more sensible, clean and symmetrical artistic representations. The painting of Jean-Baptiste Bellay, by Anne Louis Girodet-Trioson, is a symmetrical, balanced, uncluttered, natural representation of Bellay. It is interesting that the bust of the philosopher Abbe Raynal, whose writings inspired the black revolt in Haiti leading to Bellay's trip as representative to Paris, is watching closely in the background.

Suggested Teaching Sequence

1. Examine the Classical period.

Have students:

- Read the text on pages 127–129.
- Share what they know about the composers, artists, and authors listed on this page.
- Read, discuss, and answer the review questions individually, in pairs, or in small groups.
- Discuss their answers with the whole group, clarifying misunderstandings.

2. Examine the Classical period in historical perspective.

Have students:

- Turn to the time line on pages 128–129 and read the citations.
- Discuss why these events and people are considered important to the Classical period.
- Compare each of these events to what they know happened before and after the Classical period.
- Write a one- or two-sentence statement that describes the Classical period based on one of the events in the time line. (The excavation of Pompeii rekindled interest in the Classical simplicity that had previously occurred in the Renaissance period.)
- Write one additional sentence which tells how this event of the Classical period is related to the student's world. (Today, many people suggest that a return to the "good old days" when life was more simple would help resolve the troubles of our society.)

Swift's *Gulliver's Travels* published	George Washington	Thomas Jefferson	American Revolutionary War fought
▼ 1726	▼ 1732–1799	▼ 1743–1826	▼ 1775–1783

▼ 1732–1757
Franklin writes *Poor Richard's Almanac*

▼ 1775
James Watt invents the steam engine

3. Define the musical aspects of the Classical period.

Have students:

- Review the changes in music during the Classical period.
- Define *chamber music, sonata-allegro form,* and *symphony,* explaining how they reflected the changes of the Classical period.

Assessment

Informal Assessment

In this lesson, students showed the ability to:

- Identify characteristics of the Classical period and music of the Classical period.
- Compare music in the Classical period to today's world.
- Define *chamber music, sonata-allegro form,* and *symphony,* and explain how each of these terms is related to the Classical period.

Student Self-Assessment

Have students:

- Return to page 129 and answer the Check Your Understanding questions.
- Write a paragraph describing how much they understand abut the development of music during the Classical period.

Individual Performance Assessment

To further demonstrate accomplishment, have each student:

- Learn more about one aspect of music during the Classical period.
- Share information with the class in a creative way, such as in a poster, demonstration, design for the cover of a CD or video, and so on.

128

Music of the Classical Period

Like Neoclassical paintings, sculpture, and architecture, Classical music left behind the extreme drama and emotion of the Baroque period. Exaggerated embellishments and improvisations had no place in Classical compositions. Instead, Classical music emphasized precision and balance. An essential characteristic of the period was a careful balance between the content of the music and the form in which it was expressed.

During this period, middle-class people took an increasing interest in music. Composers responded by writing works that were accessible to the general public. Comic operas began to replace the serious operas of Baroque times. Dance music, including familiar folk tunes, were included in many compositions. Music, like other art forms, gradually became available to a wider range of the population.

Vocal and mixed forms, especially the opera and the oratorio, continued to develop during the Classical period. However, the most important Classical developments came in instrumental music, which gained in importance during this time.

Interest in archeology, particularly Greek and Roman models, resulted in the design of the library at Kenwood House by Robert Adam. This room combines Roman stucco ornamentation with the symmetry and geometric precision of the Classical period. Symmetry and precision are vital elements in musical compositions of the Classical period along with formal design and structure.

Begun in 1767. Robert Adam. Library at Kenwood House. London, England.

Chamber music—*music for a small group of instruments designed to be played in a room (or chamber) rather than in a public concert hall*—became significant during the Classical period. Such compositions are generally light and entertaining, both for the performers and for the listeners. The most popular Classical chamber music compositions were **string quartets**, *pieces composed for two violins, a viola, and a cello.*

Another important instrumental form of the Classical period was the **sonata form**, *a movement written in A A′ B A form.* The sonata form begins with a theme (A), which is then repeated with elaboration (A′). Then comes a contrasting development (B), and the form closes with a return to the original theme (A).

The concerto also changed and developed during the Classical period. The Baroque concerto featured an instrumental group supported by an orchestra. The Classical concerto, by contrast, became a work for an instrumental soloist—often a pianist, but also a violinist, trumpeter, clarinetist, bassoonist, or cellist—and orchestra.

128 *Choral Connections Level 3 Treble Voices*

Library at Kenwood House

The library at Kenwood House, by Robert Adam, begun in 1767, likewise reflects a return to a more clean, symmetrical, Roman style of architecture. However, signs of the Baroque and Rococo are evident here and there, as each period leaves a trace of influence on the next.

Notice the open space in both the painting and architecture, and the controlled use of design as an accent rather than as the complete style. Notice, also, the natural use of light and shadow, developed much more clearly during this period.

American Declaration of Independence signed

▼ **1776**

Federal Government established in America

▼ **1789**

▲ **1789**

French Revolution begins

▲ **1808**

Roman excavations begin at Pompeii, Italy

Extension

Networking with Your Community

Classical music is performed today frequently by vocal and instrumental groups. Large orchestras have many Classical pieces in their repertoire. Classical music is likewise performed in many church concerts, and by individuals in solo concert venues. Check with your local arts council, performing groups, and neighboring universities to discover locations and times of Classical performances for students to attend.

In a Classical concerto, the soloist and the orchestra are equals—another example of the Classical emphasis on balance.

Perhaps the most important instrumental development of the period was the **symphony**, *a large-scale piece for orchestra in three or more movements*. A Classical symphony usually consisted of four movements in this order: 1) A dramatic, fast movement; 2) A slow movement, often in sonata form; 3) A dance-style movement; 4) An exciting, fast movement.

Major Classical Composers

The Classical period was dominated by two composers, Franz Joseph Haydn and Wolfgang Amadeus Mozart. Both were popular and respected musicians in their time, and both remain among the best loved and most widely performed composers of our time. Haydn composed more than 100 symphonies and 68 string quartets, as well as sonatas, operas, masses, and other works. Although Mozart died just before he reached the age of 36, he composed more than 600 musical works, including over 40 symphonies and 20 concertos, which are considered among his greatest achievements.

A third major composer of the time, Ludwig van Beethoven, belongs both to the Classical period and to the next era, the Romantic period. Beethoven's compositions began in Classical style, but the texture, emotion, and new forms of his later music belong more to the Romantic period.

Notation in the Classical Period

Have students:

* Find copies of notation written by the hand of Mozart, Handel, or Telemann, and study the notation to get a feel for what had become standard by the time of the Classical period.
* Seek a local antique store, book store, or document gallery to find out how available or rare certain manuscripts are, and how much they might be worth.

Check Your Understanding

Recall

1. To whom did artists of the Classical period look for standards and ideals?

2. What were the central attitudes of the Classical period?

3. What is chamber music?

4. For which instruments is a string quartet composed?

5. What is a symphony? Which four movements are usually included in a Classical symphony?

6. Who are the two major composers of the Classical period? What kinds of works did each compose?

Thinking It Through

1. Describe a Classical composition you have listened to. What characteristics mark the work as coming from the Classical period?

2. What do you think led Classical composers, other artists, and society in general to want less freedom and more structure?

Classical Period **129**

Native American, Asian, and African Cultures and the Classical Period

Have students:

* Explore the music that was being performed and created in other cultures from 1750 to 1820, using the following questions as guides: What music was occurring in the culture during this time period? What was the music like? Was there any influence from or to European Classical music? If so, how did these music types change each other, if at all?

ANSWERS TO RECALL QUESTIONS

1. Ancient Greece and Rome.
2. People trusted reason and thought, and they believed in the equality of all people.
3. Music for a small group of instruments designed to be played in a room (or chamber) rather than in a public concert hall.
4. Violins, viola, and cello.
5. A large-scale piece for orchestra in three or more movements; a dramatic, fast movement; a slow movement, often in sonata form; a dance-style movement; an exciting, fast movement.
6. Franz Joseph Haydn (symphonies, string quartets, sonatas, operas, and masses) and Wolfgang Amadeus Mozart (symphonies and concertos).

Listening to...
Classical Music

This feature is designed to expand students' appreciation of choral and instrumental music of the Classical period.

CHORAL SELECTION: "Là Ci Darem la Mano" from *Don Giovanni* by Mozart

Have students:
- Read the information on this page to learn more about "Là Ci Darem la Mano."
- Watch as you follow a transparency of Blackline Master, Listening Map 5.

Using the Listening Map

Start in the upper left-hand corner and follow words of libretto and melodic patterns of instrumental interludes. Notice that each of the two singers is represented by a different heart. When they sing together, the hearts are entwined. Have students:
- Take notes as you define the terminology of the opera excerpt being played and the musical controls used: opera, libretto, duet, pianoforte, triplet, tied notes, baritone, soprano. (See your Blackline Master for definitions.)
- Note that the interplay between solo (one singer) or duet (two singers) changes the texture of the melody.
- Understand the translation of the Italian text to understand the story. (See your Blackline Master.)
- Listen to the choral selection as you point to the transparency.

Listening to...
Classical Music

CHORAL SELECTION

Mozart — *Don Giovanni*, Act I, "Lá Ci Darem la Mano"

Born in Salzburg, Austria, Wolfgang Amadeus Mozart (1756–1791), whose full name is Johann Chrysostom Wolfgang Theophilus, began his musical career at an extremely early age. By the time he was four years old, Mozart had already mastered the keyboard and by age five had written his first musical piece. He became a master of the violin quickly thereafter. Mozart's father, Leopold Mozart, recognized Amadeus's talent and began a tour through Europe, exhibiting his son's extraordinary abilities. By age 16, Mozart had already written nearly 25 symphonies.

Don Giovanni is an opera in two acts. The characters are: Don Giovanni, a young nobleman; Leporello, his servant; the Commendatore Seville; Donna Anna, Seville's daughter; Don Ottavio, her fiancé; Donna Elvira, a lady of Burgos; Zerlina, a country girl; and Masetto, her fiancé.

In this aria, "Lá Ci Darem la Mano," Don Giovanni sings to Zerlina, whom he meets at her engagement party. His flirtation is interrupted by the entrance of Donna Elvira, an old flame he had deserted. In the end of the opera, he receives just retribution for his actions when a supernatural fire destroys him and his palace.

INSTRUMENTAL SELECTION

Haydn — Symphony No. 94 in G major (*Surprise*)

Franz Joseph Haydn (1732–1809), a child prodigy and nine-year member of the Vienna Boys' Choir, spent most of his adult life working for Prince Esterhazy in Austria. While there, he wrote music for many occasions and experimented with music in new and different ways. He composed new forms and introduced touches of folk and gypsy music that he picked up from the country people. He was close friends with Mozart and was one of Beethoven's teachers. The *Surprise Symphony* was written for an evening concert after a dinner party. He put the loud (surprise) chord in to wake up the too-full, sleepy audience.

130 *Choral Connections   Level 3 Treble Voices*

TEACHER'S RESOURCE BINDER
Blackline Master, Listening Map 5
Blackline Master, Listening Map 6
Optional Listening Selections:
Music: An Appreciation, 6th edition
"Là Ci Darem la Mano": CD 3, Track 61
Symphony No. 94 in G Major (*Surprise*):
    CD 3, Track 35

National Standards
This lesson addresses the following National Standard:
6. Listening to, analyzing, and describing music. **(b)**

♪ CLASSICAL CONNECTIONS

Introducing...
"Holy, Holy, Holy"

Wolfgang Amadeus Mozart

Setting the Stage

The most impressive feature of "Holy, Holy, Holy" is its overall clarity. You will see an uncluttered page, relatively simple rhythms, and a very chordal structure—all features of the Classical period. Also notice that the dynamic requirements are very precise and clearly defined between forte and piano, with no indications of crescendo or diminuendo. This is not to imply that there is not to be a musical "arch to the phrase" in the performance; it merely means that the style of the period does not include the highly emotional "rise-and-fall" that marks the music of the Romantic period.

Listen perceptively and you will hear all the elements coming together to create a clean, crisp style that is unmistakably Mozart!

Meeting the Composer
Wolfgang Amadeus Mozart

Mozart (1756–1791) is very familiar to all musicians for his many compositions in virtually every performance medium, from concerto to opera to symphony. He was a gifted child, and from the age of five he began to write music of such quality that it astounded the adults around him. As with many gifted individuals, he was misunderstood and did not receive the recognition he deserved while he was alive. His contributions to music history have now been duly noted and Mozart is ranked alongside Bach, Beethoven, and Brahms as one of the greatest composers to have ever lived.

Classical Connections **131**

ASSESSMENT
Individual Performance Assessment
Have each student:
- Create a game that has one student calling out the definitions of operatic terms while the other students answer in the form of a question. (e.g., *libretto:* what are the words to an opera selection?)
- Translate any assigned phrase of "Là Ci Darem la Mano."
- Continue the answer/question game with the terms associated with Haydn's *Surprise* Symphony.
- Write descriptions of Haydn's symphony using the technical terminology given in the lesson.
- Perform the theme and as many variations as possible on a keyboard instrument.

INSTRUMENTAL SELECTION: Symphony No. 94 in G Major (*Surprise*) by Haydn
Have students:
- Read the information on page 130 to learn more about Haydn's Symphony No. 94 in G Major.
- Watch as you point to a transparency of Blackline Master, Listening Map 6.

Using the Listening Map
Start in the upper left-hand corner. Follow the melodic patterns for the theme and each variation, noting repeat signs as they appear. Have students:
- Listen as you explain that the style and form of this piece is theme and variations. The theme is repeated over and over and is changed each time it is repeated. Each variation is about the same length as the theme. Changes of melody, rhythm, harmony, accompaniment, dynamics, or tone color give a variation its own identity. The core melody may appear in the bass, or it may be repeated in a minor key instead of a major one. It may be heard together with a new melody (countermelody). The variations may be connected or separated.
- Take notes as you describe the specific musical terminology that is used in this movement: theme, variations, countermelody, polyphonic, major, minor, staccato, andante, and solo.
- Listen as you point to the transparency.

INTRODUCING . . . "Holy, Holy, Holy"
This feature is designed to introduce students to the Classical Lesson on the following pages. Have students:
- Read Setting the Stage on this page to learn more about "Holy, Holy, Holy."
- Read Meeting the Composer to learn more about Wolfgang Amadeus Mozart.
- Turn the page and begin the Classical Lesson.

Holy, Holy, Holy

COMPOSER: Wolfgang
Amadeus Mozart (1756–1791)
ARRANGER: Arthur Hardwicke

Focus

OVERVIEW
Contrasting dynamics; Latin text.

OBJECTIVES
After completing this lesson, students should be able to:
- Identify and perform contrasting dynamics.
- Sing in three parts with homophonic and polyphonic (imitative) textures.
- Sing correct Latin pronunciation.

CHORAL MUSIC TERMS
Define the Choral Music Terms for students, giving pronunciation, and answering any questions that may arise.

Warming Up

Vocal Warm-Up
This Vocal Warm-Up is designed to prepare students to:
- Read and sing pitches of the tonic triad with vocal flexibility.
- Sing a stressed marking followed by a marcato-staccato one, using the diaphragm.
- Sing with a relaxed throat and free jaw.

Have students:
- Read through the Vocal Warm-Up directions.
- Sing, following your demonstration.

CLASSICAL LESSON

Holy, Holy, Holy

COMPOSER: *Wolfgang Amadeus Mozart* (1756–1791)
ARRANGER: *Arthur Hardwicke*
ENGLISH TEXT: *Arthur Hardwicke*

CHORAL MUSIC TERMS
contrast
da capo
dynamics
fine
forte
homophony
marcato
piano
polyphony (imitation)
staccato

VOICING
SSA

PERFORMANCE STYLE
Adagio
Accompanied by piano or organ

FOCUS
- Identify and perform contrasting dynamics.
- Sing in three parts with homophonic and polyphonic (imitative) textures.
- Sing correct Latin pronunciation.

Warming Up

 Vocal Warm-Up

Sing this warm-up using the text provided. Notice the stressed and marcato-staccato markings, and use your diaphragm to make this articulation happen. Keep your throat relaxed and jaw free at all times.

Neh - ah, neh - ah, neh - ah, neh - ah, neh - ah, neh - ah, neh - ah, neh - ah, neh.

TEACHER'S RESOURCE BINDER
Blackline Master 20, *Translation and Pronunciation Guide for "Holy, Holy, Holy"*

National Standards
1. Singing, alone and with others, a varied repertoire of music. **(a, c, f)**
5. Reading and notating music. **(a, b)**
6. Listening to, analyzing, and describing music. **(a, b)**
7. Evaluating music and music performances. **(a)**
8. Understanding relationships between music, the other arts, and disciplines outside the arts. **(c)**
9. Understanding music in relation to history and culture. **(a, c, d)**

Sight-sing this exercise using solfège and hand signs or numbers, with solid style and well-defined dynamics. How would you describe the movement of voice parts in relationship to one another? Is it consistent throughout the exercise? Notice the indication at the end to go back to the beginning (*da capo*) and sing to the double bar (*Fine*, meaning end).

Singing: "Holy, Holy, Holy"

Compare the sound of a basketball and a golf ball, both bounced with the same amount of energy on the same surface. Which sound would you call *forte*? Which would you call *piano*?

The amount of sound for piano and forte may differ, but the amount of breath support remains the same.

Now turn to the music for "Holy, Holy, Holy" on page 134.

HOW DID YOU DO?

?
?

With lots of support, you have learned this classical piece by Mozart. Think about your preparation and performance of "Holy, Holy, Holy."

1. Describe the dynamics in "Holy, Holy, Holy" and tell how they are or are not characteristic of Classical period style.

2. How is your Latin pronunciation? What is easy? What needs more work?

3. Describe the vocal textures included in "Holy, Holy, Holy," pointing them out in the notation. How are these related to the dynamics indicated for the piece?

Sight-Singing

This Sight-Singing exercise is designed to prepare students to:
- Read and sing in three parts.
- Sing homophonic passages with alternating sections of dynamic contrast.
- Sing imitative passages.
- Read and follow *da capo* and *Fine* instructions.

Have students:
- Read through the Sight-Singing exercise directions.
- Read through each voice part rhythmically, using rhythm syllables.
- Sight-sing through each part separately using solfège and hand signs or numbers.
- Sing all parts together.

Singing: "Holy, Holy, Holy"

Identify and practice dynamics. Have students:
- Read the text on page 133.
- Compare the dynamics of a basketball and golf ball bounced on the same surface, identifying the basketball as having a louder sound than the golf ball. (*forte* and *piano*)
- Recall that although dynamics may change, the amount of breath support remains the same.
- Look at the notation for "Holy, Holy, Holy," finding all dynamic markings.

Holy, Holy, Holy **133**

Suggested Teaching Sequence

1. Review Vocal Warm-Up.

Warm-up voice. Sing stress followed by marcato-staccato markings. Have students:

- Review the Vocal Warm-Up on page 132.
- Identify the markings for each set of eighths as a stressed note followed by a marcato-staccato, requiring double diaphragmatic pushes.
- Practice until this becomes familiar.

2. Review Sight-Singing.

Read and sing in three parts, using dynamic variation. Sing homophonic and imitative passages. Have students:

- Review the Sight-Singing exercise on page 133.
- Identify the dynamic markings and tell what they mean. (*f* = loud, *mf* = medium loud, *mp* = medium soft, *p* = soft)
- Recall that all dynamics require the same amount of solid breath support and a full breath before each entry.
- Identify the voice part relationships as homophonic, with passages of imitation at measures 9 and 13.
- Sing the exercise, demonstrating dynamic contrast with solid energy for both *piano* and *forte*.

Holy, Holy, Holy

(Sanctus)

Wolfgang Amadeus Mozart
Edited and arr. by Arthur Hardwicke
English text by A.H.

SSA with Piano or Organ Accompaniment

134 *Choral Connections   Level 3 Treble Voices*

MUSIC LITERACY

Classical Simplicity and Sight-Singing

The Classical style consists of simple and clean rhythms, straightforward melodic lines, and clear structure, all of which are good qualities for sight-singing material. Have students:

- Sight-sing any or all of this piece to test their own sight-singing ability.

- Practice once each day as part of rehearsal, tracking their improvement. Stop when the practice "falls apart," returning the next class to try again.

3. Sight-sing "Holy, Holy, Holy" using solfège and hand signs or numbers.
Have students:
- Divide into voice sections (SSA) and read each part rhythmically, using rhythm syllables.
- Clap and speak the rhythm in full ensemble, following dynamic markings.
- Again in sections, sing with solfège and hand signs or numbers, identifying and working on problem areas.
- Sing the piece through using solfège and hand signs or numbers with full ensemble, building part independence.
- Sing the piece in full ensemble, with correct dynamic contrast.

4. Learn the Latin pronunciation.
Have students:
- Using Blackline Master 20, *Translation and Pronunciation Guide for "Holy, Holy, Holy,"* echo or read the words slowly.
- Speak the text in Latin in rhythm.
- Sing the piece in Latin, using correct pronunciation.

TEACHING STRATEGY

Texture

Have students:
- Recall the textures that are found in this piece: homophonic and polyphonic.
- Identify the concept of a chord sequence that underlies this type of writing, with each voice singing one of the chord tones.
- Compose short exercises, up to 16 measures, using one or the other texture.
- Share these exercises in small groups as sight-singing practice. Assess their strengths and weaknesses.
- Discuss how difficult it is to write a truly fine, simple exercise in parts.

5. Identify the texture of each section of "Holy, Holy, Holy."

Have students:

- Review the piece, describing the textures found (homophonic = all parts moving together chordally; polyphonic = all parts moving independently, sometimes in imitative style).
- Notice that the homophonic sections are marked *forte,* and the polyphonic ones are marked *piano.*
- Sing the piece with dynamic balance between the parts, equal during the homophonic sections, and bringing the melody out during polyphonic or imitative sections.

VOCAL DEVELOPMENT
Phrases and Dynamics

To encourage vocal development, have students:

- Identify the phrases throughout the piece.
- Identify ways to shape the phrase using dynamics to build tension and release.
- Find the dynamic markings in the piece, and relate them to the phrase shapes and the overall shape of the piece.

- Discuss how breath support helps shape and sustain phrases.
- Perform the piece adding the phrasing through the dynamics marked on the notation.

Assessment

Informal Assessment
During this lesson, students showed the ability to:
- Use the diaphragm to control articulation in the Vocal Warm-Up exercise.
- Identify and sing dynamic contrast in the Sight-Singing exercise.
- Sight-sing using solfège and hand signs or numbers in three homophonic and imitative parts in the Sight-Singing exercise.
- Sing independently in three homophonic and polyphonic parts, using correct dynamic contrast, in "Holy, Holy, Holy."
- Sing in Latin with correct pronunciation in "Holy, Holy, Holy."

Student Self-Assessment
Have students:
- Evaluate their performance with the How Did You Do? section on page 133.
- Answer the questions individually. Discuss them in pairs or small groups and/or write their responses on a sheet of paper.

Individual Performance Assessment
To further demonstrate accomplishment, have each student:
- In a trio, sing the Sight-Singing exercise into a tape recorder in a isolated space, demonstrating part independence and dynamic contrast.
- Individually sing her voice part from measure 29 for five measures, demonstrating correct Latin pronunciation.

Extension

Arranging the Accompaniment for Another Instrument

Have students:

- Listen to someone play the piano or organ accompaniment for "Holy, Holy, Holy."
- Suggest other instruments that might be appropriate for this accompaniment. (possibly a brass ensemble)
- Write the accompaniment for a different instrument group.
- Perform the piece with this new accompaniment.

Comparing Your Performance to Another

Have students:

- Listen to a different Mozart vocal piece.
- Identify any characteristics of Classical music, and critique the performance, telling what was especially good, and what could have been better.
- Compare their performance of "Holy, Holy, Holy" to the recorded performance, describing what was similar and what was different.
- Determine any changes to be made in their performance, and then sing "Holy, Holy, Holy" again.

National Standards

The following National Standards are addressed through the Extension and bottom-page activities:

1. Singing, alone and with others, a varied repertoire of music. **(a, c)**
4. Composing and arranging music within specified guidelines. **(a, b)**
5. Reading and notating music. **(a, b)**
6. Listening to, analyzing, and describing music. **(a, b, c, e, f)**
7. Evaluating music and music performances. **(a, b)**
9. Understanding music in relation to history and culture. **(a, c, d)**

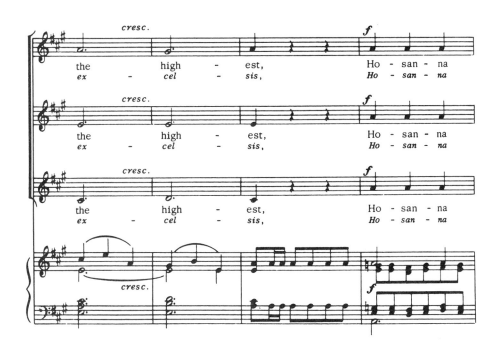

Composing in the Classical Style

In groups or individually, have students:

- Analyze this composition by Mozart, writing down the most important characteristics.
- Choose or write a text modeled after the Mozart text, either sacred or secular.
- Compose a short piece that follows the characteristics found in the Mozart piece.
- Revise, practice, and perform their piece.

Classical Characteristics

Have students:

- Describe the musical characteristics of "Holy, Holy, Holy."
- Recall characteristics of Classical music.
- Construct a Venn diagram, demonstrating the overlapping characteristics of the two that define the piece as an example of Classical music.

in the high - est, Ho - san - na
in ex - cel - sis, Ho - san - na

in the high - est, Ho - san - na
in ex - cel - sis, Ho - san - na

in the high - est, Ho - san - na
in ex - cel - sis, Ho - san - na

in the high - est.
in ex - cel - sis.

in the high - est.
in ex - cel - sis.

in the high - est.
in ex - cel - sis.

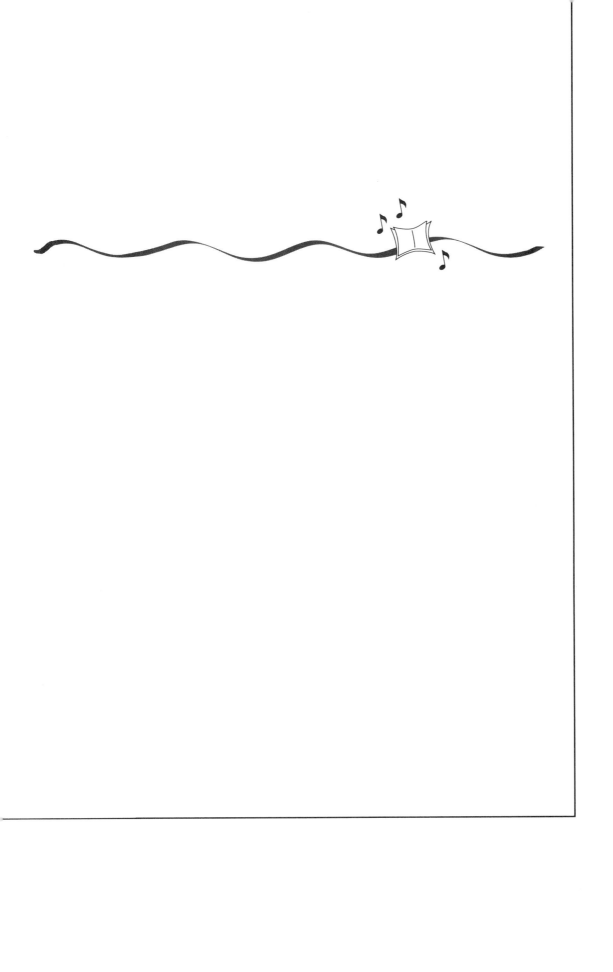

Romantic Period

Focus

OVERVIEW
Understanding the development of choral and instrumental music during the Romantic period.

OBJECTIVES
After completing this lesson, students should be able to:
- Describe characteristics of architecture, fine art, and music during the Romantic period.
- Identify several musical forms of the Romantic period.
- Define *art song, music critic,* and *nationalism;* explain how each of these terms is related to the Romantic period.
- Identify some of the key musical figures of the Romantic period.

CHORAL MUSIC TERMS
Define the Choral Music Terms for students, giving pronunciation, and answering any questions that may arise.

Introducing the Lesson

Introduce the Romantic period through visual art.
Analyze the artwork and pavilion on pages 142 and 145.
Have students:
- Study the painting and architecture.
- Discuss the information about each artwork provided at the bottom of pages 143 and 144 in your Teacher's Wraparound Edition.

An episode in the lives of the middle and lower classes of the nineteenth century is reflected in the realism of *Concert in the Tuileries* by Edouard Manet (1832–1883). The realistic treatment is also obvious in the dramatic subject matter that appeared in the operas of the Italian composers of the Romantic period, such as Rossini, Bellini, and Verdi.

1862. Edouard Manet. *Concert in the Tuileries.* Oil on canvas. 75 x 118 cm (30 x 46 1/2"). National Gallery, London.

TEACHER'S RESOURCE BINDER
Fine Art Transparency 5, *Concert in the Tuileries,* by Edouard Manet

Optional Listening Selections:
Music: An Appreciation, 6th edition
"Quartet" from *Rigoletto:* CD 6, Track 22
Romance in G Minor for Violin and Piano: CD 4, Track 62

National Standards
This lesson addresses the following:
6. Listening to, analyzing, and describing music. **(a, b, c)**
7. Evaluating music and music performances. **(a)**
8. Understanding relationships between music, the other arts, and disciplines outside the arts. **(a, b, c, d, e)**
9. Understanding music in relation to history and culture. **(a, c, d, e)**

Romantic Period

After completing this lesson, you should be able to:

- Discuss the most important developments of the Romantic period.
- Identify the major musical forms of the Romantic period.
- Explain the importance of nationalism in Romantic music.
- Identify at least three major Romantic composers.

Emotion, imagination, and a concern for the individual returned to the arts with the Romantic period, which defined most of the nineteenth century, from about 1820 until around 1900. A new sense of political and artistic freedom emerged, as artists, including musicians, became impatient with established rules and tradition.

A Time of Freedom and Imagination

In many ways, the Romantic period was a reaction against the constraints of the Classical period. People became less interested in the balance and clarity of earlier times. Rather, their interests focused on adventure, a love of nature, and freedom of expression.

The Romantic period coincided with the Industrial Revolution, which created many new nonagricultural jobs and contributed to the growth of cities. The middle class grew in numbers, as well as in confidence and power. More and more people took an active part in their culture and their nation. A new sense of patriotism grew among citizens of individual European countries and of the United States.

Visual artists of the Romantic period reflected the era's attitudes with bolder, more colorful works. The enthusiasm for nature was reflected in the growing popularity of landscape paintings. The Romantic paintings of William Turner and John Constable express the movements and moods of nature. Later, Impressionist painters, including Edouard Manet, Claude Monet, and Pierre Auguste Renoir, developed new techniques to bring the sense and feeling of nature alive for the viewer.

Romantic Musical Developments

Romantic composers worked primarily with the same forms that had developed and become popular during the Classical period. However, Romantic composers treated these forms in ways that made new statements about music and about their own attitudes toward life. Romantic compositions, focused on both the heights and depths of human emotion, were characterized by complexity, exploration, and excitement. The interests of the period were expressed in larger, more complex vocal melodies and more colorful harmonies. In addition, instrumentation was expanded to enhance the overall possibilities of tone color in the music, and the rhythms became more free and more flexible.

COMPOSERS

Ludwig van Beethoven (1770–1827)
Franz Schubert (1797–1828)
Hector Berlioz (1803–1869)
Felix Mendelssohn (1809–1847)
Frédéric Chopin (1810–1849)
Robert Schumann (1810–1856)
Franz Liszt (1811–1886)
Richard Wagner (1813–1883)
Giuseppe Verdi (1813–1901)
Clara Schumann (1819–1896)
Johann Strauss (1825–1899)
Johannes Brahms (1833–1897)
Peter Ilyich Tschaikovsky (1840–1893)
Giacomo Puccini (1858–1924)

ARTISTS

Élisabeth Vigée-Lebrun (1755–1842)
Joseph Mallard William Turner (1775–1851)
John Constable (1776–1837)
Rosa Bonheur (1822–1899)
Edouard Manet (1832–1883)
James A. McNeill Whistler (1834–1903)
Edgar Degas (1834–1917)
Paul Cezanne (1839–1906)
Claude Monet (1840–1926)
Berthe Morisot (1841–1895)
Pierre Auguste Renoir (1841–1919)
Mary Cassatt (1845–1926)
Vincent van Gogh (1853–1890)
Georges Seurat (1859–1891)

AUTHORS

Noah Webster (1758–1843)
Sir Walter Scott (1771–1832)
Mary Wollstonecraft Shelley (1797–1851)
Ralph Waldo Emerson (1803–1882)

CHORAL MUSIC TERMS

art song

music critic

nationalism

Romantic Period **143**

Suggested Teaching Sequence

1. Examine the Romantic period.

Have students:

- Read the text on pages 143–145.
- Share what they know about the composers, artists, and authors listed on this page.
- Read, discuss, and answer the review questions individually, in pairs, or in small groups.
- Discuss their answers with the whole group, clarifying misunderstandings.

2. Examine the Romantic period in historical perspective.

Have students:

- Turn to the time line and read the citations.
- Discuss why these people and events are considered important dates during the Romantic period.
- Compare each of these events to what they know occurred before and after the Romantic period.
- Write a statement of one or two sentences in length that describes the Romantic period, based on one of the events of the time line. (President Abraham Lincoln abolished slavery, encouraging individuals to be in control of their own lives.)
- Write one additional sentence which tells how this Romantic period event is related to the student's world. (Today, some people suggest that there needs to be less government involvement in everyday life, and people need more freedom to make their own choices.)

3. Define the musical aspects of the Romantic period.

Have students:

- Review the changes in music during the Romantic period.
- Define *art song, music critic,* and *nationalism.*

MORE ABOUT... Concert in the Tuileries

Manet's *Concert in the Tuileries* is an example of a new, reactionary type of art called Realism, which began to appear in the 1840s. Realists focused on everyday people and occurrences for their subjects, and tried to represent what they saw in an accurate, unsentimental way. Manet was the first artist in Western history to curve the hallowed horizon line, and he obscures the guiding verticals and camouflages the horizon. Every tree trunk is curved; every man's hat tilts. Just as Manet attempts to revise the viewer's notion of space, so composers of the Romantic period continually experimented with new forms, scales, harmonies, and styles—consistent with their search for new audiences.

Assessment

Informal Assessment
In this lesson, students showed the ability to:
- Identify characteristics of the Romantic period and music of the Romantic period.
- Compare music in the Romantic period to today's world.
- Define *art song, music critic,* and *nationalism,* and explain how each of these terms is related to the Romantic period.

Student Self-Assessment
Have students:
- Return to page 145 and answer the Check Your Understanding questions.
- Write a paragraph describing how much they understand about the development of music during the Romantic period.

Individual Performance Assessment
To further demonstrate accomplishment, have each student:
- Learn more about one aspect of music during the Romantic period.
- Share information with the class in a creative way, such as in a poster, demonstration, design for the cover of a CD or video, and so on.

Louisiana Purchase transacted
1803

Abraham Lincoln
1809–1865

Frederick Douglass
c. 1817–1895

Mary Baker Eddy
1821–1910

1804
Napoleon crowned Emperor

1812–1814
War of 1812

1821
Jean Champollion deciphers Egyptian hieroglyphics using the Rosetta Stone

1823
Monroe Doctrine created

Many Romantic compositions reflect the period's spirit of **nationalism**, *pride in a country's historical and legendary past.* Composers used traditional legends, as well as nationalistic dramas and novels, as the basis for both vocal and instrumental works.

Nationalism is seen perhaps most clearly in the operas of Richard Wagner and Giuseppe Verdi. Wagner's works, including the series of four operas known as *The Ring of the Nibelung*, are based on epic sagas and are intended to preserve German legends and folk music. Verdi, who has become the most popular of all opera composers, emphasized the importance of following Italian historical and cultural traditions.

Other musical forms of the Romantic period also reflect the era's nationalism. There was an increased interest in the traditional folk tunes and folk dances of specific nations or regions; these folk tunes were often used or imitated in serious compositions. German folk songs can be heard in Robert Schumann's piano pieces and symphonies, for example. In the United States, the songs composed by Stephen Foster express his understanding of and special pride in the southern United States.

As the Romantic period progressed, the most important vocal form became the **art song**, *an expressive song about life, love, and human relationships for solo voice and piano.* Art songs are known in German as *lieder*, and the most famous composers of these Romantic works were German-speakers. Austrian Franz Schubert composed more than 600 songs, as well as symphonies, string quartets, and other works, before his death at the age of 31. German composers Robert Schumann and Johannes Brahms are also known for their *lieder*.

Instrumental music became more elaborate and expressive during the Romantic period. Symphonies gained in popularity. Symphony orchestras increased in size, and percussion held a new place of importance. The most famous symphonies of the period—and perhaps of all time—are those composed by Ludwig van Beethoven. Some symphonies, including Beethoven's *Ninth Symphony*, added a chorus to the instrumental music.

Dance music also grew in importance during this time. Great social occasions became popular and required new dance compositions. The waltzes of Johann Strauss were played throughout Europe; new polonaises and other dance forms were also composed.

Modern Innovations of the Romantic Period

During the Romantic period, musicians and other artists received less support from wealthy or aristocratic patrons. As a result, composers began to think about "selling" their music to an audience. For several Romantic musicians, a colorful and controversial private life was part of "the package"; it sparked public interest in the composer and his works.

Another innovation of the period was the emergence of the **music critic**, *a writer who explains composers and their music to the public and who helps set standards in musical taste.* As music became more diverse and as increasing numbers of people listened to and appreciated new compositions, critics often sought to guide the direction new music might take.

144 *Choral Connections Level 3 Treble Voices*

Royal Pavilion

Romanticism was characterized by a heightened sense of the dramatic, but also strove for an idealized vision of the world through the arts. In John Nash's Royal Pavilion, characteristics of all architectural styles of the past are incorporated, but then idealized, embellished, and transformed into a fantasy vision of symmetrical beauty with great elaboration. An awareness of other cultures is evident in the domes and lattice work, as well as in the shapes of openings.

This idealized and elaborated style is represented in music by the increasingly elaborate operas and larger orchestral pieces, as well as the increased ranges, tone colors, harmonies, rhythms, and forms that allowed composers to explore the depths of emotion through music.

Mary Mason Lyon founds Mt.
Holyoke Female Seminary

1837

American Civil War

1861–1865

Wireless telegraph developed by
Guglielmo Marconi

1895

1835–1910   **1844–1900**

Mark Twain   Friedrich Nietzsche

1889   **1898**

Jane Addams and   Motion picture camera
Ellen Starr found   patented by Thomas Edison;
Hull House   sound recording developed

▲ **John Nash (1752–1835) reaches for originality in his design of the Royal Pavilion in Brighton, England. The combination of Oriental onion domes and minarets with an interior in the Classical style is totally unique. Interest in the exotic was also a hallmark of Romantic composers who dealt with foreign lands as well as legends and mysticism in their works.**

1815–23. John Nash. Royal Pavilion, Brighton, England.

Check Your Understanding

Recall

1. In what ways was the Romantic period a reaction against the Classical period?

2. What is nationalism? How is it important in Romantic music?

3. What are art songs? Which Romantic composers are especially noted for this kind of composition?

4. How did symphonies change during the Romantic period?

5. Why did composers of the Romantic period have to start thinking about "selling" their music to an audience?

6. What is a music critic?

Thinking It Through

1. Review what you know about the musical ideals of the Renaissance period, the Baroque period, the Classical period, and the Romantic period. What cycle or trend can you identify? What implications do you think that cycle or trend might have?

2. What relationship do you think might exist between the decline of the patronage system and the emergence of the music critic?

Romantic Period **145**

Extension

North America and the Romantic Period

What was going on in North America during the Romantic period?
Have students:

- Look at the time line and discover any citations that relate to North America.

- Research what music was being sung, played, and created in North America. Was there any contact between Europe and North America that affected music? Was Romantic music played in North America? Did the Romantic spirit foster any new musical inventions in North America?

- What non-European music was being performed and created in North America?

ANSWERS TO RECALL QUESTIONS

1. People became less interested in balance and clarity and focused on adventure, love of nature, and freedom of expression.

2. Pride in a country's historical and legendary past. Composers used traditional legends as the basis for both vocal and instrumental works.

3. Expressive songs about life, love, and human relationships for solo voice and piano. Franz Schubert, Robert Schumann, and Johannes Brahms.

4. They increased in size, and percussion held a new place of importance.

5. They received less support from wealthy or aristocratic patrons.

6. A writer who explains composers and their music to the public and who helps set standards in musical taste.

ROMANTIC CONNECTIONS

Listening to...
Romantic Music

This feature is designed to expand students' appreciation of choral and instrumental music of the Romantic period.

CHORAL SELECTION: Quartet from Act III of *Rigoletto* by Verdi

Have students:

• Read the information on this page to learn more about Verdi's *Rigoletto.*

• Watch as you follow a transparency of Blackline Master, Listening Map 7.

Using the Listening Map

Start in the upper left-hand corner. Follow the melody and words of the Duke's first solo; then follow the melody lines of other characters until they go into ensemble singing (all 4 together). Follow the Duke's melody; then follow the iconic notation for Gilda's melody line. Finally, follow the last line at bottom of map. Have students:

• Listen as you explain how Verdi's operas display tension and release in the melody line. (making the melody go higher on emotional words, having notes held longer when strong feelings shown, using trills and runs to heighten suspense)

• Listen as you explain that the picture on the map is the house where the "Quartet" scene is performed, with Gilda and Rigoletto outside while the Duke and Maddalena are inside.

• Listen to the recording as you point to the transparency.

Listening to...
Romantic Music

CHORAL SELECTION

Verdi — *Rigoletto*, Act III, Quartet

Rigoletto was first performed at Venice on March 11, 1851. It was based on Victor Hugo's *Le Roi s'amuse.* Giuseppe Verdi (1813–1901) chose librettos that show his deep sense of theater. For his texts, he usually chose plays with dramatic situations and forceful confrontations. Many of the librettos of the early opera use condensed, violent stories interspersed with bloody elements. *Rigoletto* is such an example.

INSTRUMENTAL SELECTION

Schumann — Romance in G Minor for Violin and Piano No. 2

Clara Schumann (1819–1896) is universally regarded as one of the most distinguished musicians of the nineteenth century. She was admired in Europe as an outstanding pianist, but never acknowledged in her lifetime as the outstanding composer that she was. Her main works are solo pieces, variations, chamber music (including the selection you will hear, a lied written in 1855–1856), cadenzas for Mozart and Beethoven piano concertos, and one piano concerto.

146 *Choral Connections Level 3 Treble Voices*

TEACHER'S RESOURCE BINDER

Blackline Master, Listening Map 7
Blackline Master, Listening Map 8

Optional Listening Selections:

Music: An Appreciation, 6th edition
"Quartet" from *Rigoletto:* CD 6, Track 22
Romance in G Minor for Violin and Piano:
    CD 4, Track 62

National Standards

This lesson addresses the following National Standard:

6. Listening to, analyzing, and describing music. **(c)**

♪ ROMANTIC CONNECTIONS

Introducing...

"Gruss"

Felix Mendelssohn

Setting the Stage

The soaring piano introduction you will hear in "Gruss" brings an audience to the entry of the singers with an anticipation of movement, of being lifted upward in the melody of the song. One is not disappointed; the voices quickly move to the highest pitch of the entire piece in only the third measure of the vocal lines! This is Romantic music at its best, bringing one to heights before experiencing depths. While the rhythmic content of the piece is not difficult, the calculation of the phrases presents a great challenge. The singer is asked to sing relatively long phrases that contain wide leaps and demanding dynamics.

Meeting the Composer

Felix Mendelssohn

Felix Mendelssohn-Bartholdy (1809–1847) was a Romantic composer who was highly influenced by Classical ideals. An accomplished pianist, he wrote music for piano requiring fluent technique, but in an elegant, sensitive style that was not as flamboyant as other composers of his time. His works closely follow the standard musical forms of the Classical period—for example, the sonata, the concerto, and the symphony—giving Romantic themes to these established vehicles of composition.

Romantic Connections **147**

INSTRUMENTAL SELECTION: Romance in G Minor for Violin and Piano by Clara Schumann
Have students:
• Read the information on page 146 to learn more about Schumann's Romance in G Minor for Violin and Piano.
• Watch as you follow a transparency of Blackline Master, Listening Map 8.

Using the Listening Map
Start in the upper left-hand corner. Follow the melody of violin part using the form of selection: ABA coda. Have students
• Listen as you explain the use of tension in this performance by violin and piano. (The melody passes back and forth between instruments; the melody line builds more tension with the shape of the melody—builds to high pitches, uses ample chromaticism, changes dynamics, and uses trills.)
• Listen as you explain the way "release" is shown. (use of repeated melody, use of ABA form-returns to first idea, ritards)
• Listen to the recording as you point to the transparency.

INTRODUCING . . . "Gruss"
This feature is designed to introduce students to the Romantic Lesson on the following pages. Have students:
• Read Setting the Stage on this page to learn more about "Gruss."
• Read Meeting the Composer to learn more about Felix Mendelssohn.
• Turn the page and begin the Romantic Lesson.

ASSESSMENT

Individual Performance Assessment

Have each student:
• Identify the measures in the first section of "Quartet" where the melody line illustrates the emotional content of the words.
• Look at Gilda's melody line inside the "house" and discuss how it shows tension from the text. (short repeated notes getting higher and louder)
• List three ways that Schumann builds tension and release in the violin part of her Romance in G Minor. (large leaps in melody line, changes in dynamics, trills, tied notes)
• Individually perform the melody line of the first eight measures vocally, using the musical controls written.

ROMANTIC LESSON

Gruss

COMPOSER: Felix Mendelssohn (1809–1847)

ENGLISH TEXT: J. Von Eichendorff

EDITED BY: Robert Carl

Focus

OVERVIEW
Melodic steps and leaps; melodic repetition; German language.

OBJECTIVES
After completing this lesson, students should be able to:
- Identify and sing melodic steps and leaps.
- Identify melodic repetition between voice parts and sections of a piece.
- Sing using correct German pronunciation.

CHORAL MUSIC TERMS
Define the Choral Music Terms for students, giving pronunciation, and answering any questions that may arise.

Warming Up

Vocal Warm-Up
This Vocal Warm-Up is designed to prepare students to:
- Sing an active rhythmic line with clear articulation.
- Articulate with both diction and diaphragmatic support.
- Sing skips and leaps in tune.

Have students:
- Read through the Vocal Warm-Up directions.
- Sing, following your demonstration.

ROMANTIC LESSON

Gruss

COMPOSER: Felix Mendelssohn (1809–1847)

ENGLISH TEXT: J. Von Eichendorff

EDITED BY: Robert Carl

CHORAL MUSIC TERMS
melodic leaps
melodic repetition
melodic steps
sections
teneramente
voice parts

VOICING
SA

PERFORMANCE STYLE
Teneramente, non legato
(sustained, but not connected)
Accompanied by piano

FOCUS
- Identify and sing melodic steps and leaps.
- Identify melodic repetition between voice parts and sections of a piece.
- Sing using correct German pronunciation.

Warming Up

Vocal Warm-Up
Sing this warm-up using the text. Make sure to enunciate clearly throughout this exercise, using effective breath support. Tune the pitches carefully—especially on the big leaps.

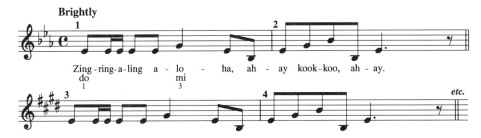

Zing - ring-a-ling a - lo - ha, ah - ay kook-koo, ah - ay.

Sight-Singing
Sight-sing this exercise with a flowing style, using solfège and hand signs or numbers. How would you describe this melodic line? Do you find any repetition within this exercise?

TEACHER'S RESOURCE BINDER
Blackline Master 21, *Translation and Pronunciation Guide for "Gruss"*

National Standards
1. Singing, alone and with others, a varied repertoire of music. **(a, c, f)**
3. Improvising melodies, variations, and accompaniments. **(b)**
5. Reading and notating music. **(a, b)**
6. Listening to, analyzing, and describing music. **(a, b)**
7. Evaluating music and music performances. **(a)**
8. Understanding relationships between music, the other arts, and disciplines outside the arts. **(c)**
9. Understanding music in relation to history and culture. **(a, c, d)**

Singing: "Gruss"

Echoes (or repetition) are a fundamental element of musical composition. Working with a partner, say a sentence and have your partner repeat it as soon as you finish. Take turns practicing this skill.

Next, repeat the same process, but sing the short phrases, with the other person repeating as soon as the pattern is finished. Switch roles.

Now turn to the music for "Gruss" on page 150.

HOW DID YOU DO?

?
?

Is your singing merely imitation, or did you make decisions about your performance based on analysis? Think about your preparation and performance of "Gruss."
1. The melody of "Gruss" has steps and leaps. Point out what these look like in your voice part. Which is easier for you to sing? Why?
2. Describe the two types of melodic repetition that occur in "Gruss." Did the repetition help you learn the piece? How?

3. Assess your ability to sing in German with correct pronunciation.
4. Describe the musical and text characteristics of "Gruss" that give clues to the period in which it was written. Are there any characteristics that you have seen or heard in music of prevous periods?

Gruss **149**

Sight-Singing

This Sight-Singing exercise is designed to prepare students to:
- Sing in unison using solfège and hand signs or numbers.
- Identify and sing stepwise melodic phrases.
- Identify melodic repetition.

Have students:
- Read through the Sight-Singing exercise directions.
- Read through each voice part rhythmically, using rhythm syllables.
- Sight-sing through each part separately using solfège and hand signs or numbers.
- Sing all parts together.

Singing: "Gruss"

Identify and practice repetition of phrases. Have students:
- Read the text on page 149.
- In pairs, first echo the spoken phrases, then the sung phrases.
- Look at the notation for "Gruss" to find places where one part repeats the other; for example, measures 12, 13, and 14. (Notice that in the alto part, the pitches are in the same configuration, but at a lower pitch.)

Suggested Teaching Sequence

1. Review Vocal Warm-Up.
Warm up the voice. Sing melodic leaps. Have students:

- Review the Vocal Warm-Up on page 148.
- Identify and sing the melodic leaps, particularly the octave leap downward toward the end.
- Look at the notation for "Gruss," pointing out melodic leaps in their voice part, upward and downward.
- Practice each of these leaps three times.

2. Review Sight-Singing.
Read and sing in unison. Identify melodic repetition. Have students:

- Review the Sight-Singing exercise on page 148.
- Describe the melodic line as stepwise.
- Identify the repetition of phrases, citing exact and approximate repetition. (Each four-measure section is repeated approximately.)
- Discuss how the repetition affects sight-singing. (It should make it easier, because the patterns have been seen and heard before, and the singer can focus on the differences.)
- Look at the notation of "Gruss," finding repetition of larger sections. (two nearly identical verses, the third begins with contrasting material and ends with material identical to the first two)

(Greeting)

Felix Mendelssohn
(Op. 63, No. 3)
Edited by Robert Carl
English Text by J. Von Eichendorff

TEACHING STRATEGY

Singing Melodic Steps and Leaps in Tune

Have students:

- Use an upward-lifting motion with the right hand, palm up, as the melodic leap occurs in the repetitions.
- Discuss what affect this physical motion has on the ability of the singers to execute the leap to the higher pitches.

3. Sight-sing "Gruss" using solfège and hand signs or numbers.

Have students:

- Divide into voice sections (SA) and read each part rhythmically, using rhythm syllables.
- Clap and speak the piece in full ensemble, adding dynamics as marked on the score. (Shift weight from side to side on the downbeat of each measure to feel the meter together.)
- Again in sections, read through the piece using solfège and hand signs or numbers, tuning the intervals carefully.
- Sing the piece through slowly with solfège and hand signs or numbers as a full ensemble.
- Sing the piece in full ensemble, with correct dynamic contrast.

4. Learn the German pronunciation.

Have students:

- Using Blackline Master 21, *Translation and Pronunciation Guide for "Gruss,"* echo or read the words slowly.
- Speak the German text in rhythm.
- Sing the piece in German, using correct pronunciation.

MUSIC LITERACY

Phrasing

One characteristic of this piece that is particularly "Romantic" is the long phrases, which are demanding of singers when there are large leaps. Have students:

- Discuss and decide where the text and music suggest phrase endings for breaths.
- Try out their plan, determining if it is musical.

- Notice the long flowing phrases, and prepare by breathing deeply, controlling the breath, and supporting the tone through the phrase while shaping it dynamically.
- Sing the piece through, adding increased awareness of phrase structure.

Romantic Characteristics

Have students:
- Describe the musical characteristics of "Gruss."
- Recall characteristics of Romantic music.
- Construct a Venn diagram, demonstrating the overlapping characteristics of the two that define the piece as an example of Romantic music.

Assessment

Informal Assessment

During this lesson, students showed the ability to:

- Identify phrase imitation.
- Identify and sing melodic leaps in the Vocal Warm-Up exercise.
- Identify and sing melodic steps and sectional repetition in the Sight-Singing exercise.
- Sing a piece with phrase and sectional repetition, with melodic steps and leaps in "Gruss."
- Sing with correct German pronunciation in "Gruss."

Student Self-Assessment

Have students:

- Evaluate their performance with the How Did You Do? section on page 149.
- Answer the questions individually. Discuss them in pairs or small groups and/or write their responses on a sheet of paper.

Individual Performance Assessment

To further demonstrate accomplishment, have each student:

- In a trio or double trio, sing one section of "Gruss" into a tape recorder in a isolated space, demonstrating in-tune singing of steps and leaps.
- Speak a section of "Gruss," demonstrating correct German pronunciation.
- Write a paragraph discussing the use of repetition in "Gruss."

Extension

Composing with Two Kinds of Repetition

This piece has both repetition of short phrases and of whole sections. Have students:

- Work in pairs or groups to experiment with imitative phrases, composing a two-part imitative piece of 16 measures or less in 3/4 meter.

- Create a longer piece by repeating this section at least twice, but changing each repetition through dynamics, rhythm, pitch, contrast, tempo, or style.

- Perform their pieces for the ensemble, first describing in words what will be heard and the process through which the piece emerged.

- Use one of these compositions as a concert piece to prepare the audience for listening to "Gruss."

Repetition Across Historical Periods and Styles

Have students:

- Compare the repetition found in "Gruss" to repetition in "I Go Before, My Charmer" in the Renaissance Lesson (page 106), "O Death, None Could Conquer Thee" in the Baroque Lesson (page 118), and "Holy, Holy, Holy" in the Classical Lesson (page 132).

- Discuss how repetition remained the same and how it changed over historical periods.

- Think of other well-known musical pieces from any of the historical periods that used repetition as a structural device. (Beethoven's Fifth Symphony)

- Listen to popular music on the radio or recordings, identifying how repetition is used.

National Standards

The following National Standards are addressed through the Extension and bottom-page activities:

1. Singing, alone and with others, a varied repertoire of music. **(a, c)**

4. Composing and arranging music within specified guidelines. **(a)**

5. Reading and notating music. **(a, b)**

6. Listening to, analyzing, and describing music. **(a, b, c, e, f)**

7. Evaluating music and music performances. **(a, b)**

8. Understanding relationships between music, the other arts, and disciplines outside the arts. **(c)**

9. Understanding music in relation to history and culture. **(a, c, d, e)**

Compar...
Performa...

Have studen...
- Listen to a...
  Mendelssoh...
- Identify any...
  Romantic mu...
  tique the perfo...
  telling what wa...
  good, and what...
  been better.
- Compare their perf...
  of "Gruss" to the rec...
  performance, descri...
  what was similar and...
  was different.
- Determine any changes...
  made in their performanc...
  and then sing "Gruss" aga...

Composing in the
Romantic Style

In groups or individually, have
students:
- Analyze the composition by
  Mendelssohn, writing down
  the most important characteristics.
- Choose or write a text modeled after the Mendelssohn
  text, with a Romantic theme.
- Compose a short piece that
  follows the characteristics
  found in the Mendelssohn
  piece.
- Revise, practice, and perform
  their piece.

ng Your
nce to Another
ts:
different
vocal piece.
characteristics of
sic, and cri-
mance.
especially
ould have
mance
orded
g
what
o be

sic
eriod.

this lesson,
be able to:
characteristics of
cture, fine art, and
c during the Contempo-
ry period.
Identify several musical
forms of the Contemporary
period.
- Define *abstract, aleatoric music, dissonance, fusion,* and *Impressionism,* identifying what motivated the creation of these styles.
- Identify some of the key musical figures of the Contemporary period.

CHORAL MUSIC TERMS
Define the Choral Music Terms for students, giving pronunciation, and answering any questions that may arise.

Introducing the Lesson

Introduce the Contemporary period through visual art.
Analyze the artwork and building on pages 156 and 159.
Have students:
- Study the painting and architecture.
- Discuss the information about each artwork provided at the bottom of pages 157 and 158 in your Teacher's Wraparound Edition.

 Individuals in contemporary society are increasingly interested in expressing their ethnic backgrounds. Palmer Hayden (1890–1973) shows this interest by juxtaposing the comedy, tragedy, and pleasures of the African-American painter who works during the day as a janitor, yet aspires to be a great artist. Music of the twentieth century is influenced by many different cultures as well as by technology and experimentation.

1937. Palmer Hayden. *The Janitor Who Paints.* Oil on canvas. 99.4 x 83.5 cm (39 ⅛ x 32 ⅞"). National Museum of American Art, Washington, D.C.

156 *Choral Connections Level 3 Treble Voices*

TEACHER'S RESOURCE BINDER
Fine Art Transparency 5, *The Janitor Who Paints,* by Palmer Hayden

Optional Listening Selections:
Music: An Appreciation, 6th edition
"Lost Your Head Blues": CD 8, Track 36
The Firebird, Scene 2: CD 1, Track 8

National Standards
5. Reading and notating music. **(d)**
6. Listening to, analyzing, and describing music. **(a, b, c)**
7. Evaluating music and music performances. **(a)**
8. Understanding relationships between music, the other arts, and disciplines outside the arts. **(a, b, c, d, e)**
9. Understanding music in relation to history and culture. **(a, c, d, e)**

Contemporary Period

After completing this lesson, you should be able to:

- Identify technological advancements that have affected the involvement of the general public in the music of the Contemporary period.
- Discuss at least five musical developments of the Contemporary period.
- Identify at least four Contemporary composers.
- Explain the importance of fusion in Contemporary music.

The twentieth century has been a period of rapid change. The developments in transportation may typify the rate at which change has taken place in all aspects of modern life. In 1900, the first automobiles were coming into use, and the first successful airplane was yet to be built. Today, highways are jammed with automobiles, commercial flights take off regularly from large and small airports, and unmanned spaceflights explore the farthest reaches of the solar system.

Political events have brought repeated and often radical changes in the lives and ideas of people around the world. Among the major political events of the twentieth century have been two world wars, many localized wars, revolutions in Russia and China, the Great Depression, the Cold War, and the rise and fall of communism in many countries. All these changes and more have been part of the Contemporary period, the time from 1900 to right now.

Technology and Contemporary Music

Technological advancements have affected many aspects of twentieth-century life, including the musical interests and involvement of the general public. First, phonographs and records made music readily available to everyone who wanted to hear it. Then, radio brought live musical performances and a wide variety of musical recordings into people's homes. By now, television has replaced radio as a source of news and entertainment—including news about music and musical entertainment—in most homes. Audiotapes, CDs, and computers with interactive software have also become popular, bringing higher quality sounds and images to the public. In addition, synthesizers now make it easier and less expensive for everyone to become involved in making and listening to music.

During the Contemporary period, music and musicians have had to rely much more on the general public for support than during any past time. Composers or musicians may still be employed by religious

COMPOSERS

Richard Strauss (1864–1949)
Ralph Vaughan Williams (1872–1958)
Arnold Schoenberg (1874–1951)
Charles Ives (1874–1954)
Pablo Casals (1876–1973)
Béla Bartók (1881–1945)
Igor Stravinsky (1882–1971)
Sergei Prokofiev (1891–1953)
Bessie Smith (1894–1937)
Paul Hindemith (1895–1963)
George Gershwin (1898–1937)
Aaron Copland (1900–1990)
Samuel Barber (1910–1981)
Gian Carlo Menotti (1911–)
Benjamin Britten (1913–1976)
Leonard Bernstein (1918–1990)
Philip Glass (1937–)

ARTISTS

Henri Rousseau (1844–1910)
Edvard Munch (1863–1944)
Wassily Kandinsky (1866–1944)
Henri Matisse (1869–1954)
Pablo Picasso (1881–1973)
Georgia O'Keeffe (1887–1986)
Palmer Hayden (1890–1973)
Jackson Pollock (1912–1956)
Andrew Wyeth (1917–)
Andy Warhol (1930–1987)

AUTHORS

George Bernard Shaw (1856–1950)
Sir Arthur Conan Doyle (1859–1930)
Edith Wharton (1862–1937)

CHORAL MUSIC TERMS

abstract

aleatoric music

dissonance

Expressionism

fusion

Impressionism

twelve-tone music

Contemporary Period **157**

Sugge... Sequen...

1. Examine t... Contemporar...

Have students:

- Read the text o... 157–161.
- Share what they k... the composers, art... authors listed on thi...
- Read, discuss, and a... the review questions i... ually, in pairs, or in sm... groups.
- Discuss their answers wit... the whole group, clarifying... misunderstandings.

2. Examine the Contemporary period in historical perspective.

Have students:

- Turn to the time line on pages 158–161 and read the citations.
- Discuss why these people and events are significant to the Contemporary period.
- Compare each of these events to those they know occurred before.
- Write a statement of one or two sentences in length that describes the Contemporary period, based on one of the events in the time line.
- Devise one additional sentence which tells how this Contemporary event is related to the student's world.

The Janitor Who Paints

The Contemporary period is indeed a period with a style for everyone, where form, function, and art are sometimes inextricably bound together. Old ideas are often used, but are many times abandoned for a new way of looking at the world. Palmer Hayden's *The Janitor Who Paints,* a self-portrait, is symbolic rather than realistic, and com-municates that the self is intertwined with the world, not separate from it. Hayden com-municates what he feels like and thinks, rather than what he looks like. The painting finds its parallel in the natural musical forms that come out of the African-American tra-dition—jazz, blues, and soul music.

sted Teaching
ce

he
y period.

n pages

now about
sts, and
s page.
swer
ndivid-
all

Wright Brothers' flight
1903

Model-T Ford introduced
1908

Leopold Stokowski named conductor of
the Philadelphia Symphony Orchestra
1912

1905
First motion picture
theater opens

1909
Sergei Diaghilev presents
"Ballet Russe" for the first
time in Paris

1914–1918
World War I

1919
Observations of the total eclipse
of the sun confirm Albert Einstein's
theory of relativity

organizations, city orchestras, or schools, but most support themselves through the sale of concert tickets, published music, and professional recordings. Music also receives some support from nonprofit organizations, but the era of the patronage system is clearly over.

Musical Developments of the Contemporary Period

The twentieth century has been a time of musical changes. Many composers have continued to use forms from the Romantic period, such as the opera, symphony, and art song, but they have adapted these forms to express new musical ideas. Many compositions from the early part of the century are considered **Impressionism**, *works that create a musical picture with a dreamy quality through chromaticism.* Many later works are considered examples of **Expressionism**, *bold and dynamic musical expression of mood with great dissonance.*

Composers of the Contemporary period have experimented with many different approaches to music. Some have worked in an objective style, creating works that stress music for its own sake. Their compositions are **abstract**, *focusing on lines, rows, angles, clusters, textures, and form.*

Many composers have also experimented with music that lacks a tonal center and a scale-oriented organization of pitch. Rather than using traditional chords built on intervals of a third, these modern compositions feature **dissonance**, *chords using seconds, fourths, fifths, and sevenths.*

Another new development is **twelve-tone music**. *In this organization, the twelve tones of the chromatic scale are arranged in a tone row, then the piece is composed by arranging and rearranging the "row" in different ways—backward, forward, in clusters of three or four pitches, and so on.* Twelve-tone compositions can be approached mathematically, and the possible combinations are nearly limitless, especially when arrangements are layered, instrument over instrument. Although this approach to composition fascinates some composers, not all listeners find the resulting works satisfying.

Some Contemporary composers have also created **aleatoric**—or chance—**music**, *works that have only a beginning and an end, with the rest left to chance.* An aleatoric work usually does have a score, but each performer is given the freedom to make many choices, including which pitch to begin on, how long to hold each pitch, how fast to play, and when to stop playing.

Other compositional elements of the Contemporary period include more angular contour of the melody, different concepts of harmony, which may emphasize dissonance, complex rhythms, and specific performance markings. These musical innovations are most evident in the secular music of the twentieth century, but they can be seen in many sacred works as well. The number of sacred compositions has decreased

First complete talking film
1928

Television begins under
commercial license
1939

First atomic bomb exploded
1945

1927
Lindbergh's solo flight
across the Atlantic

1929
New York stock market collapses;
Great Depression begins

1939–1945
World War II

1950–1953
Korean War

▲ Just as new compositional techniques in various formats are prevalent in Contemporary music, the architecture in the Opera House in Sydney, Australia, incorporated new materials and construction techniques. Award-winning Danish architect Jørn Utzon (1918–) called for segmented, precast concrete in the construction of the white tiled shells that form the roof of this imaginative and poetic building.

1959–72. Jørn Utzon. Opera House, Sydney, Australia.

during this century. However, important Contemporary musicians, including Leonard Bernstein, Paul Hindemith, Benjamin Britten, Charles Ives, and Gian Carlo Menotti, have composed masses, sacred cantatas, chorales, and othe religious works.

A New Mix

Rapid improvements in communication and transportation have brought people from all parts of the world into closer touch with one another. Individuals and groups have shared many aspects of their cultures, including traditional musical techniques and new musical developments. One of the results of this sharing is **fusion**, *a blending*

Contemporary Period **159**

The Sydney Opera House

The Sydney Opera House is an imposing structure, designed to fit into its harbor home. The white shells represent sails of the boats in the harbor, and the large glass windows allow the concertgoers to experience the environment as a natural setting open to the water. This structure stands out in the landscape, beckoning all to partake and participate in the arts.

The Opera House is an experiment in design drawn from nature. It is also an experimental exploration of form, symmetry, elaboration and simplicity, grandeur, and function. Likewise, Contemporary composers may also be composing pieces that experiment with traditional musical elements.

Assessment

Informal Assessment
During this lesson, students showed the ability to:
- Identify characteristics of the Contemporary period and music of the Contemporary period.
- Explore the role of music in today's world.
- Define *abstract, aleatoric music, dissonance, fusion,* and *Impressionism,* and explain what motivated the creation of these styles.

Student Self-Assessment
Have students:
- Return to page 161 and answer the Check Your Understanding questions.
- Write a paragraph describing how much they understand about the development of music during the Contemporary period.
- Answer the questions individually. Discuss them in pairs or small groups and/or write their responses on a sheet of paper.

Individual Performance Assessment
To further demonstrate accomplishment, have each student:
- Learn more about one aspect of music during the Contemporary period.
- Share their findings with the class in a creative way, such as in a poster, demonstration, CD or video design contest, and so on.

1958	1962	1971
U.S. satellite put into orbit	U.S. astronaut John Glenn orbits the Earth	Voting age lowered from 21 to 18

1957	**1961**	**1969**	**1972**
First Earth satellite put into orbit by USSR	Soviet cosmonaut orbits the Earth	U.S. astronauts land on the moon	Robert Moog patents the Moog synthesizer

Extension

Notation in the Contemporary Period

Have students:

• Explore scores of Contemporary vocal and instrumental pieces to see the range of styles, and also the new complexities brought about by the larger pieces of work. Find copies of a magazine called *Score* to see the graphic types of representations being explored.

Using Graphic Notation

Graphic notation can be anything that graphically represents sound. It could be pictures on index cards which are arranged in a specific way. It could be the environment viewed object by object. It could be the contour of a juice bottle. Anything goes.

Have students:

• Choose a graphic representation to play in sound.
• Choose sound sources for the visual images.
• Decide how to play the "piece."
• Perform it for the ensemble.
• Discuss the result in terms of its musical elements—rhythm, melody, dynamics, form, etc. Then tell whether they liked it or not.

---

of musical styles. Tejano music, for example, is a blending of Mexican and Country styles; Zydeco is a blending of African-American, Cajun, and French Canadian styles.

The Contemporary period has also been a time of fusion between popular music styles and art music. Pop singers occasionally perform with professional orchestras and choirs, and opera singers record popular songs and traditional folk music.

Many new kinds of popular music have emerged during the Contemporary period. Some, including blues, jazz, country, rock, and reggae, continue to thrive and to blend with other kinds of popular music. Other styles, such as ragtime, seem to have become part of history rather than popular culture. Popular music styles are part of the change characteristic of the period, and new styles will continue to develop.

The Future of Music

The changes of the Contemporary period are ongoing, and the music of the period continues to evolve. Which trends will prove most significant? When will a new direction emerge that will mark the end of this period? What name will future historians give to the time we call Contemporary? As a consumer of music—and perhaps even as a music maker—you may help determine the answers to these questions.

Check Your Understanding

Recall

1. What is Impressionism?

2. What is abstract music?

3. What is dissonance?

4. List at least three choices that are left up to performers of aleatoric music.

5. What is the status of sacred music in the Contemporary period?

6. What is fusion? Give at least two examples of fusion.

Little League accepts girls
1975

Fall of the Berlin Wall
1989

1975
U.S. withdraws from Vietnam

1991
Dissolution of the Union
of Soviet Socialist Republics

1976
U.S. celebrates its 200th birthday

Thinking It Through

1. How do you think the change from a patronage system to a reliance on public support has affected the development of music? Explain your ideas.

2. What forms of Contemporary music do you like best? Why? Be specific.

3. Which previous period—Renaissance, Baroque, Classical, or Romantic—do you consider most like the Contemporary period? What similarities can you identify? What do you consider the most important differences?

Abstract Art Styles of the Contemporary Period

Abstract art can be represented in sound, visual images, or dance. Have students:

- Choose a piece of abstract art, for example a work by: Jackson Pollock, Joan Miro, Alexander Calder, Louise Nevelson, or Mondrian.
- Using the work as a model, create their own painting, sculpture, or mobile in the style of the artist.
- Using their art as a graphic notation, create a sound composition that follows the notation provided by the painting, mobile, or sculpture.
- Using their music as a guide, create a dance that shows the elements of color and sound through movement.
- Perform the sound composition and dance as the art is exhibited on a large screen behind the performers.

ANSWERS TO RECALL QUESTIONS

1. Works that create a musical picture with a dreamy quality through chromaticism.
2. Musical works that focus on lines, rows, angles, clusters, textures, and form.
3. Chords using seconds, fourths, fifths, and sevenths.
4. Any three: which pitch to begin on; how long to hold each pitch; how fast to play; and when to stop playing.
5. It has decreased during this century; however, important Contemporary musicians have composed masses, sacred cantatas, chorales, and other religious works.
6. A blending of musical styles. Tejano and zydeco.

**CONTEMPORARY
CONNECTIONS**

Listening to...
Contemporary Music

This feature is designed to expand students' appreciation of choral and instrumental music of the Contemporary period.

CHORAL SELECTION:
"Lost Your Head Blues" by Smith
Have students:

- Read the information on this page to learn more about "Lost Your Head Blues."
- Watch as you follow a transparency of Blackline Master, Listening Map 9.

Using the Listening Map
Start at introduction. Progress to verse 1, verse 2, and continue through verse 5. Have students:

- Listen while you explain the blues form: statement phrase, repetition of the statement, then a conclusion phrase in each verse.
- Listen while you explain the standard blues chord progression: I—statement; IV—repetition, returning to I chord; V₇—conclusion, then back to I chord.
- Listen while you explain improvisation.
- Spontaneously create melodies that fit the chord and words being used, not written down but composed as you play along, based on the blues scale.
- Listen as you discuss the vocal style found in blues: use of dialect and/or slang; use of heavier vocal tone; lyrics that dictate how the voice will sound; expression of lyrics is more important than vocal technique.
- Listen as you point to the transparency.

Listening to...
Contemporary Music

CHORAL SELECTION

Smith—"Lost Your Head Blues"

Bessie Smith (1894–1937) was known as the "Empress of the Blues" Raised in an impoverished background, she became famous for singing of hopelessness and despair. Tragically, she died of complications from an auto accident; after being turned away from a white hospital in this period of rigid segregation. She died en route to a black hospital in Mississippi.

INSTRUMENTAL SELECTION

Stravinsky—Firebird Suite, Scene 2

Igor Stravinsky (1882–1971) is considered one of the most influential composers of the 1900s. His most famous works include *The Firebird*, *Petrouchka*, and *The Rite of Spring*. Since *The Firebird* is a ballet based on a Russian legend, many versions of the story can be found. The basic fairy tale begins with Prince Ivan, the Czar's son, hunting in a forest. He captures a magical golden bird with wings of fire. The firebird gives Ivan a feather in return for its freedom. Ivan continues his walk through the woods when suddenly he sees King Katschei's castle. The evil King has turned many prisoners into stone and is holding princesses as captives. Ivan enters the sinister castle. With the help of the magic feather, he conquers King Katschei, the castle sinks into the ground, and the 13 princesses and prisoners are freed. Prince Ivan falls in love with one of the princesses and, as in most fairy tales, they live happily ever after.

TEACHER'S RESOURCE BINDER
Blackline Master, Listening Map 9
Blackline Master, Listening Map 10

Optional Listening Selections:
Music: An Appreciation, 6th edition
"Lost Your Head Blues": CD 8, Track 36
The Firebird, Scene 2: CD 1, Track 8

National Standards
This lesson addresses the following National Standard:

7. Evaluating music and music performances. **(a)**

♪♪ CONTEMPORARY CONNECTIONS

Introducing...

"Nigra Sum"

Pablo Casals

Setting the Stage

Though composers of the twentieth century are constantly seeking new ways to present musical composition, there are also the traditionalists. These composers are recognized for their creativity based on traditional harmonies: harmonies with some twentieth-century dissonance, but not a far stretch from the harmonies enjoyed by the composers of the Romantic period. Casals demonstrates such traditionalism in this work; Neo-Romantic is its basic style. However, the Neo-Romantic composers used percussion more predominately. This work of Casals, "Nigra Sum," is written for piano and choir, and the choir has all the rich quality of the cello, cast in lyricism rather than percussive verticalism.

Meeting the Composer

Pablo Casals

Pablo Casals is known as one of the great Spanish cellists. He was born in Vendrell, Catalonia, on December 29, 1876. He died in San Juan, Puerto Rico, on October 22, 1973. His father, the parish organist and choirmaster in Vendrell, gave Casals instruction in piano, violin, and organ. When Casals was eleven, he first heard the cello performed by a group of traveling musicians and decided to study the instrument. In 1888, his mother took him to Barcelona, where he enrolled in Escuela Municipal de Música. There, his progress as a cellist was nothing short of prodigious and he gave a solo recital in Barcelona at the age of fourteen. By 1956, he had moved to San Juan, Puerto Rico, which became his permanent home.

Winner of the United Nations Peace Prize, Casals played at the General Assembly Hall in 1958 to celebrate the United Nations' thirteenth anniversary. In 1961, he performed for President Kennedy at the White House. Many significant twentieth-century works have been dedicated to him, and the Monks of Montserrat perform his sacred works extensively, valuing their simplicity, conviction, and traditional style.

Contemporary Connections **163**

INSTRUMENTAL SELECTION: *The Firebird,* **Scene 2, by Stravinsky**
Have students:
- Read the information on page 162 to learn more about *The Firebird* Suite.
- Watch as you follow a transparency of Blackline Master, Listening Map 10.

Using the Listening Map
Start at the bottom left corner of the map and follow the numbers of 1 to 24.
Have students:
- Listen as you describe what happens at the end of the ballet. (Everone is freed from the evil spell of King Katschei; Ivan falls in love with one of the princesses; the Firebird is freed; everyone lives happily ever after.
- Develop a list of descriptors to predict what might be heard in the conclusion of the ballet, based on the ending described above. (climactic, joyful, happy, uplifting, and so on)
- Listen to the recording as you point to the transparency.

INTRODUCING . . . "Nigra Sum"
This feature is designed to introduce students to the Contemporary Lesson on the following pages.
Have students:
- Read Setting the Stage on this page to learn more about "Nigra Sum."
- Read Meeting the Composer to learn more about Pablo Casals.
- Turn the page and begin the Contemporary Lesson.

ASSESSMENT
Individual Performance Assessment
To further demonstrate understanding of Contemporary music, have each student:
- Evaluate the performance of "Lost Your Head Blues" with an assessment rubric of their own creation or one supplied to them.
- Use the word list created for *The Firebird* to evaluate whether or not the composition accomplished its purpose.

Nigra Sum

COMPOSER: Pablo Casals
(1876–1973)

ENGLISH TEXT: Kenneth Sterne

Focus

OVERVIEW

Reading rhythm and pitch; rich tone quality; posture and breathing; Latin language.

OBJECTIVES

After completing this lesson, students should be able to:

- Read and sing familiar rhythms and pitches using a rich tone quality.
- Use correct posture and breathing.
- Sing using correct Latin pronunciation.

CHORAL MUSIC TERMS

Define the Choral Music Terms for students, giving pronunciation, and answering any questions that may arise.

Warming Up

Vocal Warm-Up

This Vocal Warm-Up is designed to prepare students to:

- Sing with a rich, warm tone.
- Breathe deeply.
- Sing well-formed, rounded vowels.

Have students:

- Read through the Vocal Warm-Up directions.
- Sing, following your demonstration.

Nigra Sum

COMPOSER: *Pablo Casals* (1876–1973)
ENGLISH TEXT: *Kenneth Sterne*

CHORAL MUSIC TERMS
breathing
pitch
posture
rhythm

VOICING

Three-part chorus

PERFORMANCE STYLE

Moderato
Accompanied by piano or organ

FOCUS

- Read and sing familiar rhythms and pitches using a rich tone quality.
- Use correct posture and breathing.
- Sing using correct Latin pronunciation.

Warming Up

 Vocal Warm-Up

Using rich vocal tones, sing this warm-up on *yah-oh-e-ah*. Take a deep breath and concentrate on singing tall vowels, providing a lot of room toward the back of the mouth. Hold your index finger about an inch from your lips and feel the warm air the tone is using. If the air is cool, the breath was shallow. If the air is warm the breath was deep. Move up or down by half steps on the repeat.

TEACHER'S RESOURCE BINDER

Blackline Master 22, *Translation and Pronunciation Guide for "Nigra Sum"*
Blackline Master 23, *Sight-Singing Melodies in 2/4 Meter*

 National Standards

1. Singing, alone and with others, a varied repertoire of music. **(a, c)**
5. Reading and notating music. **(a, b)**
6. Listening to, analyzing, and describing music. **(a, b)**
7. Evaluating music and music performances. **(a)**
8. Understanding relationships between music, the other arts, and disciplines outside the arts. **(c)**
9. Understanding music in relation to history and culture. **(a, c)**

Sight-Singing

Sight-sing this exercise using solfège and hand signs or numbers. Sing the pitches richly. The melody is easy so you are free to concentrate on the tone you are producing. Make your voice sound like a cello.

Singing: "Nigra Sum"

Can you tell, just by looking, if an athlete is good? What clues might you look for? Can you tell, just by looking, if a singer is good? What clues might you look for?

Now turn to the music for "Nigra Sum" on page 166.

HOW DID YOU DO?

If someone were watching you sing, would they know you are a good singer? Think about your preparation and performance of "Nigra Sum."

1. Did you use correct posture and breathing? How would the observer know? What would they see? What do you feel?

2. Could you read the rhythms and pitches of the piece? What was easy? What needed practice?

3. Was your Latin pronunciation correct? What was good? What could be better?

4. Could you make your voice sound rich like a cello? How did you do it?

Sight-Singing

This Sight-Singing exercise is designed to prepare students to:
- Sight-sing using solfège and hand signs or numbers.
- Sing with excellent tone quality, even when sight-singing.
- Sustain long phrases with a good breath.

Have students:
- Read through the Sight-Singing exercise directions.
- Read through each voice part rhythmically, using rhythm syllables.
- Sight-sing through each part separately using solfège and hand signs or numbers.
- Sing all parts together.

Singing: "Nigra Sum"

Identify characteristics of a good singer. Have students:
- Read the text on page 165.
- Identify visual clues typical of a good athlete. (the way he or she runs, throws a ball, catches a ball, and so on)
- Identify visual clues typical of a good singer. (posture, breathing, relaxed jaw, lifted mask, gestures and/or expression)
- Use these characteristics to sing the Vocal Warm-Up and Sight-Singing exercises while looking "like a singer."

Nigra Sum **165**

Suggested Teaching Sequence

1. Review Vocal Warm-Up.
Breathe deeply. Sing rich, warm tones. Shape vowels. Have students:
- Review the Vocal Warm-Up on page 164.
- Review posture and breathing techniques.
- Shape the vowels for a rich, warm sound.
- Check the warmth of breath as suggested.

2. Review Sight-Singing.
Read and sing in unison. Sing with a rich, warm tone. Have students:
- Review the Sight-Singing exercise on page 165.
- Listen to, or describe, the tone of a cello as warm and rich.
- Sing the exercise, creating that same warm, rich tone vocally through deep breathing and a round mouth cavity.

3. Sight-sing "Nigra Sum" using solfège and hand signs or numbers.
Have students:
- Divide into voice sections and read each part rhythmically, using rhythm syllables.
- Clap and speak the piece in full ensemble.
- Again in sections, sing with solfège and hand signs or numbers, identifying and working on problem areas.
- Identify staggered breathing (members of the ensemble take breaths at staggered times so the tone is always sustained), and practice from measures 83–100 using staggered breathing technique.
- Sing the piece through using solfège and hand signs or numbers with full ensemble, tuning the intervals.

Nigra Sum
I am Black
(Decepta ex Canticis)

Pablo Casals
English version by Kenneth Sterne

Three-part Chorus of Treble Voices
with Piano or Organ Accompaniment

166 *Choral Connections   Level 3 Treble Voices*

A.B. 120

4. Learn the Latin pronunciation.

Have students:
- Using Blackline Master 22, *Translation and Pronunciation Guide* for "Nigra Sum," echo or read the words slowly.
- Speak the Latin text in rhythm.
- Sing the piece in Latin, using correct pronunciation.

5. Practice phrasing and dynamics.

Have students:
- Review the notation for phrasing and dynamic markings.
- Practice "Nigra Sum" section by section.
- Sing the piece with correct phrasing and dynamics.

MUSIC LITERACY

The Sound of the Cello and Well-Known Cellists

Have students:
- Listen to a live performance or recording of the cello sound.
- Describe the characteristics of the sound in their own words.
- Identify Pablo Casals, the composer of this piece, as a famous cellist.

- Identify any other well-known cellists; for example, Yo-Yo Ma.
- Imitate the sound of the cello to create a rich, warm vocal sound.

TEACHING STRATEGY

Posture and Breathing

Tell students that posture and breathing are the foundation of good tone in singing.

To establish good posture, have students:

- Stand with feet apart, one foot slightly ahead of the other, weight evenly distributed, knees unlocked.
- Tuck in abdomen; body should be held firmly.
- Roll the shoulders forward and backward while counting aloud. Let shoulders drop easily and naturally.
- Turn head from side to side gently *without* moving any other part of the body. Tip head forward to chest and backward in the same manner. Head should rest comfortably on shoulders with chin level.

To promote proper breath support, have students:

- Begin with good body alignment.
- Sip in a long (deep) breath of air, as if sipping through a straw. Hold it with a good facial expression; release with an energetic long hiss.
- Sip in a long breath, hold, and release with short hisses.

To practice breath control in many different ways, have students:

- Sip in a long breath, releasing the air as if blowing on a candle, without blowing it out.
- Sip in a long breath; sing "America" on one breath.
- Sip in a long breath; count as high as possible while exhaling slowly.
- Energize sound with hisses followed by vocalizations on *hoo, whoo, whoa,* and *wow* sounds.
- Vocalize sounds from the head register downward.

A.B. 120

sur - ge et ve - ni a - mi -
rise up, my fair_____ one; a - rise,_____

- ca me - a,
my love.____

jam_____ hi - ems tráns - i - it,_____
Lo, for the win - ter is past and gone,_____

A.B. 120

VOCAL DEVELOPMENT

Unified Vowels

To encourage vocal development, have students:

- Speak the text saying only the vowel sounds.
- Listen to those around, and be sure the vowels are unified, with an open sound focused forward in the facial mask.
- Add the consonants crisply and clearly, moving quickly to the vowel sound, and adding ending consonants just before the release.

TEACHING STRATEGY

Staggered Breathing

Have students:

- Understand that staggered breathing is a technique used by an ensemble to carry over a long phrase with singers breathing at different times.
- Whenever possible, take a breath within a longer note to maintain vowel color.
- When taking the breath, soften the pitch before and after the breath to avoid an audible break in the tonal line.
- Sing two and four measures on *ahs,* assigning singers to different measures to take their breath.
- Leave the mouth in the open singing position when taking the staggered breath—no one will know when the breath is taken!

A.B. 120

Contemporary Characteristics

Have students:
- Describe the musical characteristics of "Nigra Sum."
- Recall the many types of musical characteristics possible in Contemporary music.
- Construct a Venn diagram, demonstrating the overlapping characteristics of

the two that define the piece as an example of Contemporary music.
- Identify the characteristics of music of other periods that have been used by Casals in this piece.

A.B. 120

Nigra Sum **171**

Informal Assessment

During this lesson, students showed the ability to:

- Identify visual characteristics of a good singer.
- Practice deep breathing and rich vocal production in the Vocal Warm-Up exercise.
- Sight-sing with a rich, warm tone in the Sight-Singing exercise.
- Read and sing using good posture and breath support, producing a rich, warm tone in "Nigra Sum."
- Sing with correct Latin pronunciation in "Nigra Sum."

Student Self-Assessment

Have students:

- Evaluate their performance with the How Did You Do? section on page 165.
- Answer the questions individually. Discuss them in pairs or small groups and/or write their responses on a sheet of paper.

Individual Performance Assessment

To further demonstrate accomplishment, have each student:

- In a trio or double trio, sing measures 83–100 into a tape recorder in an isolated space, demonstrating good breath support and staggered breathing.
- In a small group, sight-sing from Blackline Master 23, *Sight-Singing Melodies in 2/4 Meter,* into a tape recorder in an isolated space.
- Individually speak measures 1–20 in rhythm and in Latin, demonstrating correct pronunciation.

Extension

Back to the Basics

Have students:

- Look at the Choral Music Terms for this lesson on page 164.
- Identify these terms as common to music of most periods and very basic.
- Identify the character of "Nigra Sum" as using basic musical elements in fairly traditional ways.
- Discuss whether "Nigra Sum" is then a basic piece, or if it has emotional power and aesthetic integrity. Ask: Might it be both? Why or why not?

Comparing Your Performance to Another

Have students:

- Listen to a different Casals vocal or cello piece.
- Identify any characteristics of Contemporary music, and critique the performance, telling what was especially good, and what could have been better.
- Compare their performance of "Nigra Sum" to the recorded performance, describing what was similar and what was different.
- Determine any changes to be made in their performance, and then sing "Nigra Sum" again.

A.B. 120

National Standards

The following National Standards are addressed through the Extension and bottom-page activities:

1. Singing, alone and with others, a varied repertoire of music. **(a, c)**
4. Composing and arranging music within specified guidelines. **(a, b)**
5. Reading and notating music. **(a, b)**
6. Listening to, analyzing, and describing music. **(a, b, c, e, f)**

7. Evaluating music and music performances. **(a, b)**
8. Understanding relationships between music, the other arts, and disciplines outside the arts. **(c)**
9. Understanding music in relation to history and culture. **(a, c, d, e)**

A.B. 120

Nigra Sum **173**

Could a Cello Play This Piece?

Have students:

- Consider these questions:
- — Could a cello (or two or three cellos) play the vocal lines of this piece?
- — What other instrument groups could play this piece?
- — Which do you think would be particularly effective?
- — What would be missing from the vocal performance? Is it essential to the piece?
- Optional: Arrange the piece for an instrumental ensemble with piano or organ accompaniment.

Arranging the Melody for a Nonvocal Duet

Have students:

- Arrange the two vocal parts as a duet for orchestral instruments; for example, two trumpets or two clarinets.
- Perform the piece vocally and instrumentally, or extend the vocal piece by adding instrumental sections.

Additional Performance Selections

Gloria

COMPOSER: Joseph Haydn
(1732–1809)
EDITED BY: Bennett Williams

Warming Up

Vocal Warm-Up

Have students:

- Read through the Vocal Warm-Up directions.
- Sing the pattern using solfège and hand signs or numbers, then with the text.
- Sing with great energy, focusing on both consonants and vowels.
- Sing, following your demonstration.

Now turn to page 180.

I Wonder As I Wander

Appalachian Carol
ARRANGER: Richard Osborne

Warming Up

Vocal Warm-Up

Have students:

- Read through the Vocal Warm-Up directions.
- Sing the pattern using solfège and hand signs or numbers, then on *loo.*
- Use a very legato, connected articulation and slow tempo.
- Sing, following your demonstration.

Now turn to page 187.

176

VOICING
Two-part chorus

PERFORMANCE STYLE
Vivace
Accompanied by piano or organ

Gloria

Warming Up

Vocal Warm-Up
   Sing this exercise using solfège and hand signs or numbers. Then sing it using the text provided. Sing it with a good bounce on the breath. There's plenty of action for both consonants and vowels. Move up by half steps as you repeat. Notice that this is the main theme of "Gloria."

Zing-ring-a-ling, a-lo-ha, eh - ah.

Now turn to page 180.

VOICING
Three-part treble voices

PERFORMANCE STYLE
Andante
Accompanied by harp or piano

I Wonder As I Wander

Warming Up

Vocal Warm-Up
   Sing this exercise using solfège and hand signs or numbers, then on *loo*. Move up by half steps on each repeat. This will give you a feel for the tonality and meter of "I Wonder As I Wander."

Loo

Now turn to page 187.

Native American Spring Songs

Warming Up

Vocal Warm-Up

Sing this exercise tuning the parallel thirds carefully. Sing one vowel sound for each note, keeping each vowel completely focused throughout the exercise. Use a deep breath to expand your waistline, which you can feel by putting your hands on your sides, turned toward your stomach.

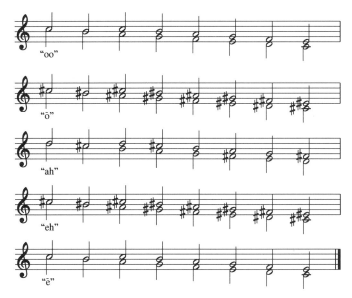

Now turn to page **196.**

Native American Spring Songs

COMPOSER: Nancy Grundahl

Warming Up

Vocal Warm-Up

Have students:

- Read through the Vocal Warm-Up directions.
- Sing the pattern using solfège and hand signs or number, then with the vowel sounds.
- Tune the thirds carefully, and keep the vowels focused and unified.
- Sing, following your demonstration.

Now turn to page **196.**

Festival Alleluia

COMPOSER: Allen Pote

Warming Up

Vocal Warm-Up

Have students:
- Read through the Vocal Warm-Up directions.
- Sing the pattern using solfège and hand signs or numbers, swaying on the first and fourth eighth note in each measure.
- Sing, following your demonstration.

Now turn to page **201**.

Wisdom and Understanding

Job 28: 20–21, 23–28
COMPOSER: Kent A. Newbury

Warming Up

Vocal Warm-Up

Have students:
- Read through the Vocal Warm-Up directions.
- Sing the pattern with vowel sounds, tuning the chords, and blending the vowels carefully.
- Sing, following your demonstration.

Now turn to page **207**.

178

VOICING
| Unison or two-part choir

PERFORMANCE STYLE
| With sparkle
| Accompanied by keyboard

Festival Alleluia

Warming Up

Vocal Warm-Up

Sing this exercise using solfège and hand signs or numbers, swaying to the two beats felt in each measure. Notice the 6/8 meter. Move up by half steps on each repeat.

do re mi
1 2 3

Now turn to page **201**.

VOICING
| SSA

PERFORMANCE STYLE
| Excitedly
| A cappella

Wisdom and Understanding

Warming Up

Vocal Warm-Up

Sing this exercise using each vowel (a, e, i, o, u) for the whole exercise, then use the next vowel, moving up or down a half step. First get the pitches tuned in each chord. Then work on choral blend by singing uniform vowels. Keep each vowel focused through the lower, middle, and upper range.

1. Ah
2. Eh
3. ee
4. ō
5. o͞o

Now turn to page **207**.

Beautiful Yet Truthful

Warming Up

Vocal Warm-Up

Sing this exercise using solfège and hand signs or numbers. Move up or down by half steps. Sing it faster and faster, but articulate the syllables with the utmost precision. Find this pattern in "Beautiful Yet Truthful." Is it exactly the same?

Now turn to page **214.**

Beautiful Yet Truthful

A Folk Song Elaboration
ARRANGER: Lloyd Pfautsch

Warming Up

Vocal Warm-Up

Have students:

- Read through the Vocal Warm-Up directions.
- Sing the pattern using solfège and hand signs or numbers. Sing faster with accurate diction and clarity.
- Sing, following your demonstration.

Now turn to page **214.**

Gloria

Performance Tips

Rhythmic Focus

Explain to students:
- From the opening statement in the accompaniment, there is a trumpetlike rhythmic figure that recurs throughout the piece.
- The rhythms are straightforward throughout, with some interesting interplay between the parts.
- Count the rest carefully, so they get their full value. While the piece moves along quickly, it should not have a feeling of rushing ahead.

Melodic Focus

Tell students:
- The melody centers round the tonic triad (*do-mi-so*) in G major.
- The very martial feeling relaxes just a bit after measure 15, but still has a strong pulse and moves along.
- Notice the upward leaps from measures 21–23 and again at 28 and 30.
- There are melismatic scalewise passages at measures 51 and 59.

Gloria

From the Heiligmesse (1796)

Joseph Haydn (1732–1809)
Edited by Bennett Williams

Two-part Chorus (SA or TB) Piano or Organ

Glo-ri-a in ex-cel-sis De - o, Glo-ri-a in ex-cel-sis,
Glo-ry to God in heav-en, glo - ry! Glo-ry to God in heav - en,

Glo-ri-a in ex-cel-sis De - o, Glo-ri-a in ex-cel-sis,
Glo-ry to God in heav-en, glo - ry! Glo-ry to God in heav - en,

More Ideas
- This piece is divided into sections, dictated by the phrases of the "Gloria" text from the liturgical mass, and separated by short instrumental interludes.
- The Latin vowels will allow a bright vocal sound.

Hot Spots
- Keep the higher pitches well-supported and open.
- Perform the dynamics with accuracy. Classical dynamics are terraced rather than gradual.
- Change to legato articulation at measure 17.

Glo-ri-a in ex-cel-sis, in ex-cel-sis De - o.
Glo-ry to God in heav-en, to the Lord in heav-en!

Glo-ri-a in ex-cel-sis, in ex-cel-sis De - o.
Glo-ry to God in heav-en, to the Lord in heav-en!

Glo-ri-a, glo-ri-a in ex-cel-sis, in ex-cel-sis
To the Lord, glo-ry to God in heav-en, to the Lord in

Glo-ri-a, glo-ri-a in ex-cel-sis, in ex-cel-sis
To the Lord, glo-ry to God in heav-en, to the Lord in

De - o.
heav - en.

De - o.
heav - en.

Gloria **181**

Program Ideas

- This piece is exciting as is, performed with rhythmic and melodic accuracy, and unified vowels.

"Peace Today Descends from Heaven"—Grandi

"Gloria"—Haydn

"Behold, a Tiny Baby!"—Lightfoot

"Arruru"—Dwyer/Gerber

I Wonder As I Wander

Appalachian Carol
Arranged and adapted by Richard Osborne

Three-part Treble Voices with Harp

I Wonder As I Wander **187**

TEACHING STRATEGY

Folk Tradition

"I Wonder As I Wander" is a folk song, shared for generations by aural and oral tradition rather than by reading.

Have students:

• After learning the piece, sing it without the notation in front of them, shaping the phrases and feeling the rhythm as a natural extension of the text.

• Keep the performance fluid and flowing, deciding where to stretch the beat a bit, or have a little forward motion. Remind students that they must all do it together.

I Wonder as I Wander

Performance Tips

Rhythmic Focus

Explain to students:

• The rhythm is in slow 6/8 meter, felt in a slow and flowing 2.

• There are brief shifts to 3/8 or 9/8 meter near the end of phrases.

• The rhythm must be accurate, even though this is a folk melody with a legato feel.

Melodic Focus

Tell students:

• The melody is set in minor, and can be sung in unison following the upper voice line.

• Each verse has a bit more complexity, but never gets too complex, maintaining the folk quality of the piece.

More Ideas

- Although this piece is written for harp accompaniment, it can be sung with piano or electronic keyboard quite successfully. It also might be adapted for dulcimer, acoustic guitar, or hammered dulcimer.

Have students:

- Perform this piece in a small ensemble; for example, a trio or double trio.
- Listen to the difference between the quality of individual voices, and the blended voices of an entire performing ensemble.
- Perhaps have the small ensemble perform verse 3 by themselves.

Hot Spots

- The rhythmic shift to a three-quarter note feel at measures 10, 22, 34, 46, and 49 provide rhythmic interest, but also a challenge.
- Notice the key change at measure 41, and practice the unison F♯, which can be picked up from the accompaniment earlier in the measure.
- Be certain the parts are in balance, with the melody emerging slightly.

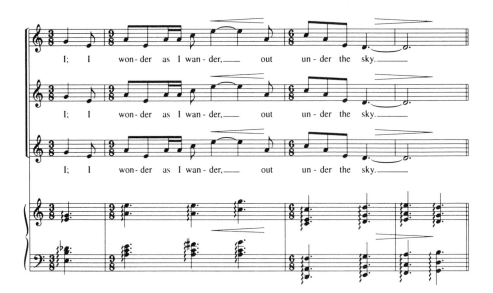

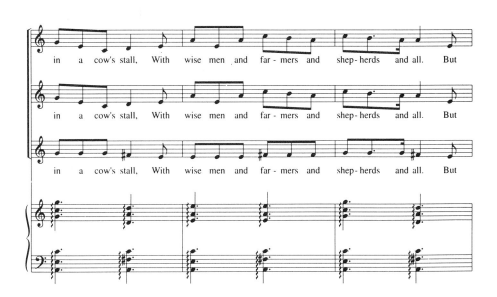

Program Ideas

- This melody may be familiar enough that the audience could sing along on the last verse. Display the words on their program, or from a transparency onto a screen.

"Peace Today Descends from Heaven"—Grandi
"I Wonder as I Wander"—Osborne
"Os Justi"—Daley
"Behold, a Tiny Baby!"—Lightfoot

I Wonder As I Wander **189**

high from God's heav - en a star's light did fall, The

high from God's heav - en a star's light did fall, The

high from God's heav - en a star's light did fall, The

prom - ise of a - ges_____ it then did re - call._____

prom - ise of a - ges_____ it then did re - call.

prom - ise of a - ges_____ it then did re - call.

star in the sky or a bird on the wing, Or

star in the sky or a bird on the wing, Or

loo_____ Or

all of God's an - gels in heav'n for to sing. He

all of God's an - gels in heav'n for to sing. He

all of God's an - gels in heav'n for to sing. He

sure - ly could have it.____ 'Cause He was the King.____

sure - ly could have it.____ 'Cause He was the King.____

sure - ly could have it.____ 'Cause He was the King.____

I won - der as I wan - der, out

I won - der as I wan - der, out

I won - der as I wan - der, out

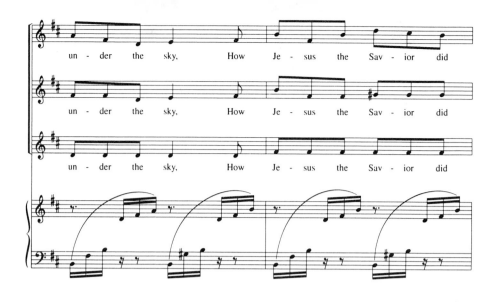

un - der the sky, How Je - sus the Sav - ior did

un - der the sky, How Je - sus the Sav - ior did

un - der the sky, How Je - sus the Sav - ior did

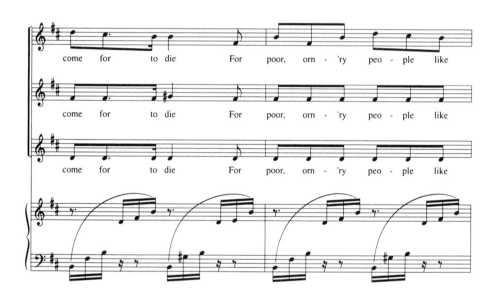

come for to die For poor, orn - 'ry peo - ple like

come for to die For poor, orn - 'ry peo - ple like

come for to die For poor, orn - 'ry peo - ple like

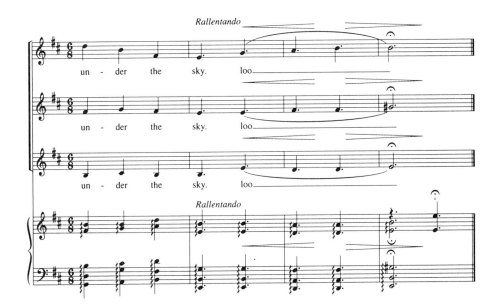

Performance Tips

Rhythmic Focus
Explain to students:
- The rhythm of this piece is through-composed to give a free feeling. However, it must be performed together exactly to be effective.
- Upbeat entrances are prevalent. Practice these by isolating the parts.

Melodic Focus
Tell students:
- Though the melodic line is linear in motion, the pitches contained in the line are unconventional, creating poignant and dissonant harmony between parts.
- This dissonant tension enhances the beautiful consonant sonority at the close of the work.

Native American Spring Songs
1. As My Eyes Search

Chippewa
By Nancy Grundahl

Arranger Nancy Grundahl

With advanced degrees in vocal performance, Nancy Grundahl has applied her training and education to the world of choral performance. She has served as interim choir director at Augsburg College in Minneapolis, Minnesota, director of music at Mayflower, UCC, and conductor of the Anglican Cantanti Concert Choir. Currently she resides in Minneapolis.

More Ideas
- Add the flute part for an additional haunting sound.
- Read the text first as a poem; then sing.

Hot Spots
- Tuning the open fifths at measures 16 and 17 and measures 21–23 will be a challenge.

Program Ideas
- Capture the mystique of this piece by singing it on *oo* with the lights dimmed. This will allow the ears to hear what the eyes cannot see.
- "As My Eyes Search" should be performed with "All Winter Long." Neither of these pieces should be performed without the other.

 VOCAL DEVELOPMENT

Have students:
- Demonstrate good vocal tone by singing with tall vowels and clear consonants.
- Energize sustained tones by increasing the breath support and dynamic level.
- Energize repeated notes by making a crescendo with added breath support.
- Sustain phrases by staggering the breathing through the phrases.

- Listen for diphthongs in *my, eyes,* and *I.*
- Demonstrate the correct singing of the *r* consonant after a vowel, as in *search* and *summer.*
- The dynamics should reflect the melodic contour and meaning of the text.
- Follow the melodic line between the parts, noting the places that join in unison and those that are imitative (measures 8–12).

All Winter Long

Performance Tips

Rhythmic Focus
Explain to students:
- Speak the text in rhythm, one section at a time, until the rhythms are secure.
- Identify measures that are rhythmically similar; for example, measures 5–6, 18–19, and 25–26.
- Speak the whole piece accurately before adding the melody.

Melodic Focus
Tell students:
- The melody is sometimes stepwise, and other times has wide leaps.
- Identify and practice the unusually wide leaps, first in isolation, then in context by singing the notes immediately preceding and following the interval.

2. All Winter Long

By Nancy Grundahl

More Ideas

- Add the flute part for an additional haunting sound.
- Read the text first as a poem, then sing the piece.

Hot Spots

- The piece has unusually large leaps in the melody.
- Cross-voicing at measures 13 and 16 could be troublesome.
- Tune the parallel fifths carefully, beginning at measure 23.
- The high A♭ in the last few measures, reached from a leap of a 12th, will be difficult to achieve without screeching. Hold back a little, and use good breath support.

Program Ideas

- This piece should be performed with "As My Eyes Search." Neither of these pieces should be performed without the other.

Native American Spring Songs **199**

VOCAL DEVELOPMENT

To encourage vocal development, have students:

- Demonstrate good vocal tone by singing with tall vowels and clear consonants.

- Energize the melodic line by increasing the breath support and observing the dynamic levels. Soft singing is supported with the same intensity as loud singing.

- Energize repeated notes by making a crescendo with added breath support.

- Energize sustained tones by increasing the breath support and dynamic level.

- Emphasize the intervallic leaps and slurred two-note phrases without a "scooping" effect. "Arch over" the melodic leap by thinking of how a bird lands on a branch—it alights, rather than scrambling upward.

- Demonstrate the correct singing of the *r* consonant after a vowel when singing in English. It should be almost silent, as in *winter, thunder, heard, bird, where,* and *guardsman.*

- Feel the arched contour of each musical phrase as it begins, builds, then tapers off. The dynamics should reflect the melodic contour and meaning of the text.

- Follow the melodic line between the parts, noting the places that join in unison and those that are imitative.

Where did we run, run be-yond gate and guardsman?

Where did we run, run be-yond gate and guardsman?

Guess if you can, we ran to the sun,

Guess if you can, we ran to the sun,

the dance of the sun.

the dance of the sun.

For the Greater Detroit Chapter Choristers Guild

Festival Alleluía

Allen Pote

Unison or Two-part Choir with Keyboard

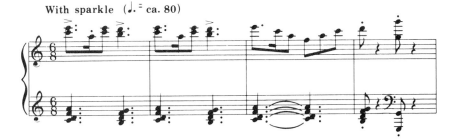

With sparkle (♩. = ca. 80)

Sing ——— un-to God ——— all the heav-ens and earth, ———

—— Al-le-lu - ia, clap your hands, (clap, clap) re-joice and

Festival Alleluia **201**

Festival Alleluía

Performance Tips

Rhythmic Focus
Explain to students:
- The rhythm is made up of basic rhythmic patterns in 6/8 and 4/4.
- Practice clapping the rhythm, working on difficult combinations until they become familiar.

Melodic Focus
Tell students:
- The melody has many scale-wise patterns and is not difficult.
- The skips are scale tones and normal.
- The harmony sections and soprano descant on page 205 are not difficult.

More Ideas

- This is a high-energy piece.
- The 6/8 section should be sung with smoothly pulsed energy. Swaying will get this feel.
- The 4/4 section needs a more energized feel than the beginning section. Marching in place can be effective, if the marching is done with lifting feet, so students don't pound and cover the voices.

Hot Spots

- The dotted quarter tied to the eight in 6/8 meter, as in measure 5, must still reflect the flow of 6/8 meter. Work to pulse on the eighth-note that is tied, so the feeling of a pulse is not lost.
- Make sure sopranos have their beginning note on page 205.
- At measure 37, have students lean forward and lift their eyebrows to enter the 4/4 section with energy.
- The echo section at the end needs to stress the *lu* rather than *ia.* It also needs tall, open vowel sounds.
- Do not slow down until the last measure and a half.

cel - e-brate, *(snap, snap)* and with a cheer - ful voice sing

al - le - lu - ia, sing it from your heart. _____

Make your life a song to God.

with articulation

mf

Lis-ten to the rhy-thm, to the rhy-thm of cre - a - tion,

Program Ideas

- Use movement to enhance the energetic feeling of the piece. Sway slightly during the 6/8 section, and quietly march in place on the 4/4 section.
- Use silk scarves or streamers in a patterned, planned movement, to enhance the strong feeling of beat. (Use either movement or scarves, not both at the same time.)
- Enter the concert stage to this piece. Perhaps a small group could be on the risers, and the others enter during the first part. The piano introduction can be doubled in length. Students need to watch carefully, and listen to stay together as they enter.

"Festival Alleluia"—Pote
"Arruru"—Dwyer/Gerber
"Joseph's Lullaby"—Schulz-Widmar
"Dance on My Heart"—Koepke
"Behold, a Tiny Baby!"—Lightfoot
"Nigra Sum"—Casals
"Wisdom and Understanding"—Newbury

VOCAL DEVELOPMENT

To encourage vocal development, have students:

- Demonstrate good vocal tone by singing with tall vowels and clear consonants.
- Energize sustained tones by increasing the breath support and dynamic level.
- Modify vowel sounds from *uh* or *ay* to *awh* on words such as *unto, God, alleluia, from, creation, above,* and *love.* Feel and hear a full resonant sound on the *oo* sounds of *allelu,* and *alleluia.*
- Energize repeated notes by articulating or overexaggerating the words. Sing lightly and clearly, making a crescendo with added breath support. Emphasize the consonants.
- Sustain phrases by staggering the breathing and moving forward through the phrases.
- Listen for diphthongs (two vowel sounds when one vowel is written) in words when singing in English, such as *rejoice, joyful, voice, life,* and *light.* Sing or sustain the first vowel sound and barely sing the second vowel sound with the next syllable.
- Demonstrate the correct singing of the *r* consonant after a vowel when singing in English. It sould be almost silent, as in *earth, your, heart, world, wonder,* and *Lord.*
- Feel the arched contour of each musical phrase as it begins, builds, then tapers off. The dynamics should reflect the melodic contour.
- Tune the unison sections with identical vowel sounds and precise rhythms. Tune the fourths at measure 39 and the parts at measure 48 carefully.

sing it from your heart. _____ Make your life a

sing it from your heart. _____ Make your life a

song to God. Al-le-lu - ia, _____

song to God. Al-le-lu - ia, al-le-

_____ al-le-lu - ia, al-le-lu, al-le-lu, al-le-lu - ia!

lu - ia, al-le-lu, al-le-lu, al-le-lu, al-le-lu - ia!

To Dottie and Cary Sue

Wisdom and Understanding

Kent A. Newbury
Job 28: 20–21, 23–28 (RSV)

SSA Chorus A cappella

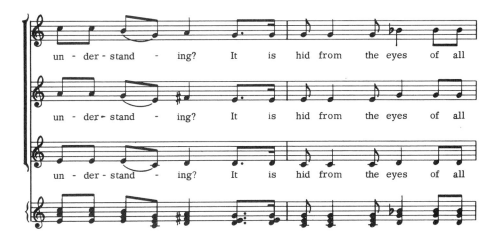

Wisdom and Understanding **207**

"Wisdom and Understanding"

The text of this piece is taken from the Bible's Book of Job. Have students:

- Share what they know about this story, or look it up and read it.
- Identify the lesson taught through the story of Job.
- Relate the message of the text in their own words.

Wisdom and Understanding

Performance Tips

Rhythmic Focus
Explain to students:
- The rhythm is the focus of this piece and is a perfect match with the text.
- You will find word painting, sharply accented sounds, syncopation, and imitative rhythmic patterns.
- Work on one section at a time, and enjoy learning the rhythms securely before adding the pitch.

Melodic Focus
Tell students:
- The melody is not terribly difficult, but is more complex because of the quick tempo and rhythmic challenge.
- The pitches are conceived in patterns.
- Each section has a different texture.
- Sequential progressions are generally the rule.

More Ideas

- The brisk tempo and syncopated rhythms throughout are sometimes difficult, but very exciting.
- Drill the rhythms with and without words and pitches.

Hot Spots

- The slower section beginning on page 211, pickup of measure 21, can be deceptively difficult to tune.
- This number requires vocal stamina. Once started, there are very few moments to relax, but it's worth it.

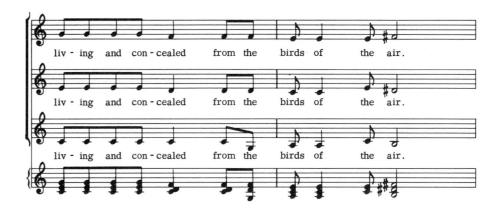

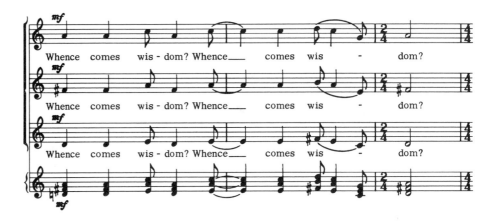

Program Ideas

- Divide the piece into sections; for example: measures 1–13, 13–20, 20–23, 24–27, 28–29, 29–38, 38–43, 43–end. Standing in mixed voice groups, each group sings one or more of the sections, with all singing measures 28–29 and 43–end. The mixture of groups will allow everyone a bit of breathing time, and add even more excitement to an already exciting piece.
- Use facial expression and bodily gesture to add to the excitement of the text and rhythm.

"Wisdom and Understanding"—Newbury

"O Death, None Could Conquer Thee"—Bach/Kjelson

"Who Has Seen the Wind?"—Kreutz

"Dance on My Heart"—Koepke

VOCAL DEVELOPMENT

To encourage vocal development, have students:

- Demonstrate good vocal tone by singing with tall vowels and clear consonants.
- Modify vowel sounds in such words as *God, comes, wisdom,* and *from* to create a resonant *awh* sound rather than an *uh* sound.
- Energize sustained tones and accented notes by increasing the breath support and dynamic level.
- Sustain phrases by staggering the breathing and moving forward through the phrases.
- Listen for diphthongs (two vowel sounds when one vowel is written) in words when singing in English, as in *eyes, way,* and *out.* Sing or sustain the first vowel sound and barely sing the second vowel sound with the next syllable.
- Demonstrate the correct singing of the *r* consonant after a vowel when singing in English. It should be almost silent, as in *where, understanding, birds, air, earth, under, waters, thunder, searched, fear, Lord,* and *depart.*
- Perform the rhythms, accents, and mixed meters precisely by conducting and speaking the rhythm, or speaking the text in rhythm.
- Note the imitative sections at the top of page 210, contrasting with the syllabic section at the top of page 211.
- Tune the chords by listening carefully to the balance of the three parts.

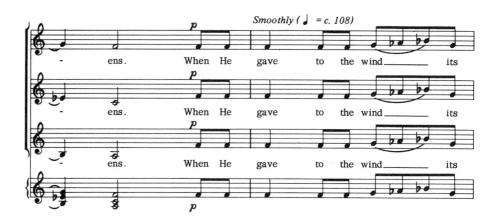

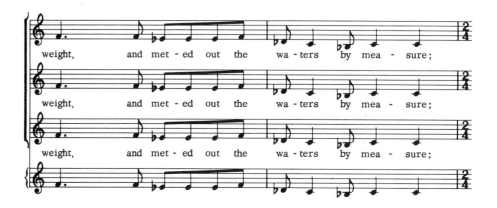

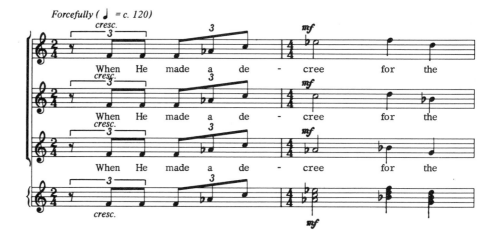

rain _____ and a way for the light - ning of the

rain _____ and a way for the light - ning of the

rain _____ and a way for the light - ning of the

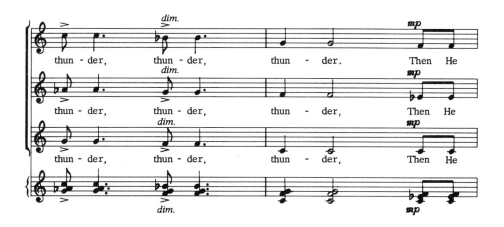

thun - der, thun - der, thun - der. Then He

thun - der, thun - der, thun - der, Then He

thun - der, thun - der, thun - der, Then He

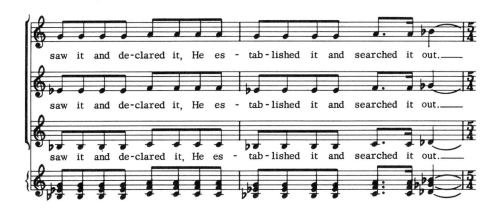

saw it and de-clared it, He es - tab-lished it and searched it out. _____

saw it and de-clared it, He es - tab-lished it and searched it out. _____

saw it and de-clared it, He es - tab-lished it and searched it out. _____

Lord, that is wis - dom, And to de -

part from e - vil is un - der - stand - ing, un - der - stand - ing,

Wis - dom and un - der - stand - ing." That is wis - dom.

Beautiful Yet Truthful

Performance Tips

Rhythmic Focus
Explain to students:
- The rhythms in the piece are straightforward.
- The tempo is quite fast, so the rhythm and words must be well practiced.
- Notice the stresses on almost every other measure. Be sure to practice them as you practice the rhythm.

Melodic Focus
Tell students:
- The melody is within an octave and quite singable.
- Have fun with this one.

Beautiful Yet Truthful

A Folksong Elaboration*
By Lloyd Pfautsch

Three-part Chorus of Female Voices
with Piano Accompaniment

* From *American Ballads and Folksongs* by John Lomax, used by permission

214 *Choral Connections   Level 3 Treble Voices*

Arranger Lloyd Pfautsch

Dr. Lloyd Pfautsch is Professor of Sacred Music and Director of Choral Music Emeritus at the Southern Methodist University. Since 1979 he has annually received an ASCAP award for excellence in composition, as well as numerous other honors. Throughout the country he is known as a guest conductor and clinician at music camps, all-state and regional high school choral festivals, church music workshops and festivals, choral conductors' clinics, and both national and international music conventions. Dr. Pfautsch has published over 300 music compositions, arrangements, and editions.

More Ideas

- This is a humorous piece, so sing it "tongue in cheek."
- There are three verses, the first two being similar, and the third changing character by going from 2/2 to 3/2.

Hot Spots

- The rhythm is the tricky element of this piece.
- Watch the staggered entrances on page 221.

sin-gle hour, Some-bod-y's sure to send me flow'rs.

Ain't it fierce to be so beau-ti-ful. beau-ti-ful, Ain't it fierce to be so

beau-ti-ful?

Soprano

Ain't it fierce to be so brain-y, brain-y So

Alto

Ain't it fierce to be so brain-y, brain-y So

rar-in', tear-in', brain-y! Ain't it fierce to be so brain-y, brain-y,

rar-in', tear-in', brain-y! Ain't it fierce to be so brain-y, brain-y,

Ain't it fierce to be so brain-y! I ain't got no

Ain't it fierce to be so brain-y! I ain't got no

peace of mind, The teach-ers are so aw-ful-ly kind, Out-

peace of mind, The teach-ers are so aw-ful-ly kind, Out-

Beautiful Yet Truthful **217**

side of their doors they stand, stand, Wait-in' there to shake my

side of their doors they stand, stand, Wait-in' there to shake my—

hand,— Out - side of their doors they stand,— stand.—

hand,— Out - side of their doors they stand. stand,

Wait'- in there to shake my hand!——— Al - most ev'- ry

Wait'- in there to shake my hand!——— Al - most ev'- ry

Ain't it fierce to be so truth - - - ful?

Ain't it fierce to be so truth - ful?

Ain't it fierce to be so truth - ful!

Ev'-ry-one says my hon-es-ty— Is on-ly matched by my

Ev'-ry-one says my hon-es-ty Is on-ly matched by my

Ev'-ry-one says my hon-es-ty Is on-ly matched by my

Beautiful Yet Truthful **221**

truth-ful, truth-ful? Ain't it fierce___ to be beau - ti -ful,

truth-ful, truth-ful? Ain't it fierce___ to be beau - ti -ful,

truth-ful, truth-ful? Ain't it fierce___ to be beau - ti -ful,

brain - y yet truth - - - ful?

brain - y yet truth - - ful?

brain - y yet truth - - ful?

Bloomington, Illinois
March 12, 1955

Glossary

A

a cappella (ah-kah-PEH-lah) [It.] Unaccompanied vocal music.

accelerando (*accel.*) (ah-chel-leh-RAHN-doh) [It.] Gradually increasing the tempo.

accent Indicates the note is to be sung with extra force or stress. (>)

accidentals Signs used to indicate the raising or lowering of a pitch. A sharp (♯) alters a pitch by raising it one-half step; a flat (♭) alters a pitch by lowering it one-half step; a natural (♮) cancels a sharp or a flat.

accompaniment Musical material that supports another; for example, a piano or orchestra accompanying a choir or soloist.

adagio (ah-DAH-jee-oh) [It.] Slow tempo, but not as slow as largo.

ad libitum (ad. lib.) [Lt.] An indication that the performer may vary the tempo, add or delete a vocal or instrumental part. Synonymous with a *piacere*.

al fine (ahl FEE-neh) [It.] To the end.

alla breve Indicates cut time; duple meter in which there are two beats per measure, the half note getting one beat. (¢)

allargando (*allarg.*) (ahl-ahr-GAHN-doh) [It.] To broaden, become slower.

aleatoric or chance music Music in which chance is deliberately used as a compositional component.

allegro (ah-LEH-groh) [It.] Brisk tempo; faster than moderato, slower than *vivace*.

allegro assai (ah-LEH-groh ah-SAH-ee) [It.] Very fast; in seventeenth-century music, the term can also mean "sufficiently fast."

altered pitch A note that does not belong to the scale of the work being performed.

alto The lower female voice; sometimes called contralto or mezzo-soprano.

anacrusis (a-nuh-KROO-suhs) [Gk.] *See* upbeat.

andante (ahn-DAHN-teh) [It.] Moderately slow; a walking tempo.

andante con moto (ahn-DAHN-teh kohn MOH-toh) [It.] A slightly faster tempo, "with motion."

animato Quick, lively; "animated."

anthem A choral composition in English using a sacred text. *See also* motet.

antiphonal Music performed by alternating ensembles, positioned in opposing locations, as in choirs or brass; first brought to prominence by Giovanni Gabrielli at St. Mark's Cathedral, Venice, in the Baroque period.

appassionato (uh-pah-shun-NAHT-oh) [It.] With deep feeling, passionately.

appoggiatura (uh-pah-zhuh-TOOR-uh) [It.] A nonharmonic tone, usually a half or whole step above the harmonic tone, performed on the beat, resolving downward to the harmonic tone.

aria (AHR-ee-uh) [It.] A song for a solo singer and orchestra, usually in an opera, oratorio, or cantata.

arpeggio (ahr-PEH-jee-oh) [It.] A chord in which the pitches are sounded successively, usually from lowest to highest; in broken style.

art song Expressive songs about life, love, and human relationships for solo voice and piano.

articulation Clarity in performance of notes and diction.

a tempo (ah TEM-poh) [It.] Return to the established tempo after a change.

atonality Music not organized around a key center.

augmentation A technique used in composition by which the melody line is repeated in doubled note values; opposite of *diminution*.

augmented The term indicating that a major or perfect interval has been enlarged by one-half step; as in C-F♯ (augmented fourth) or C-G♯ (augmented fifth).

B

balance and symmetry Even and equal.

baritone The male voice between tenor and bass.

bar line (measure bar) A vertical line drawn through the staff to show the end of a measure. Double bar lines show the end of a section or a piece of music.

Bar Line   Double Bar Line

Baroque period (buh-ROHK) [Fr.] Historic period between c. 1600 and c. 1750 that reflected highly embellished styles in art, architecture, fashion, manners, and music. The period of elaboration.

bass The lowest male voice, below tenor and baritone.

bass clef Symbol at the beginning of the staff for lower voices and instruments, or the piano left hand; usually referring to pitches lower than middle C. The two dots lie on either side of the fourth-line F, thus the term, F clef.

beat A steady pulse.

bel canto (bell KAHN-toh) [It.] Italian vocal technique of the eighteenth century with emphasis on beauty of sound and brilliance of performance.

binary form Defines a form having two sections (A and B), each of which may be repeated.

bitonality The designation of music written in two different keys at the same time.

breath mark A mark placed within a phrase or melody showing where the singer or musician should breathe. (')

C

cadence Punctuation or termination of a musical phrase; a breathing break.

caesura (si-ZHUR-uh) [Lt.] A break or pause between two musical phrases. (//)

call and response A song style that follows a simple question-and-answer pattern in which a soloist leads and a group responds.

calypso style Folk-style music from the Caribbean Islands with bright, syncopated rhythm.

cambiata The young male voice that is still developing.

canon A compositional form in which the subject is begun in one group and then is continually and exactly repeated by other groups. Unlike the round, the canon closes with all voices ending together on a common chord.

cantata (kan-TAH-tuh) [It.] A collection of vocal compositions with instrumental accompaniment consisting of several movements based on related secular or sacred text segments.

cantabile In a lyrical, singing style.

cantor A solo singer in the Jewish and Roman Catholic traditions who leads the congregation in worship by introducing responses and other musical portions of the services.

cantus firmus (KAHN-tuhs FUHR-muhs) [Lt.] A previously-composed melody which is used as a basis for a new composition.

chance music See aleatoric music.

chantey (SHAN-tee) [Fr.] A song sung by sailors in rhythm with their work.

chant, plainsong Music from the liturgy of the early church, characterized by free rhythms, monophonic texture, and sung *a cappella*.

chorale (kuh-RAL) [Gr.] Congregational song or hymn of the German Protestant (Evangelical) Church.

chord Three or more pitches sounded simultaneously.

chord, block Three or more pitches sounded simultaneously.

chord, broken Three or more pitches sounded in succession; *see also* arpeggio.

chromatic (kroh-MAT-ik) [Gr.] Moving up or down by half steps. Also the name of a scale composed entirely of half steps.

Classical period The period in Western history beginning around 1750 and lasting until around 1820 that reflected a time when society began looking to the ancient Greeks and Romans for examples of order and ways of looking at life.

clef The symbol at the beginning of the staff that identifies a set of pitches; *see also* bass clef and treble clef.

coda Ending section; a concluding portion of a composition. (⊕)

common time Another name for 4/4 meter; *see also* cut time. (**c**)

composer The creator of musical works.

compound meter Meter whose beat can be subdivided into threes and/or sixes.

con (kohn) [It.] With.

con brio (kohn BREE-oh) [It.] With spirit; vigorously.

concerto Composition for solo instrument and an orchestra, usually with three movements.

con moto (kohn MOH-toh) [It.] With motion.

consonance A musical interval or chord that sounds pleasing; opposite of dissonance.

Contemporary period The time from 1900 to right now.

continuo A Baroque tradition in which the bass line is played "continuously," by a cello, double bass, and/or bassoon while a keyboard instrument (harpsichord, organ) plays the bass line and indicated harmonies.

contrapuntal See counterpoint.

counterpoint The combination of simultaneous parts; *see* polyphony.

crescendo (*cresc.*) (kreh-SHEN-doh) [It.] To gradually become louder.

cued notes Smaller notes indicating either optional harmony or notes from another voice part.

cut time 2/2 time with the half note getting the beat. (**¢**)

D

da capo (*D.C.*) (dah KAH-poh) [It.] Go back to the beginning and repeat; *see also* dal segno and al fine.

dal segno (*D.S.*) (dahl SAYN-yoh) [It.] Go back to the sign and repeat. (𝄋)

D. C. al fine (dah KAH-poh ahl FEE-neh) [It.] Repeat back to the beginning and end at the "fine."

decrescendo (*decresc.*) (deh-kreh-SHEN-doh) [It.] To gradually become softer.

delicato Delicate; to play or sing delicately.

descant A high, ornamental voice part often lying above the melody.

diaphragm The muscle that separates the chest cavity (thorax) from the abdomen. The primary muscle in the inhalation/exhalation cycle.

diction Clear and correct enunciation.

diminished The term describing an interval that has been descreased by half steps; for example, the *perfect fourth* (3 whole and one half steps) becomes a *diminished fourth* (3 whole steps). Also used for a triad which has a minor third (R, 3) and a diminished fifth (R, 5); for example, C, E♭, G♭.

diminuendo (*dim.*) (duh-min-yoo-WEN-doh) [It.] Gradually getting softer; *see also* decrescendo.

diminution The halving of values; that is, halves become quarters, quarters become eighths, etc. Opposite of *augmentation.*

diphthong A combination of two vowel sounds consisting of a primary vowel sound and a secondary vowel sound. The secondary vowel sound is (usually) at the very end of the diphthong; for example, in the word *toy*, the diphthong starts with the sound of "o," then moves on to "y," in this case pronounced "ee."

dissonance Discord in music, suggesting a state of tension or "seeking"; chords using seconds, fourths, fifths, and sevenths; the opposite of consonance.

divisi (*div.*) (dih-VEE-see) [It.] Divide; the parts divide.

dolce (DOHL-chay) [It.] Sweet; *dolcissimo*, very sweet; *dolcemente*, sweetly.

dominant The fifth degree of a major or minor scale; the triad built on the fifth degree; indicated as V in harmonic analysis.

Dorian mode A scale with the pattern of whole-step, half, whole, whole, whole, half, and whole. For example, D to D on the keyboard.

dotted rhythm A note written with a dot increases its value again by half.

double bar Two vertical lines placed on the staff indicating the end of a section or a composition; used with two dots to enclose repeated sections.

double flat (♭♭) Symbol showing the lowering of a pitch one whole step (two half steps).

double sharp (𝄪) Symbol showing the raising of a pitch one whole step (two half steps).

doubling The performance of the same note by two parts, either at the same pitch or an octave apart.

downbeat The accented first beat in a measure.

D. S. al coda (dahl SAYN-yoh ahl KOH-dah) [It.] Repeat from the symbol (𝄋) and skip to the coda when you see the sign. (⊕)

D. S. al fine (dahl SAYN-yoh ahl FEE-neh) [It.] Repeat from the symbol (𝄋) and sing to fine or the end.

duple Any time signature or group of beats that is a multiple of two.

duet Composition for two performers.

dynamics The volume of sound, the loudness or softness of a musical passage; intensity, power.

E ——————————

enharmonic Identical tones that are named and written differently; for example, C sharp and D flat.

ensemble A group of musicians or singers who perform together.

enunciation Speaking and singing words with distinct vowels and consonants.

espressivo (*espress.*) (es-preh-SEE-vo) [It.] For expression; *con espressione*, with feeling.

expressive singing To sing with feeling.

exuberance Joyously unrestrained and enthusiastic.

F ——————————

fermata (fur-MAH-tah) [It.] A hold; to hold the note longer. ( )

fine (FEE-neh) Ending; to finish.

flat Symbol (accidental) that lowers a pitch by one half step. (♭)

folk music Uncomplicated music that speaks directly of everyday matters; the first popular music; usually passed down through the oral tradition.

form The structure of a musical composition.

forte (*f*) (FOR-teh) [It.] Loud.

fortissimo (*ff*) (for-TEE-suh-moh) [It.] Very loud.

freely A direction that permits liberties with tempo, dynamics, and style.

fugue (FYOOG) [It.] A polyphonic composition consisting of a series of successive melody imitations; *see also* imitative style.

fusion A combination or blending of different genres of music.

grandioso [It.] Stately, majestic.

grand staff Two staves usually linked together by a long bar line and a bracket.

grave (GRAH-veh) [It.] Slow, solemn.

grazioso (grah-tsee-OH-soh) [It.] Graceful.

H

half step The smallest distance (interval) between two notes on a keyboard; the chromatic scale is composed entirely of half steps, shown as (∨).

half time *See* cut time.

harmonic interval Intervals that are sung or played simultaneously; *see also* melodic interval.

harmony Vertical blocks of different tones sounded simultaneously.

hemiola (hee-mee-OH-lah) [Gk.] A metric flow of two against a metric flow of three.

homophonic (hah-muh-FAH-nik) [Gk.] A texture where all parts sing similar rhythm in unison or harmony.

homophony (hah-MAH-fuh-nee) [Gk.] Music that consists of two or more voice parts with similar or identical rhythms. From the Greek words meaning "same sounds," homophony could be described as "hymn-style."

hushed A style marking indicating a soft, whispered tone.

I

imitation, imitative style Restating identical or nearly identical musical material in two or more parts.

improvised Invented on the spur of the moment.

improvisation Spontaneous musical invention, commonly associated with jazz.

interval The distance from one note to another; intervals are measured by the total steps and half steps between the two notes.

intonation The degree to which pitch is accurately produced in tune.

introduction An opening section at the beginning of a movement or work, preparatory to the main body of the form.

inversion May be applied to melody and harmony: *melodic inversion* occurs in an exchange of ascending and descending movement (for instance, a third becomes a sixth, a fourth becomes a fifth, etc.); *harmonic inversion* occurs in the position of the chord tones (that is, root position with the root as lowest tone, first inversion with the third as lowest tone, and second inversion with the fifth as the lowest tone).

K

key The way tonality is organized around a tonal center; *see also* key signature.

key change Changing an initial key signature in the body of a composition.

key signature Designation of sharps or flats at the beginning of a composition to indicate its basic scale and tonality.

L

leading tone The seventh degree of a scale, so called because of its strong tendency to resolve upward to the tonic.

legato (leh-GAH-toh) [It.] Smooth, connected style.

ledger lines Short lines that appear above, between treble and bass clefs, or below the bass clef, used to expand the notation.

leggiero (leh-JEH-roh) [It.] Articulate lightly; sometimes nonlegato.

lento Slow; a little faster than *largo*, a little slower than *adagio*.

linear flow, line Singing/playing notes in a flowing (smooth) manner, as if in a horizontal line.

liturgical Pertaining to prescribed forms of worship or ritual in various religious services. Western music contains much literature written for the liturgy of the early Roman Catholic Church.

lullaby A cradle song; in Western music, usually sung with a gentle and regular rhythm.

M

madrigal A secular vocal form in several parts, popular in the Renaissance.

maestoso (mah-eh-STOH-soh) [It.] Perform majestically.

major (key, scale, mode) Scale built on the formula of two whole steps, one half step, three whole steps, one half step.

Letter Names:	G	A	B	C	D	E	F♯	G
Movable Do:	do	re	mi	fa	so	la	ti	do
Numbers:	1	2	3	4	5	6	7	1

Major 2nd The name for an interval of one whole step or two half steps. For example, from C to D.

Major 6th The name for an interval of four whole steps and one-half step. For example, from C to A.

Major 3rd The name for an interval of two whole steps or four half steps. For example, from C to E.

major triad Three tones that form a major third *do* to *mi* and a minor third *mi* to *so* as in C E G.

marcato (mahr-KAH-toh) [It.] Long but separated pitches; translated as marked.

mass The main religious service of the Roman Catholic Church. There are two divisions of mass: the Proper of the Mass in which the text changes for each day, and the Ordinary of the Mass in which the text remains the same for every mass. Music for the mass includes the Kyrie, Gloria, Credo, Sanctus, and Agnus Dei as well as other chants, hymns, and psalms. For special mass occasions composers through the centuries have created large musical works for choruses, soloists, instrumentalists, and orchestras.

measure The space from one bar line to the next; also called bars.

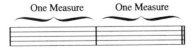

One Measure   One Measure

medieval Historical period prior to the Renaissance, c. 500-1450.

medley A group of tunes, linked together and sung consecutively.

melisma (n.) or melismatic (adj.) (muh-LIZ-mah or muh-liz-MAT-ik) [Gk.] A term describing the setting of one syllable of text to several pitches.

son, e - le - - i - son._____
us, On - us - - mer - cy._____

melodic interval Intervals that are performed in succession; *see also* harmonic interval.

melody A logical succession of musical tones; also called tune.

meter The pattern into which a steady succession of rhythmic pulses (beats) is organized.

meter signature The divided number at the beginning of a clef; 4/4, 3/4, and so forth; *see also* time signature.

metronome marking A sign that appears over the top line of the treble clef staff at the beginning of a piece indicating the tempo. It shows the kind of note that will get the beat and the numbers of beats per minute as measured by a metronome; for example, ♪ = 100.

mezzo forte (*mf*) (MEHT-soh FOR-teh) [It.] Medium loud.

mezzo piano (*mp*) (MEHT-soh pee-AH-noh) [It.] Medium soft.

mezzo voce (MET-soh VOH-cheh) [It.] With half voice; reduced volume and tone.

middle C The note that is located nearest the center of the piano keyboard; middle C can be written in either the treble or bass clef.

minor (key, scale) Scale built on the formula of one whole step, one half step, two whole steps, one half step, two whole steps.

Letter Names:	D	E	F	G	A	B♭	C	D
Movable Do:	la	ti	do	re	mi	fa	so	la
Numbers:	6	7	1	2	3	4	5	6

minor mode One of two modes upon which the basic scales of Western music are based, the other being major; using W for a whole step and H for a half step, a minor scale has the pattern W H W W H W W.

minor triad Three tones that form a minor third (bottom) and a major third (top), such as A C E.

minor third The name for an interval of three half steps. For example, from A to C.

mixed meter Frequently changing time signatures or meters.

moderato Moderate.

modulation Adjusting to a change of keys within a song.

molto Very or much; for example, *molto rit.* means "much slower."

monophonic (mah-nuh-FAH-nik) [Gk.] A musical texture having a single melodic line with no accompaniment; monophony.

monophony (muh-NAH-fuh-nee) [Gk.] One sound; music that has a single melody. Gregorian chants or plainsongs exhibit monophony.

motet Originating as a Medieval and Renaissance polyphonic song, this choral form of composition became an unaccompanied work, often in contrapuntal style.

motive A shortened expression, sometimes contained within a phrase.

musical variations Changes in rhythm, pitch, dynamics, style, and tempo to create new statements of the established theme.

mysterioso Perform in a mysterious or haunting way; to create a haunting mood.

N

nationalism Patriotism; pride of country. This feeling influenced many Romantic composers such as Wagner, Tchaikovsky, Dvořák, Chopin, and Brahms.

natural (♮) Cancels a previous sharp (♯) lowering the pitch a half step, or a previous flat (♭), raising the pitch a half step.

no breath mark A direction not to take a breath at a specific place in the composition. (♪ ⌢ ♪ or N.B.)

non-harmonic tones Identifies those pitches outside the harmonic structure of the chord; for example, the *passing tone* and the *appoggiatura*.

non troppo (nahn TROH-poh) [It.] Not too much; for example, allegro non troppo, not too fast.

notation Written notes, symbols, and directions used to represent music within a composition.

nuance Subtle variations in tempo, phrasing, dynamics, etc., to enhance the musical performance.

O

octave An interval of twelve half steps; 8 or 8va = an octave above; 8vb = an octave below.

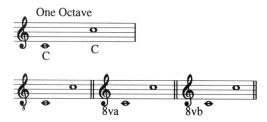

One Octave

opera A combination of singing, instrumental music, dancing, and drama that tells a story.

operetta A lighter, "popular" style of operatic form, including sung and spoken dialogue, solo, chorus, and dance.

optional divisi (*opt. div.*) Indicating a split in the music into optional harmony, shown by the smaller cued note.

opus, Op. The term, meaning "work," used by composers to show the chronological order of their works; for example, Opus 1, Op. 2.

oratorio A piece for solo voices, chorus, and orchestra, that is an expanded dramatic work on a literary or religious theme presented without theatrical action.

ostinato (ahs-tuh-NAH-toh) [It.] A rhythmic or melodic passage that is repeated continuously.

overtones The almost inaudible higher pitches which occur over the fundamental tone, resulting from the division of the vibrating cycle into smaller segments; compare to partials, harmonics.

P

palate The roof of the mouth; the *hard palate* is forward, the *soft palate* (*velum*) is at the back.

parallel major and minor keys Major and minor keys having the same tonic, such as A major and A minor (A major being the parallel major of A minor and A minor the parallel minor of A major).

parallel motion The movement of two or more voice parts in the same direction, at the same interval from each other.

peak The high point in the course of a development; for example, the high point of a musical phrase or the high point in a movement of instrumental music.

pentatonic scale A five-tone scale constructed of *do, re, mi, so, la* (degrees 1, 2, 3, 5, 6) of a corresponding major scale.

Perfect 5th The name for an interval of three whole steps and one half step. For example, C to G.

Perfect 4th The name for an interval of two whole steps and one half step. For example, C to F.

phrase A musical sentence containing a beginning, middle, and end.

phrase mark In music, an indicator of the length of a phrase in a melody; this mark may also mean that the singer or musician should not take a breath for the duration of the phrase. (⌢)

phrasing The realization of the phrase structure of a work; largely a function of a performer's articulation and breathing.

pianissimo (*pp*) (pee-uh-NEE-suh-moh) [It.] Very soft.

piano (*p*) (pee-ANN-noh) [It.] Soft.

Picardy third An interval of a major third used in the final, tonic chord of a piece written in a minor key.

pick-up *See* upbeat.

pitch Sound, the result of vibration; the highness or lowness of a tone, determined by the number of vibrations per second.

piu (pew) [It.] More; for example, *piu forte* means "more loudly."

poco (POH-koh) [It.] Little; for example, *poco dim.* means "a little softer."

poco a poco (POH-koh ah POH-koh) [It.] Little by little; for example, *poco a poco cresc.* means "little by little increase in volume."

polyphony (n.) or polyphonic (adj.) (pah-LIH-fuh-nee or pah-lee-FAH-nik) [Gk.] The term that means that each voice part begins at a different place, is independent and important, and that sections often repeat in contrasting dynamic levels. Poly = many, phony = sounds.

presto (PREH-stoh) [It.] Very fast.

program music A descriptive style of music composed to relate or illustrate a specific incident, situation, or drama; the form of the piece is often dictated or influenced by the nonmusical program. This style commonly occurs in music composed during the Romantic period. For example, "The Moldau" from *Má Vlast*, by Bedřich Smetana.

progression A succession of two or more pitches or chords; also melodic or harmonic progression.

R

rallentando (*rall.*) (rahl-en-TAHN-doh) [It.] Meaning to "perform more and more slowly." *See also* ritardando.

recitative (res-uh-TAY-teev) [It.] A speechlike style of singing used in opera, oratorio, and cantata.

register, vocal A term used for different parts of a singer's range, such as head register (high notes) and chest register (low notes).

relative major and minor keys The relative minor of any major key or scale, while sharing its key signature and pitches, takes for its tonic the sixth scale degree of that major key or scale. For example, in D major the sixth scale degree is B (or *la* in solfège), *la* then becomes the tonic for A minor.

D major   B minor

Renaissance period The historic period in Western Europe from c. 1430 to 1600; the term means "rebirth" or "renewal"; it indicates a period of rapid development in exploration, science, art, and music.

repeat sign A direction to repeat the section of music (‖:‖); if the first half of this sign is omitted, it means to "go back to the beginning" (:‖).

repetition The restatement of a musical idea; repeated pitches; repeated "A" section in ABA form.

resolution (*res.*) A progression from a dissonant tone or harmony to a consonant harmony; a sense of completion.

resonance Reinforcement and intensification of sound by vibrations.

rest Symbols used to indicated silence.

rhythm The pattern of sounds and silences.

rhythmic motif A rhythmic pattern that is repeated throughout a movement or composition.

ritardando (*rit.*) The gradual slowing of tempo; also called "ritard."

Rococo Music of the Baroque period so elaborate it was named after a certain type of fancy rock work.

Romantic period A historic period starting c. 1820 and ending c. 1900 in which artists and composers attempted to break with classical music ideas.

rondo form An instrumental form based on an alternation between a repeated (or recurring) section and contrasting episodes (ABACADA).

root The bottom note of a triad in its original position; the note on which the chord is built.

round A composition in which the perpetual theme (sometimes with harmonic parts) begins in one group and is strictly imitated in other groups in an overlapping fashion. Usually the last voice to enter becomes the final voice to complete the song.

rubato (roo-BAH-toh) [It.] Freely; allows the conductor or the performer to vary the tempo.

S

sacred music Of or dealing with religious music; hymns, chorales, early masses; *see* secular music.

scale A pattern of pitches arranged by whole steps and half steps.

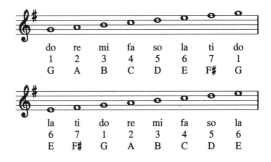

do	re	mi	fa	so	la	ti	do
1	2	3	4	5	6	7	1
G	A	B	C	D	E	F♯	G

la	ti	do	re	mi	fa	so	la
6	7	1	2	3	4	5	6
E	F♯	G	A	B	C	D	E

score   The arrangement of instrumental and vocal staffs that all sound at the same time.

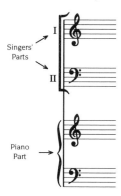

secular music   Music without religious content; *see* sacred music.

sempre   (SEHM-preh) [It.] Always, continually.

seventh chord   By adding a seventh above the root of a triad (R, 3, 5), the result is a four-tone chord (R, 3, 5, 7).

sforzando   (*sfz*) (sfohr-TSAHN-doh) [It.] A sudden strong accent on a note or chord.

sharp   A symbol (accidental) that raises a pitch by one half step. (♯)

sight-sing   Reading and singing of music at first sight.

simile   (*sim.*) (SIM-ee-leh) [It.] To continue in the same way.

simple meter   Meter in which each beat is divisible by 2.

skip   Melodic movement in intervals larger than a whole step.

slur   Curved line placed over or under a group of notes to indicate that they are to be performed without a break. (   )

solfège   (SOHL-fehj) [Fr.] A method of sight-singing, using the syllables *do, re, mi, fa, so, la, ti*, etc. for pitches of the scale.

solo   Composition for one featured performer.

sonata-allegro form   (suh-NAH-tuh ah-LEH-groh) [It.] Large A B A form consisting of three sections: exposition, development, and recapitulation.

soprano   The higher female voice.

sostenuto   (SAHS-tuh-noot-oh) [It.] The sustaining of a tone or the slackening of tempo; the right pedal of a piano, which, when depressed, allows the strings to vibrate.

sotto voce   In a quiet, subdued manner; "under" the voice.

spirito   (SPEE-ree-toh) [It.] Spirited; for example, *con spirito*, with spirit.

spiritual   A type of song created by African Americans who combined African rhythms with melodies they created and heard in America.

staccato   (stah-KAH-toh) [It.] Performed in a short, detached manner, as opposed to legato.

staff   Series of five horizontal lines and four spaces on which music is written to show pitch.

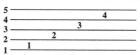

staggered entrances   Voice parts or instruments begin singing or playing at different points within the composition.

steady beat   A metrical pulse; *see also* beat, meter, rhythm.

step   Melodic movement from one note to the next adjacent note, either higher or lower.

stepwise melodic movement   Motion from one note to an adjacent one.

stress   Emphasis on certain notes or rhythmic elements.

strong beat   Naturally accented beats; beats 1 and 3 in 4/4 meter, beat 1 in 3/4 meter.

strophic   Description of a song in which all the stanzas of the text are sung to the same music; opposite of *through-composed*.

style   The particular character of a musical work; often indicated by words at the beginning of a composition, telling the performer the general manner in which the piece is to be performed.

subito   (sub.) (SOO-bee-toh) [It.] Suddenly; for example, *sub. piano* means "suddenly soft."

suspension or suspended tone   The tone or tones in a chord that are held as the remainder of the notes change to a new chord. The sustained tones often form a *dissonance* with the new chord, into which they then resolve.

sustained tone   A tone sustained in duration; sometimes implying a slowing of tempo; *sostenuto* or *sostenendo*, abbreviated *sost.*

swing   This is a performance style in which a pair of eighth notes ( ) are no longer performed evenly, but instead like a triplet ( ), yet they are still written ( ); usually indicated at the beginning of a song or a section.

symphony   An extended work in several movements, for orchestra; also an orchestra configured to perform symphonic music.

syncopation   Deliberate shifts of accent so that a rhythm goes against the steady beat; sometimes referred to as the "offbeat."

T

tactus (TAKT-us) [Lt.] The musical term for "beat" in the fifteenth and sixteenth century; generally related to the speed of the human heart.

tempo A pace with which music moves, based on the speed of the underlying beat.

tempo I or tempo primo Return to the first tempo.

tenor A high male voice, lower than the alto, but higher than bass.

tenuto (teh-NOO-toh) [It.] Stress and extend the marked note. ($\bar{\rho}$)

text Words, usually set in a poetic style, that express a central thought, idea, moral, or narrative.

texture The thickness of the different layers of horizontal and vertical sounds.

theme and variation form A musical form in which variations of the basic theme comprise the composition.

tie A curved line connecting two successive notes of the same pitch, indicating that the second note is not to be articulated. ($\rho \frown \rho$)

timbre Tone color; the unique quality produced by a voice or instrument.

time signature The sign placed at the beginning and within a composition to indicate the meter; for example, 4/4, 3/4; *see also* cut time, meter signature.

to coda Skip to the ⊕ or CODA.

tonality The organized relationships of pitches with reference to a definite key center. In Western music, most tonalities are organized by the major and minor scales.

tone A sound quality of a definite pitch.

tone color, quality, or timbre That which distinguishes the voice or tone of one singer or instrument from another; for example, a soprano from an alto or a flute from a clarinet.

tonic chord (TAH-nik kord) [Gk.] The name of a chord built on the tonal center of a scale; for example, C E G or *do, mi, so* for C major.

tonic or tonal center The most important pitch in a scale; *do*; the home tone; the tonal center or root of a key or scale.

tonic triad A three-note chord comprising root, third, and fifth; for example, C E G.

transposition The process of changing the key of a composition.

treble clef The symbol that appears at the beginning of the staff used for higher voices, instruments, or the piano right hand; generally referring to pitches above middle C, it wraps around the line for G, therefore it is also called the G-clef.

triad A three-note chord built in thirds above a root tone.

trill A rapid change between the marked note and the one above it within the same key. (*tr⌇*)

triplet A group of notes in which three notes of equal duration are sung in the time normally given to two notes of equal duration.

troppo (TROHP-oh) [It.] Too much; for example, *allegro non troppo*, not too fast.

troubadour A wandering minstrel of noble birth in southern France, Spain, and Italy during the eleventh to thirteenth centuries.

tuning The process of adjusting the tones of voices or instruments so they will sound the proper pitches.

tutti (TOO-tee) [It.] Meaning "all" or "together."

twelve-tone music Twentieth-century system of writing music in which the twelve tones of the chromatic scale are arranged into a tone row (numbered 1 to 12), and then the piece is composed by arranging and rearranging the "row" in different ways; for example, backward, forward, or in clusters of three or four pitches.

U

unison Voice parts or instruments sounding the same pitches in the same rhythm simultaneously.

upbeat A weak beat preceding the downbeat.

V

variation *See* theme and variation form, musical variations.

vivace (vee-VAH-chay) [It.] Very fast; lively.

voice crossing (or voice exchange) When one voice "crosses" above or below another voice part.

W

whole step The combination of two successive half steps. (⌷)

whole tone scale A scale consisting only of whole steps.